Mission in Marginal Places

T0346457

Introducing the Mission in Marginal Places series

Christian mission is facing critical challenges. Diverse, complex and rapidly changing contexts raise fundamental questions about the theology and practice of mission. The vision behind this series is to engage afresh with these questions in a way that will help equip Christian communities of all kinds to develop mission in their own particular situation.

The series incorporates a number of distinctive elements that are critical for contemporary mission. Firstly, Christian mission must give priority to those on the margins of society and questions of 'difference' must therefore be a guiding consideration in all aspects. Secondly, mission must be predicated on a practical or 'lived' theology which grapples with the actual experiences of life in a broad range of contexts. And thirdly, to be both rigorous and credible, mission studies must be in dialogue with the social sciences where much can be learned about the context for mission in relation to, for example, globalization, shifting experiences of 'place' and 'space', self-other relationships, urban studies and changing patterns of marginalization.

At heart, our intention is to help readers ground such theology and understandings into their own personal journey; to reflect on the character and spiritualities needed to sustain such an embodied and highly contextual approach to mission; and to help develop rhythms and practices that will enable such engagement.

The books:
Paul Cloke and Mike Pears (eds), *Mission in Marginal Places: the Theory* (2016)
Paul Cloke and Mike Pears (eds), *Mission in Marginal Places: the Praxis* (2016)
Paul Cloke and Mike Pears (eds) *Mission in Marginal Places: the Stories* (2017)
Paul Cloke and Mike Pears, *Exploring Spiritual Landscapes: Mission in Marginal Places* (2017)
Mike Pears, *The Peaceful Way: Mission in Marginal Places* (2018)
Mike Pears, *Placing the Powers: Mission in Marginal Places* (2018)

Mission in Marginal Places

The Theory

Paul Cloke and Mike Pears (eds)

Paternoster:
thinking faith

Reprinted 2018

First published 2016 by Paternoster
Paternoster is an imprint of Authentic Media Ltd
PO Box 6326, Bletchley, Milton Keynes MK1 9GG
authenticmedia.co.uk

British Library Cataloguing in Publication Data

A catalogue record for this book is available from the British Library

ISBN 978-1-84227-909-0
978-1-84227-915-1 (e-book)

Cover design by David McNeill revocreative.co.uk
Printed and bound by CPI Group (UK) Ltd., Croydon, CR0 8YY

Contents

Introduction

Mike Pears and Paul Cloke

Spatial and Social Margins

The focus of this book is on how the Christian community might explore more thoughtful and effective responses to marginalized people in marginal places. Our hope is that new and helpful approaches and resources can emerge from a re-evaluation of the theological and social scientific principles that underpin Christian mission. Our frank concern is that without thoughtful consideration of the mechanisms that sustain marginalization and exclusion in our everyday places, Christians involved in mission will inevitably find themselves, at least to some extent, collaborating with the very structures of society and patterns of living that tend to maintain or even increase the marginalization of the poor.

The UK is the world's sixth largest economy, and yet one in five people live below the official poverty line, and therefore experience the daily turmoil of living below the breadline. In 2014, 3.7 million children were living in poverty, a figure predicted to rise to 4.3 million by 2020.[1] These figures are both astonishing and unacceptable, according to most ethical metrics used by Christian communities to evaluate the state of their society. Yet these are simply the headlines that point to two crucial socio-political processes happening right here, right now. The first is that the situation is deteriorating rapidly due to *austerity governance*. Austerity is being directed very specifically at reforms to the welfare state that result in reductions in benefits, and punitive sanctions for minor misdemeanours or administrative failures. It is a regime that disproportionately targets the most vulnerable sectors of society, and leaves the better off relatively unscathed. Along with these benefit cuts there is an accelerating pattern of unstable and low-paid work that is producing a new category of poverty – the working poor. In 2013, for the first time in UK history, there were more people in working families living below the poverty line than in workless or retired families combined.[2] In these conditions we are seeing significant proportions of the population sliding into indebtedness, and rapidly increasing numbers of people relying on food banks for essential food supplies. We are also witnessing a remarkable Christian response; across a wide spectrum of denominations and theological convictions, the practical involvement and service of the church is making a significant difference, evidencing high levels of sacrificial service, innovation and creativity.[3] Indeed, an examination of almost any city in the UK will demonstrate that without the ongoing work of the faith communities many of the services upon which the poorer members of society depend would cease to function.

The second socio-political process at work here is that of *marginalization*. Poverty is the public face of deeper and less visible drivers that exclude and marginalize the least well off, separating them from much that might be assumed to be the 'normal' way of life in the UK. Exclusion is therefore *simultaneously social and spatial*. It causes individuals and families to 'slip outside, or even become unwelcome visitors within, those spaces which come to be regarded as the loci of "mainstream" social life (e.g. middle class suburbs, upmarket shopping malls or prime public space)'.[4] As a result it congregates such people increasingly into what might be thought of as marginal places such as separated-off housing estates. As a result, marginalized people residing within different quarters of UK cities are being shaped in such a way that they live increasingly in different worlds with different norms and expectations. Jon May[5] identifies five key marginalizing characteristics of social exclusion:

1. Exclusion is simultaneously material and symbolic, each reinforcing the other. For example, the symbolic stigmatization of individuals or groups is often closely associated with the experience of exclusion.

2. Exclusion is an active process, involving acts of deliberate distancing by other, supposedly more 'mainstream' social groups.
3. Exclusion is irretrievably intertwined with practices of *inclusion*. The social and spatial boundaries of who is included necessarily dictate who is excluded.
4. Exclusion occurs across multiple axes, including social background, socio-economic status, gender, ethnicity, sexuality and mental and physical health.
5. Exclusion is never absolute and can always to some extent be resisted.

These, then, are the characteristics of life on the margins in the UK. What Christian communities need to understand is that they are not simply responding to the individual needs of unfortunate individuals, but they are confronting complex and unjust societal practices that cause such people to be excluded from the mainstream and marginalized both socially and spatially.

As these issues of exclusion and marginalization become ever more significant, and present themselves as crucial foci for Christian mission, so other developments are underway which profoundly affect the mission of the church. The numerical decline of the church in the western world in general, and of the denominational churches in particular, is happening at a staggering rate. Congregations in the UK are closing on a daily basis so that entire areas of the country, both rural and urban, are becoming de-churched, whole denominations are facing serious questions about their own sustainability[6] and for many decline is fuelling an atmosphere of anxiety and stress. In some quarters, decline may be having the opposite effect, provoking fresh and creative approaches to mission and in many instances this mission is accompanied by a practical commitment to marginalized people in society.[7] However, too often the primary drivers or motivations for this resurgence of mission relate to the need for growth, especially numerical growth (in terms of church and denominational membership) and related financial growth.

The serious nature of this decline, and the responses to it, raise critical issues for the church's mission and its involvement in the social and geographic margins. On the one hand, if its presence in the community is characterized by an underlying anxiety, it will be less attentive to the gentle presence and work of the Spirit of God especially among the most vulnerable and marginalized. On the other hand, if the church's presence is predicated on growth, whether growth in the numbers attending its food banks and social projects or growth in its congregations, it is likely to embody practices that continue to disadvantage and exclude the most vulnerable. While we do not suggest that growth of itself should not be welcomed or encouraged, we do want to draw attention to the way in which a growth agenda can unwittingly embody assumptions about success that reinforce the barriers between the 'haves' and 'have-nots'. Without a thoughtful and self-reflective consideration of this issue, we are as a Christian community in danger of becoming complicit, through our mission, with the very forces in society which privilege the powerful and disadvantage the vulnerable. It would be ironic indeed if, in its own vulnerability, the Christian community found itself to be less empathetic with and compassionate towards the vulnerable in our society. It would be tragic if, in a period of growing disparity between the rich and poor, powerful and vulnerable, the church found that the methods of its mission reinforced such division rather than being a prophetic and reconciling presence.

Our response to these risks is to advocate a far more contextual approach to mission. In this introduction we map out the development of *ideas and concepts* in the theology of mission over the last thirty years and critically assess the trajectory of this development in terms of its relevance to social scientific concepts relating to power, exclusion and marginalization. We then evaluate how the *practice* of mission has been able to engage with excluded others in marginalized places.

Theologies of Mission: Some Key Ideas

The complex and multifaceted story of world mission over the past century has involved a series of radical shifts which have been instrumental in the development of contemporary contextual approaches. One of the most important of these shifts could be conceived of in broad terms as a movement away from the idea of mission as 'expansion' or 'taking territory' and towards a new appreciation of mission as 'encounter' and more specifically as relational, open-hearted encounter with the 'other' whether they be neighbours, strangers or enemies. In this way, the modus operandi of mission undergoes a radical challenge: previous ideas of encounter have emphasized the *needs* of the individual being encountered, but this shift suggests a re-configuration of mission as a mutual relational embrace devoid of preconceptions about who is powerful and who is not, or of who needs what.

This radical change of approach has occurred as world mission, from the 1950s onwards, sought to adapt to a post-colonial era and grapple with the legacy of the slave trade and colonial subjugation in which it was so deeply implicated.[8] In particular, the post-colonial context gave rise to searching and painful questions[9] about the assumed correlation between western culture and the gospel, and the extent to which the patterns and practices of mission were complicit with the colonizing interests of western nations to 'civilize' so-called 'natives and pagans' in foreign territories, often transposing or imposing western cultural hegemony as an integral aspect of the mission effort.[10]

To describe the movement away from these attitudes of expansion towards thinking in terms of encounter or engagement as a 'paradigm shift' is not however to imply that it has been a clearly defined or cleanly executed step that has seen the issues resolved and mission entering some kind of new and untroubled era. Rather it describes a general trend which is theologically and practically complex and which includes contrasting, even conflicting, ideas about how mission should be conceived and practised. Indeed, the continuing process of transition from expansion to engagement still defines many of the core issues that inform the shape of Christian mission today.

Engagement is not only relevant in attempts to revise or reverse the legacies of the colonial era within mission, but is also a critical praxis that grounds one of the central themes of the Christian gospel: namely that a person's relationship to their 'neighbour' is not to be one of subjugation – colonial or otherwise – but one of 'love'; that we 'love our neighbour as ourselves' (see Luke 10:27). Furthermore, the kind of engagement with our neighbour to which Jesus calls us in this parable is to be both outwardly with the places and communities around us (the socio-spatial arrangements of society) and also inwardly to search the deep inclinations of our own hearts, recognizing that (if we are really honest) the colonializing tendency is not only 'out there' but also 'in here'. The drives which relentlessly, persistently and powerfully move us towards the domination of our neighbour rather than an open-hearted vulnerable love are both corporate and individual. They are to do with the shared workings of society and the condition of our own selves, meaning that the radical call of Jesus to love and embrace relates not only to corporate social arrangements of past or present, but also to the condition of the heart.

The struggle to engage with these deep-rooted issues is expressed in the ideas that characterize a number of important movements within mission and theology and we outline some key moments here as a crucial context for the development of new conceptual bases for mission in the contemporary context.

Contextualization

The idea of context is one in which theology can learn much from socio-scientific thought about places and about how they interact with the lives of people that dwell in or visit them.[11] According to Jon Agnew[12] a place is typically considered to be either a location (a specific point in space) or a locale (a built and social space that provides a context for social relations). However, two further strands of meaning about places are of crucial significance. First, places are not just assemblages of physical and social stuff which are basically shaped by the society that lives within them. Rather they have the capacity to shape that society as well; in other words place co-constitutes society.

Second, part of the capacity of place to shape people and events is to be found in the evocation of a 'sense of place' – that is how places affect subjective feelings about themselves, leading to emotional sensitivities about feeling in place or out of place. Place, then, can be a complex arena in which inclusion / exclusion, and marginalization / acceptance are negotiated and played out in different sets of social, cultural and spiritual relations. It follows that places are crucial to the idea of context, representing the receptacles of myriad systems of contingent meaning, and therefore that mission needs to take very special notice of the places in which it is operating.

Having first appeared in the late 1950s as part of a wide-ranging discussion around growing post-colonial consciousness surrounding issues of 'difference', the concept of contextualization has since become an essential and integral discipline within theology and mission studies.[13] The importance of contextualization began to be expressed especially with reference to the manner in which difference is defined by the emerging 'first world' and 'third world' or 'majority world' settings – and the particular way that the gospel might be translated between these profoundly different situations or 'contexts'.[14] Within theology and mission studies the idea of context itself has been broadly understood in terms of 'culture', where culture refers to diverse social, political and economic environments and linguistic characteristics of a region or people group.[15] While these developments have been of critical importance for mission, they have almost completely overlooked an explicit attention to the theme of 'place' and the growing body of work within the social sciences that defines an integral relationship between culture, place and power. In fact the subject of place has been largely ignored within theology as a whole and it is this disparity between the development of place within the social sciences and theology that provides the grounds for a constructively critical voice that theologians and those involved in mission need to consider.[16] This is a theme that will run throughout the series of books and will be introduced in more depth in Chapter 1.

A critical development in relation to contextualization has been the movement towards the reading of the biblical text from particular contexts; most significantly from the context of the post-colonial or marginalized 'other'.[17] Perhaps the greatest contribution in this sense has come from South American liberation theology: 'there is no exaggeration . . . in saying . . . that one of the most outstanding features of both liberation (mostly Roman Catholic) theology and integral mission (evangelical) theology in Latin America has been a theological methodology that views the interpretation of the text as inseparable from the context of the interpreter.'[18] It is undeniable however that while this has been a significant development, readings from a non-western or 'black world' context (that is to say, the majority world context) are still very seriously under-represented within mainstream western theology and mission studies. In arguing, as we do here, for a contextualized theology of place, we are acutely aware that work remains to be done to rectify the existing lacuna of understanding mission from non-mainstream ethno-cultural perspectives.

Indeed the focus on cultural context continues to be important in the development of the study and practice of mission, as seen for example in the *Gospel in Our Culture Network* and the associated *Allelon Missional Series* which has been particularly influential in North America.[19] These series reflect significant developments in relation to contextualization away from a Global North / Global South paradigm and towards a focus on globalization as the 'new context for mission'. Globalization is fundamentally changing the context in which Christian mission connects – the astonishing increase and speed of mobility and interconnectedness (especially of urban centres) is transforming almost every aspect of life, including the experience of life in a local place or local community. Globalization is often assumed to produce standardization across different places – processes encapsulated in buzz phrases such as 'McDonaldization' or 'Disney-ization'[20] – leading to an expectation that the outworking of globalization will result in the erosion and even destruction of long-standing local 'neighbourhoods' (arrangements of place) that enable human flourishing.[21] While there is still significant lack of theological consideration of place itself, critical evaluation of this kind of expectation has evoked within mission studies a new and growing awareness of place, in particular the kinds of places that enable human flourishing, central to which is the ability to know the neighbour. In the light of these developments mission can be conceived of as participation in the recovery or development of places which are humanizing, through the fostering of interdependent community relationships within an identifiable geographical location whose scale is defined in terms of walkable distances. Such places are defined variously as a 'neighbourhood'[22] or 'new parish'[23] in an approach used by John Inge to promote insightful analysis of 'a recovery of the dormant virtue of neighbourliness . . . which is vital to a recovery of community-in-place'.[24] This radical shift from colonial to globalized arenas of contextualization seems to be evoking both an instinctive sense of the importance of neighbour (now seen as the person of difference who is in close proximity) and a sense of importance of place – as neighbourhood to be nurtured rather than as 'territory to be conquered'.

Dialogue and Presence

This emphasis on neighbourliness is commensurate with another important aspect of the contextual approach to mission, namely that of dialogue. Although dialogue has been understood in a number of distinct ways[25] the underlying significance is that, while it included witness as integral to the task of mission, it also emphasized relationships of respect between people of difference (especially in relation to other faiths).[26] This conceptualizing of mission as dialogue is of critical importance as a recognition of, and potential response to the forcefulness and violence of mission as framed in the idea of colonial conquest.[27] Dialogue thus presents a reframing of the way in which mission relates to place where now the Christian community comes as a vulnerable guest dependent upon the hospitality of others.[28] Stephen Bevans and Roger Schroeder have conceptualized this approach to mission as 'entering into someone else's garden' so that the Christian's presence is that of a respectful learner, as much the recipient of knowledge as the bearer.[29]

This emphasis on hospitable dialogue has become a highly significant theme in contemporary social science.[30] It rests on achieving
new forms of self–other relation which recognizes the orthodox pri-
macy of the self, and argues that the danger of not acknowledging a
self-centred norm is that we can assume that everyone sees the same
world as we do. In this way, we can impose our 'sameness' onto others.[31] Moreover, even when moving beyond such assumptions, we can
immediately begin to stylize and stereotype the differences of others
in terms of how they deviate from ourselves. The resultant emphasis
has been on how to achieve hospitality between self and other – with
an obvious prerequisite of listening to and learning from others rather
than simply trying to convert them to our way of thinking. These
modes of thinking have been applied, for example, in areas of gender
and ethnicity as well as in research on vulnerable others such as homeless people.[32] Of particular relevance to the specific concerns of this
chapter is recent work on postsecularity,[33] which examines the possibility of partnership or rapprochement across religious and secular
divides. Can the secular other ever be anything more than a potential
convert in Christian mission? Postsecularity indicates an emerging
theo-ethic of dialogue and mutuality. In this context, hospitable dialogue involves the creation of free space where the other can enter
and become a friend instead of an enemy. The purpose here is not
to convert or change people, but to provide them with a space and a
relationship in which change can take place unencumbered by lines
of division.

Thus in mission terms, dialogue involves participation in the practice of humble, open-hearted and attentive presence; fundamentally
it requires 'a two-way exchange of gifts, between missionaries and
the people among whom they work . . . Mission is not just a matter of doing things for people, it is first a matter of being with people, of listening and sharing with them'.[34] In this manner, dialogue
becomes 'an attitude of respect and friendship, which permeates or
should permeate all those activities constituting the evangelizing mission of the church'; it is, in short 'a style of living in relationship
with neighbours'.[35] One of the key guiding principles of contextual

mission, then, is dialogue that not only emphasizes sensitivity and attentiveness towards social, cultural and religious others, but also achieves a two-way interaction between the Christian self and the other, described by Bevans and Schroeder as 'a sense of being open to be evangelized by those who we are evangelizing – a kind of "mission in reverse"'.[36]

This understanding of dialogue points to what (we will argue) is foundational for mission, and engages with some of the most critical issues that need to be considered in contemporary mission. We should stress that such an approach does not exclude or downgrade the importance of witness or of speaking prophetic truth to power. Indeed, this conception of mission as dialogue is itself a critical step, both in theory and practice, towards engaging with issues of power, in that it focuses on the self–other relationship – and the way in which power is configured through such relationships – and it connects the personal, inner-self to the external political and social realm. This relationship between the inner-self and the external world and its implications for engaging with power is surely one of the core themes in Jesus' own preparation for ministry expressed in Matthew 4:1–11 and Luke 4:1–15. Attention to these powerful connections would fundamentally challenge the hierarchies that cause exclusion and marginalization of the other, although such a focus clearly involves a costly spiritual path of humility and vulnerability.[37]

Third Space and Redemptive Places

Despite the advances described in terms of *dialogue* and *presence*, the dialogical engagement between human geography and theology suggests the need for yet further development in the conceptual space of mission. Contextual missiology, such as that presented by Bevans and Schroeder, struggles to make a complete break with the colonial spatial imagination; it still conveys a sense of binary difference between the missionary and his or her sending culture (usually imagined as 'Christian culture') and the foreign recipient or host (usually imagined as a 'non-Christian' culture). Even with the nuanced development of self–other relationship discussed in terms of 'mission as dialogue' this spatial imagination still seems to lurk as an unacknowledged presence in much discussion on mission, as seen for example in Bevans and Schroeder's model of 'coming into another's garden'.

An important development within the social sciences in this respect is that of *Third Space*, a concept developed by the American urban geographer Ed Soja.[38] According to Soja, First Space can be understood as the material urban form of buildings and infrastructure, and Second Space points to a more imagined, representational space in which the meaning of places can be perceived and argued over. Third Space takes these ideas further, combining First and Second Space to create a fully lived space which is simultaneously real and imagined, actual and virtual, individual and collective in its experience and agency. It often refers to the creation of particular spaces which are strategic locations in which new identities, new politics, new economics and new (theological) ethics can be performed, through reclaiming material and symbolic spaces and making them into something new. Indeed, Third Space typically refers to space in which marginalized people seek to redefine and occupy geographies that were made for one (often oppressive) purpose in order to transform them for new emancipatory purposes. As such, Third Space is where social categories are resisted by those they are imposed upon, in order to create spaces on the margin that provide a position from which to build more open and flexible identities in which commonalities may be emphasized and differences tolerated. So, for example, Homi Bhabha[39] develops a critique of race relations, recognizing the oppressive social spaces defined by modernist narratives of colonial, patriarchal and class-based power, and arguing for new narratives and experiences of space that better represent and practise a more 'hybrid identity'. Soja argues that these new narratives and experiences constitute a Third Space in which the previous hegemonic spatial imagination dominated by prejudice, power and control over subaltern people can be transformed into a space of new emancipatory purpose.

Among others, Chris Baker has applied the idea of Third Space to the church, and more specifically to the missional purposefulness of the Christian community which he sees as having a spatial imagination that is too often formed around just these colonial, patriarchal and class-based orthodoxies.[40] Mission in marginal places can, he argues, be given fresh Third Space perspective by finding alternatives to constructions of 'centre' and 'margins' so as to open up newly imagined places in which relationships are convened in such a way that there is no shadow or residue of the previously dominant colonial hierarchies. This is an alluringly simple idea, but one that has proved rather difficult to put into practice. To achieve the open and even relations suggested by Third Space requires a commitment to the practice of theologies of 'embrace', as presented by Miroslav Volf.[41] Against the background of war and 'ethnic cleansing' in the Balkans, Volf explores how the cross enables the meeting and reconciliation of sworn enemies divided by ethnic hatred:

> At the heart of the cross is Christ's stand of not letting the other remain an enemy and of creating space in himself for the offender to come in . . . The goal of the cross is the dwelling of human beings 'in the Spirit,' 'in Christ,' and 'in God.' Forgiveness is therefore not the culmination of Christ's relation to the offending other; it is a passage leading to embrace. The arms of the crucified are open – a sign of space in God's self and an invitation for the enemy to come in.[42]

In this way, the event of the cross, which Volf describes in terms of the relational event of embrace by the Trinity of the enemy–other, defines a new spatiality within the Godhead, a spatiality that specifically opens up a relational proximity to the 'other' who was previously defined by social and spatial 'exclusion'. This *redemptive spatiality* is the antithesis of exclusionary binary constructions of 'in-place' / 'out-of-place' which define difference and enmity. It refuses such a definition as the ultimate arrangement of place, and brings into play a new and ultimate spatiality, that of embrace. The redemptive spatiality of the cross, described here in terms of embrace, invites participation by all, the

Christian community and others alike, in the formation of radical new embodiments of place where people of difference, even those separated by ethnic hatred, might come together in reconciled relationships. We will refer to such grounded and earthed embodiments as redemptive places.

Third Space thinking has not yet been extensively explored within theology[43] nor applied in detail to ideas of mission.[44] However, from a theological perspective we suggest that it is helpful to understand the spatiality of the kingdom and of the new creation as a kind of Third Space or redemptive place, and that so doing opens up new ways of understanding the relationship of the gospel to contemporary marginal places and marginalized communities. It also fires the imagination with a creative range of possibilities by which Christian communities might engage prophetically and hopefully in society. This book, along with the rest of the book series, will explore how mission might be re-imagined in terms of Third Space thinking, moving decisively beyond binary construction of centre-margins, to the formation of new prophetic and hopeful redemptive places.

Mission in Urban Settings: A Changing Focus on Place

Urban theology, which was developed as a particular form of contextual theology from the 1970s onwards,[45] has shown a consistent concern for the poor and a particular engagement with various aspects of place.[46] The spatial characteristics that developed through the early stages of British urban theology were influenced in part by the coming together of two distinctive elements, namely a strong association with the core ideas of South American liberation theology,[47] and a deep engagement with places associated with the social, cultural and material aspects of the urban geography of the inner city.[48] Important ideas drawn from liberation theology included understandings that God has a 'bias to the oppressed', that the church is called to a 'preferential option for the poor' and that the experience of the oppressed is the primary point of departure for theology.[49] Inherent within these ideas was the notion that poverty should be conceived of, not solely as an ontological state, but as a function of hegemonic arrangements based on hierarchical structures of race and class. These social structures are seen as closely interconnected with spatial structures, such that poverty was assumed to be not only related to social, economic and political marginalization, but also critically to geographic marginalization. Consequently there was an association, or more accurately an 'expression of solidarity', between a set of theological ideals, the people who espoused them and certain types of physical location.

In terms of British urban theology during the 1970s and 1980s, such links or associations became focused around the socio-political location of the inner city.[50] In this way, theological ideas and practices became related to specific places and the people who lived in them. Through this arrangement the idea of the 'inner city' took on a new significance;[51] not only did it represent the locus of urban deprivation but it also became the symbolic centre for both theological and political ideals. Indeed a number of specific places assumed an almost iconic status within urban theology in that their cultural and spatial representations, such as tower blocks and estates, urban street art and music, became strongly associated with certain developments within urban theology itself and with the people who advocated them[52] – all of which conveyed meanings about material deprivation, social exclusion and structural injustice.[53]

This intrinsic sense of place within urban theology was an essential element – perhaps *the* essential element – which enabled it to develop such a distinctive theological voice and radically transformative approach to mission.[54] It shaped the practice of 'doing theology' from local places: namely those places associated with urban deprivation.[55] Kenneth Leech, for example, speaks of doing theology in response to the East End of London and says that 'theology must be localized, concretized, rooted in particular communities'.[56] Likewise Margaret Walsh gives theological voice to the communities living on urban estates.[57] The inherent sense of place which developed as an essential essence of urban theology was, at least in part, the basis upon which it went on to present a serious (and prophetic) challenge to

ecclesiological and political authorities – a challenge which is epito-
mized in the 1985 Church of England report *Faith in the City*.[58] The
report was a response to a period of urban unrest and social disorder
that has been focused by news media on inner cities and peripheral
social housing estates, and it presented a carefully assembled account
of the economic, social and infrastructural conditions existing in
these marginal spaces of the city. As a result it issued a challenge to the
church about its place and responsibilities in these marginal places,
and its duty to engage in forms of public theology so as to participate
in debates about key issues such as unemployment, housing and social
welfare. Its message was that the church, and the government, should
have faith in the city, both in terms of a continuing engagement with
these spaces, and a stronger faith-based role in meeting the needs of
the people living within them. Thinly veiled behind that message was
a critical challenge from urban theology to the institutional church,
questioning whether orthodox forms of theology risked being 'ideological expressions of the interests of the ruling class'.[59]

Despite the emergence of British urban theology as a distinctive
voice from the British inner cities of the 1970s and 1980s, it would
be misleading to suggest that it represented an organized or coherent
movement. The sense of coming together that did exist came in part
through the shared struggle of Christian groups in cities where certain areas were experiencing a climate of political and social turmoil.
However there was little evidence of integration with other Christian
voices which were rising throughout this period from groups who occupied the same urban places and were facing fundamental challenges
around issues of identity and belonging. An important example was
that of the black communities and the emerging black theologies that
were developing as a movement with its own distinctive voice.[60]

This diverse strand of missiology culminating in *Faith in the City*
bore little relation to the debates about contextual missiology discussed earlier in this chapter. Instead, it presented its own analysis of
poverty and marginalization making particularly strong associations
between deprivation and the social, political and spiritual representation of the 'inner city' imaged through high-rise estates, immigration

and black oppression, white 'underclass' and police no-go zones. As such, the missiology spawned by *Faith in the City* also had its own sense of spatiality, based on the highly mediated and politically problematized urban arrangements of the 1970s and early 1980s. It can be argued, therefore, that subsequent urban mission in Britain became rather rigidly framed around the deeply rooted notion of the problematic inner city.

Meanwhile cities have moved on. Initially, changes were associated with the regeneration of inner cities under the government of Margaret Thatcher, so that the actual territory upon which the 'inner-city' identity was dependent began to be redeveloped and fragmented.[61] This loss of territory undermined the theological and ideological foundations of British urban theology so that through the 1990s and the turn of the century it lost some of its potency and ability to critically and prophetically engage with the city.[62] Over recent decades, globalization and its attendant neoliberal politics have inexorably re-formed urban problematics.[63] Over time, new global roles for cities have been accompanied by persistent policies of deregulation and privatization as governments shed many of their previous duties and responsibilities. In particular, policies of welfare austerity are having dramatic impacts on the poorest groups in cities. The city has become a postmodern lifestyle playground for those benefitting from these globalizing tendencies, but a postindustrial wasteland for those who lose out.[64] And while the spaces of inner cities and social housing estates continue to be significant parts of this picture, the tendrils of social and economic marginalization – austerity welfare, the working poor, indebtedness, food poverty, loneliness, detachment, hopelessness, banishment from mainstream political and ethical concerns, lack of trust, lack of common purpose, social vulnerability, detachment from community, and so on – have spread out into far more complex and splintered spatialities across the city.[65] British urban theology has been slow to respond to these changes; generally speaking it has not adapted to the developments, and the challenge of any contemporary study of mission in relation to marginalization will be to account for the ways in which the complex and ever-changing patterns of urban life are affecting the way in which marginalization is configured and experienced. In many ways, urban theology has been overtaken by events, and stands bereft of a clear and critical analytical framework with which to understand and respond to the changing geographical and ideological landscape of the city.[66] The new spatial configurations of the city need to be understood in terms both of the increasingly hybrid nature of social strength and vulnerability in particular places, and of the crucial significance of mobility and on-line virtual networks in transcending traditional place-relations. As a consequence, physical distance within and between cities has been significantly reduced and the traditional association of social identity to location has been heavily fractured.[67]

The task of reorientating urban theology to these new understandings of place and space in the city is an important one, and there are encouraging signs of an emerging stream of discussion that takes contemporary urban places seriously.[68] Particularly significant contributions have been made by Chris Baker in *The Hybrid Church in the City*; Elaine Graham and Stephen Lowe in *What Makes a Good City?*;[69] Andrew Davey in *Urbanisms of Hope*[70] and most recently by Philip Sheldrake in *The Spiritual City*.[71] By presenting the themes of 'hybrid places',[72] 'liveable places'[73] and 'sacred spaces',[74] these texts take important steps in bringing alternative spatial concepts into a dialogue with previously described notions of place that have tended to predominate in mission studies, and they develop a critical challenge to models of place that are too static, rooted and bounded.[75]

Another significant move in this direction within urban theology has been its engagement with and representation of marginal voices. The emergence of a focus on marginalized voices signifies a change in, or at least a challenge to, the hegemonic arrangement of place. It also signifies the potential for new formations of place to come into existence as new co-constituted knowledge emerges from dialogical engagement between people who have been previously kept apart by hierarchical socio-spatial arrangements. This kind of dialogical engagement is suggested by Margaret Walsh who, reflecting on her work in inner-city Wolverhampton, describes 'an ecclesiology of listening and solidarity' where the task of the Christian community was to 'hear what people are saying, to see reality through their eyes and to make our response with them in the light of the gospel'.[76] However, much remains to be done to reorientate theologies of mission towards relevant frameworks of place, space and theology, and this book seeks to make a contribution to this ongoing process.

The Approach of This Book

The preceding discussion has examined a series of key signifiers of discontent with current mission orthodoxies, which in turn point to new strands of attentive hopefulness that are vested in fresh approaches to more grounded, or earthed, practices of mission. In summary, these signifiers include:

- an increasingly significant phenomenology of need in among the austerity politics of contemporary welfare provision, prompting a desire among faith-motivated people to engage in ethical and political action in these landscapes of welfare, care and justice;
- a dissatisfaction with institutionalized church priorities that tend to be inward-looking and a desire for more creative and outward-facing strategies of serving and caring for others;
- a questioning about the effectiveness of evangelistic practices that emphasize conversion to achieve deep personal and social transformation, and a concomitant embrace of reflexive theological practices that enable the living God to be encountered in praxis, especially among people in occupying social margins; and
- an openness to new forms of living and working that enable more attention to incarnational positioning and intentional community.

These contextual drivers point to new understandings of mission that draw on social geography as well as theology and missiology.

From social geography is drawn an understanding of how knowledge and discernment are situated and positioned in particular places and communities. We therefore need to understand more deeply what places are, how they function, what is in-place or out-of-place, how different place identities emerge and how these place-identities cohabit. Alongside these *material* phenomena, it is also important to grasp the *spiritual* landscapes of place where often unseen interiorities help shape the visible exterior conditions. From theology, we draw on ideas about incarnation – what it is to inhabit or dwell in places in a Jesus-centred manner. This will involve, among other virtues, different practices of radical hospitality, deeper forms of relationship, connections across different identity groups, and intentional engagement in community-building. Accordingly, mission will eschew both a tendency to change things for the sake of change, and the implementation of preformed solutions. Instead it will require an attentiveness to the multidimensional complexity of place, and a living that is both vulnerable and expectant in order to hold a watchful and creative presence that seeks encounters with God in place, and discernment of what Jesus is already doing in place.

In this first book of the *Mission in Marginal Places* series, we attend to some of the key formative ideas that we believe will underpin an alternative approach to mission. Our aim here is to outline what we believe to be important themes arising from theological principle and social scientific theory which in tandem can suggest provocative and relevant frameworks and foundations for the practice of mission. As such, we are not seeking to present dry or irrelevant 'theory'; on the contrary, we believe that mission will only come alive and be fully relevant if it inhabits the hybrid spaces and places of contemporary social marginalization with the peaceful and incarnational embrace of Jesus-centred narrative and practice. The 'theory', then, is very deliberately designed to open out new ideas about 'practice' – ideas which begin to come into view in this volume but that are explored in more depth in the second and third books in the series.

Notes

[1] See N. Brewer, J. Browne and R. Joyce, *Child and Working-Age Poverty from 2010-2020* (London: Institute for Fiscal Studies, 2014).

[2] M. O'Hara, *Austerity Bites* (Bristol: Policy Press, 2014).

[3] See for example: Paul Cloke, Justin Beaumont and Andrew Williams, *Working Faith* (Milton Keynes: Paternoster, 2013); Juliet Kilpin, ed., *Urban to the Core* (Leicester: Matador, 2013); Leeds Poverty and Truth Commission https://leedspovertytruth.wordpress.com/ (accessed 15 Sept. 2015).

[4] C. Philo, 'Social Exclusion', in *The Dictionary of Human Geography* (ed. R. Johnston, D. Gregory, G. Pratt and M. Watts; Oxford: Blackwell, 2000), pp. 751–2.

[5] J. May, 'Exclusion', in *Introducing Human Geographies* (ed. P. Cloke, P. Crang and M. Goodwin; London: Routledge, 2014), pp. 655–68.

[6] See for example, G. Davie, *Religion in Britain: A Persistent Paradox* (Chichester: Wiley-Blackwell, 2015); L. Woodhead and R. Catto, eds, *Religion and Change in Modern Britain* (London: Routledge, 2012); Stuart Murray Williams, *Church After Christendom* (London: Authentic, 2005).

[7] Michael Moynagh, *Church for Every Context: An Introduction to Theology and Practice* (London: SCM, 2012), pp. 51–96.

[8] Stephen B. Bevans and Roger P. Schroeder, *Constants in Context: A Theology of Mission for Today* (New York: Orbis, 2004), pp. 214–18; Vincent J. Donovan, *Christianity Rediscovered* (London: SCM, 3rd edn, 2001), pp. vii–xvi, 145; David J. Bosch, *Transforming Mission: Paradigm Shifts in Theology of Mission* (Maryknoll, NY: Orbis, 1991), p. 518; Ronald K. Orchard, *Missions in a Time of Testing: Thought and Practice in Contemporary Missions* (London: Lutterworth Press, 1964); James A. Scherer, *Missionary, Go Home!* (Englewood Cliffs, NJ: Prentice-Hall, 1964); Ralph Edward Dodge, *The Unpopular Missionary* (Westwood, NJ: F.H. Revell, 1964).

[9] Stephen Pickard, 'Introducing Postcolonial Articles: Church of the In-Between God: Recovering an Ecclesial Sense of Place Down-Under', *Journal of Anglican Studies* 7, no. 1 (May 2009): pp. 35–54; Myra Rivera Rivera, 'Margins and the Changing Spatiality of Power: Preliminary Notes', in *Still at the Margins: Biblical Scholarship Fifteen Years After the Voices from the Margin* (ed. R.S. Sugirtharajah; London and New York: T&T Clark, 2008), pp. 114–127.

[10] Stephen B. Bevans and Roger P. Schroeder, *Prophetic Dialogue: Reflections on Christian Mission Today* (New York: Orbis, 2011), pp. 19–22; Abbe Jean Yves, 'Mission: From Expansion to Encounter', USCMA Periodic Paper 1 (Spring 2005); Mary Eastham, 'Dreaming the Land: Practical Theologies of Resistance and Hope in New Zealand: What Are the Issues?' *Australian eJournal of Theology* 5 (August 2005): pp. 1–9.

[11] For comprehensive discussion of the geography of place see T. Cresswell, *In Place / Out of Place* (Minneapolis, MN: University of Minnesota Press, 1996); T. Cresswell, *Place: A Short Introduction* (Oxford: Blackwell, 2004). For an exploration of 'spiritual landscapes' see J.-D. Dewsbury and P. Cloke, 'Spiritual Landscapes: Existence, Performance, Immanence', *Social and Cultural Geographies* 10 (2009): pp. 695–711.

[12] J. Agnew, 'Space: Place', in *Spaces of Geographical Thought: Deconstructing Human Geography's Binaries* (ed. P. Cloke and R. Johnston; London: Sage, 2005), pp. 81–97.

[13] C. René Padilla, 'Global Partnership and Integral Mission', in *Mission in Context* (ed. John Corrie and Cathy Ross; Farnham: Ashgate, 2012), p. 47; Andrew Kirk, *What Is Mission: Theological Explorations* (London: Longman, 1999), p. 91; David J. Hesselgrave and Edward Rommen, *Contextualization: Meanings, Methods and Models* (Grand Rapids, MI: Baker, 2nd edn, 2000), pp. 28, 33–5, 131–7; Bosch, *Transforming Mission*, pp. 420–32; Donovan, *Christianity Rediscovered*, pp. 1–150; William R. Jenkinson and Helene O'Sullivan, *Trends in Mission: Toward the Third Millennium: Essays in Celebration of Twenty-Five Years of SEDOS* (Michigan: Orbis, 1991), pp. 3–85; Stephen Spencer, *Christian Mission* (London: SCM, 2007), pp. 171–5; Stan Guthrie, *Missions in the Third Millennium* (Carlisle: Paternoster, 2000), pp. 101–10; C. René Padilla, *Mission between the Times: Essays on the Kingdom* (Carlisle: Langham, 2010), pp. 103–27; Robert J. Schreiter, 'Contextualization from a World Perspective', in *Ministry and Theology in Global Perspective: Contemporary Challenges for the Church* (ed. Don A. Pittman, Ruben L.F. Habito and Terry C. Muck; Grand Rapids, MI, and Cambridge, UK: Eerdmans, 1996), pp. 315–27; Moynagh, *Church*, pp. 3–50, 168–325; Bevans and Schroeder, *Constants*, pp. 32–72; Bevans and Schroeder, *Prophetic Dialogue* (New York: Orbis, 2011), p. 22; Michael Nazir-Ali, *Mission and Dialogue: Proclaiming the Gospel Afresh in Every Age* (London: SPCK, 1995), pp. 1–152.

[14] Hesselgrave and Rommen, *Contextualization*, pp. 33–196; Padilla, *Mission*, pp. 103–4.

[15] David Hesselgrave, *Communicating Christ Cross-Culturally: An Introduction to Missionary Communication* (Grand Rapids, MI: Zondervan, 2nd

edn, 1991), pp. 95–192; Sherwood Lingenfelter, *Transforming Culture: A Challenge for Christian Mission* (Grand Rapids, MI: Baker, 2nd edn, 1998); Roger E. Hedlund, *The Mission of the Church in the World* (Grand Rapids, MI: Baker, 1991), pp. 226–35; Guthrie, *Missions*, pp. 157–66; Wilbert R. Shenk, 'Messianic Mission and the World', in *The Transfiguration of Mission: Biblical, Theological and Historical Foundations* (ed. Wilbert R. Shenk; Waterloo, Ont: Herald, 1993), pp. 153–77; Kirk, *What Is Mission*, pp. 75–95; Darrell L. Guder, *Missional Church: A Vision for the Sending of the Church in North America* (Cambridge: Eerdmans, 1998), pp. 18–45, 151; Moynagh, *Church*, pp. 151–80.

[16] See Chapter 1 for further discussion on the subject of 'place' within theology.

[17] Rasiah S. Sugirtharajah, ed., *Voices from the Margin: Interpreting the Bible in the Third World* (New York: Orbis, 2006); Rasiah S. Sugirtharajah, ed., *Still at the Margins: Biblical Scholarship Fifteen Years After Voices from the Margins* (London and New York: T&T Clark, 2008); Catherine Keller, Michael Nausner and Mayra Rivera, *Postcolonial Theologies: Divinity and Empire* (St Louis: Chalice Press, 2004); Anthony Reddie, *Black Theology* (London: SCM, 2012).

[18] Padilla, 'Global Partnership', p. 48.

[19] Alan J. Roxburgh, *Missional: Joining God in the Neighborhood* (Grand Rapids, MI: Baker, 2011), pp. 38, 51–2.

[20] A. Bryman, *The Disneyization of Society* (London: Sage, 2004); G. Ritzer, *The McDonaldization of Society* (London: Sage, 2007).

[21] Paul Sparks, Tim Soerens and Dwight J. Friesen, *The New Parish: How Neighbourhood Churches Are Transforming Mission, Discipleship and Community* (Downers Grove, IL: InterVarsity Press, 2014), pp. 21–34; C. Christopher Smith and John Pattison, *Slow Church: Cultivating Community in the Patient Way of Jesus* (Downers Grove, IL: InterVarsity Press, 2014), pp. 62–78; Michael Frost and Alan Hirsch, *The Shaping of Things to Come: Innovation and Mission for the 21st-Century Church* (Peabody: Hendrickson, 2003), pp. 148–59; Andrew Davey, 'Globalization as Challenge and Opportunity in Urban Mission', *International Review of Mission* 88, no. 351 (1999): pp. 381–9; Alan Roxburgh, 'Glocal: What is God up to in the Neighborhood?' Glocal Presentations, http://www.glocalchurch.net/ (accessed 21 Jan. 2015); Roxburgh, *Missional*, pp. 167–9; Moynagh, *Church*, pp. 88–94; Andrew Davey, *Urban Christianity and Global Order: Theological Resources for an Urban Future* (London: SPCK, 2001), pp. 88–100.

[22] Smith and Pattison, *Slow Church*, p. 74; Roxburgh, *Missional*, pp.167–9; Eric O. Jacobsen, *The Space Between: A Christian Engagement with the Built Environment* (Grand Rapids, MI: Baker, 2012), pp. 207–77; Roxburgh, *Glocal*.

[23] Sparks et al., *New Parish*, p. 23; Leonard Hjalmarson, *Introduction to a Missional Spirituality* (Charleston, SC: CreateSpace, 2014), pp. 65–72.

[24] John Inge, *A Christian Theology of Place* (Aldershot: Ashgate, 2003), p. 135.

[25] Bevans and Schroeder, *Prophetic Dialogue*, pp. 21–2.

[26] Bevans and Schroeder, *Constants*, p. 259: dialogue is 'to stand up for one's own truth but not impose it forcefully on the other'. See also J. Andrew Kirk, *Mission Under Scrutiny: Confronting Current Challenges* (London: Darton, Longman & Todd, 2006), pp. 26–45.

[27] Bevans and Schroeder, *Constants*, p. 259.

[28] For a discussion on hospitality and vulnerability see Chapter 6 of this book by Cathy Ross, 'Hospitality: It's Surprising What You Hear When You Listen'. Also see: Roxburgh, *Missional*, p. 146; Christopher L. Heuertz and Christine D. Pohl, *Friendship at the Margins: Discovering Mutuality in Service and Mission* (Downers Grove, IL: InterVarsity Press, 2010); Samuel Wells and Marcia A. Owen, *Living Without Enemies: Being Present in the Midst of Violence* (Downers Grove, IL: InterVarsity Press, 2011); Claude Marie Barbour, 'Seeking Justice and Shalom in the City', *International Review of Mission* 73 (1984): pp. 303–9.

[29] Bevans and Schroeder, *Prophetic Dialogue*, pp. 33–4.

[30] See for example, C. Barnett and D. Land, 'Geographies of Generosity: Beyond the Moral Turn', *Geoforum* 38, (2007): pp. 1065–75; M. Dikec, N. Clark and C. Barnett, 'Extending Hospitality: Giving Space, Taking Time', *Paragraph* 32 (2009): pp. 1–14.

[31] P. Cloke, 'Self-Other', in *Introducing Human Geographies* (ed. P. Cloke, P. Crang and M. Goodwin; London: Routledge, 2014), pp. 63–80.

[32] P. Cloke, S. Johnsen and J. May, *Swept Up Lives?* (Chichester: Wiley-Blackwell, 2010).

[33] See Chapter 7 of this book, and also P. Cloke and J. Beaumont, 'Geographies of Postsecular Rapprochement in the City', *Progress in Human Geography* 37 (2013): pp. 27–51.

[34] Bevans and Schroeder, *Prophetic Dialogue*, p. 20.

[35] Bevans and Schroeder, *Prophetic Dialogue*, pp. 21–2.

[36] Bevans and Schroeder, *Prophetic Dialogue*, p. 22.

[37] These themes are discussed in Chapter 2 (on incarnation), Chapter 6 (on hospitality), Chapter 9 (on cruciformity) and Chapter 10 (on *shalom*).

[38] E. Soja, *Thirdspace* (Oxford: Blackwell, 1996).

[39] H. Bhabha, *The Location of Culture* (London: Routledge, 1994).

[40] Christopher Baker, *The Hybrid Church in the City* (Farnham: Ashgate, 2007).

[41] Miroslav Volf, *Exclusion and Embrace: A Theological Exploratoin of Identity, Otherness, and Reconciliation* (Nashville, TN: Abingdon, 1996).

[42] Volf, *Exclusion*, p. 126.

[43] Baker, *Hybrid Church*; Halvor Moxnes, *Putting Jesus in His Place: A Radical Vision of Household and Kingdom* (Louisville, KY, and London: Westminster John Knox, 2003), pp. 109–24.

[44] Ray Oldenburg, *Celebrating the Third Place: Inspiring Ideas about the 'Great Good Places' at the Heart of Our Communities* (New York: Marlow, 2001).

[45] Chris Shannahan, *Voices from the Borderland: Re-Imagining Cross-Cultural Urban Theology in the Twenty-First Century* (London: Equinox, 2010), p. 5.

[46] Raymond J. Bakke, *A Theology as Big as the City* (Downers Grove, IL: InterVarsity Press, 2009), pp. 60–65; Raymond J. Bakke and Jon Sharpe, *Street Signs: A New Direction in Urban Ministry* (Birmingham, AL: New Hope, 2006), pp. 83–91, 217; John Atherton, *Marginalisation* (London: SCM, 2003), p. 113; Peter Humphrey Sedgwick, ed., *God in the City: Essays and Reflections from the Archbishop's Urban Theology Group* (London: Morehouse, 1995), pp. 119–38; Shannahan, *Voices*, pp. 47, 182–4; Eric O. Jacobsen, *The Space Between: A Christian Engagement with the Built Environment* (Grand Rapids, MI: Baker, 2012), pp. 11–28, 55–78; Eric O. Jacobsen, *Sidewalks in the Kingdom: New Urbanism and the Christian Faith* (Michigan: Brazos, 2003), pp. 75–137; Michael S. Northcott, ed., *Urban Theology: A Reader* (London: Cassell, 1998), pp. 59–78; Elaine Graham and Stephen Lowe, *What Makes a Good City? Public Theology and the Urban Church* (London: Darton, Longman & Todd, 2009), pp. 49–66; Jacques Ellul, *The Meaning of the City* (Vancouver: Eerdmans, 1993); David Sheppard, *Bias to the Poor* (London: Hodder & Stoughton, 1983), pp. 19–36; Andrew Walker and Aaron Kennedy, eds, *Discovering the Spirit in the City* (London: Continuum, 2010), pp. 1–15; Andrew Davey, ed., *Crossover City: Resources for Urban Mission and Transformation* (London and New York: Mowbray, 2010), pp. 24–37; Davey, 'Globalization', pp. 381–9; Andrew P. Davey, 'Better Place: Performing Urbanisms of Hope', *International Journal of Public Theology* 2 (2008): pp. 34–5; Kathryn Tanner, ed., *Spirit in the Cities: Searching for Soul in the Urban Landscape* (Minneapolis: Fortress, 2004), pp. 1–124; Philip Sheldrake, *The Spiritual City: Theology, Spirituality, and the Urban* (Chichester: Wiley-Blackwell, 2014), pp. 99–137; John Vincent, *Starting All Over Again: Hints of Jesus in the City* (Geneva: World Council of Churches, 1981); John Vincent, *Into the City*

(London: Epworth Press, 1982); John Vincent, *Hope from the City* (Peterborough: Epworth Press, 2000).

[47] Shannahan, *Voices*, pp. 100–23; Kari Latvus, 'The Bible in British Urban Theology', in *Reading Other-Wise: Socially Engaged Biblical Scholars Reading from Their Local Communities* (ed. Gerald O. West; Atlanta: SBL, 2007), pp. 133–40. Those influenced by liberation theology included: David Sheppard, *Built as a City: God and the Urban World Today* (London: Hodder & Stoughton, 1974); Sheppard, *Bias to the Poor*; Laurie Green, *Power to the Powerless* (Basingstoke: Marshall Pickering, 1987); Laurie Green, *Let's Do Theology: Resources for Contextual Theology* (London: Mowbray, 2009); Anthony G. Reddie, 'Exploring the Workings of Black Theology in Britain: Issues of Theological Method and Epistemological Construction', *Black Theology: An International Journal* 7, no. 1 (2009): pp. 64–85. Those who drew directly on liberation theology were: John Vincent, the founder and director of the influential Urban Theology Unit in Sheffield and author of numerous books including John Vincent, *Radical Jesus* (London: Marshall Pickering, 1986) and John Vincent, *Liberation Theology from the Inner City*, The George Jackson Lecture (Edinburgh: Edinburgh Methodist Mission, 1989); Sheppard, *Bias to the Poor*, pp. 145–58; Laurie Green, *Power*, p. 10; Kenneth Leech, *The Social God* (London: Sheldon, 1981); Kenneth Leech, *The Sky Is Red: Discerning the Signs of the Times* (London: Darton, Longman & Todd, 2006); Kenneth Leech, *The Eye of the Storm* (London: HarperCollins, 1992).

[48] Shannahan, *Voices*, pp. 8–13.

[49] Shannahan, *Voices*, p. 102.

[50] Christopher Rowland and John Vincent, eds, *Gospel from the City* (Sheffield: Urban Theology Unit, 1997), pp. 1–136; Davey, *Better Place*, p. 34.

[51] Graham and Lowe, *What Makes a Good City?*, p. 51; Shannahan, *Voices*, p.28.

[52] For example, John Vincent is linked with Sheffield, a northern city associated with heavy industry and back-to-back terraced housing; David Sheppard is associated with the working-class estates of Liverpool and also with the Mayflower Centre, Canning Town, in the East End of London (Shannahan, *Voices*, pp. 108–16); Andrew Davey with the multicultural streets and tower blocks of Peckham (Andrew Davey, 'Liberating Theology in Peckham', in *Urban Theology: A Reader* [ed. Michael Northcote; London: Cassell, 1998], pp. 8–10); Kenneth Leech with the multicultural and multi-faith East End (Kenneth Leech, *Youthquake* [London: Sheldon, 1973]); Anthony Reddie is associated the development of black theology with urban areas: Anthony Reddie, 'Exploring', pp. 64–78.

[53] Sheppard, *Bias to the Poor*, pp. 19–37, 58–78; Shannahan, *Voices*, pp. 101–14; Vincent, *Into the City*; Rowland and Vincent, *Gospel*, pp.1–136.

[54] This distinctive voice can be heard, for example, in John Vincent's critique of the suburban hegemony of the church in saying that 'we honour people who rise above their place, rather than those who belong to it and really represent it . . . We listen to voices from the top . . . rather than voices from the bottom' (Vincent, *Into the City*, p. 16). Joe Hasler makes similar observations about the church's approach to marginal white estates and argues that the 'indigenous' voice needs to be heard (Joe Hasler, 'Mind, Body and Estate: Outer Estate Ministry and Working Class Culture', National Estate Churches Network [2000] http://www.joehasler.co.uk/wp-content/uploads/2014/05/1.-Mind-body-estates-Booklet.pdf [accessed 1 Jan. 2015]).

[55] Rowland and Vincent, *Gospel*, pp.1–136; Reddie, *Exploring*, p. 64–6.

[56] Leech, *Sky Is Red*, p. 51. Localized approaches to theology are also seen in Vincent, *Radical Jesus*, pp. 23–5; Sheppard, *Built as a City* and *Bias to the Poor*.

[57] Margaret Walsh, 'Here's Hoping: The Hope Community, Wolverhampton', in *God in the City: Essays and Reflections from the Archbishop of Canterbury's Urban Theological Group* (ed. Peter Sedgwick; London: Mowbray, 1995), pp. 52–71; Margaret Walsh, 'Organising for Action' in *Urban Theology: A Reader* (ed. Michael Northcott; London: Cassell, 1998), pp. 135–7; Hasler, 'Mind, Body and Estate'.

[58] Archbishop's Commission on Urban Priority Areas, *Faith in the City: A Call for Action by Church and Nation* (London: Church House, 1985).

[59] Shannahan, *Voices*, p. 102.

[60] The distinctive black voice was being presented through theologians such as Robert Beckford, *Jesus Is Dread: Black Theology and Black Culture in Britain* (London: Darton, Longman & Todd, 1998); Robert Beckford, *God and the Gangs* (London: Darton, Longman & Todd, 2004); Anthony Reddie, *Growing into Hope: Volume 1* (Peterborough: Methodist Publishing, 1998); Anthony Reddie, *Faith Stories and Experience of Black Elders* (London: Jessica Kingsley, 2001). While the concerns of the black community were articulated by some urban theologians (Sheppard, *Bias to the Poor*, pp. 58–78), the development of black theology should not be confused with British urban theology (as implied by Shannahan, *Voices*, pp. 124–57), and from the perspective of 'place' it is important to acknowledge the distinct spatiality of first- and second-generation migrants in relation, for example, to home, identity and belonging. These are explored by authors such as Anthony Reddie (in *Out of Place: Doing*

Theology on the Crosscultural Brink [ed. Jione Havea and Clive Pearson; London and New York: Routledge, 2011], pp. ix–xi); and Edward Said (Edward W. Said, *Out of Place: A Memoir* [London: Granta, 1999]).

[61] See Doreen Massey, *World City* (Cambridge: Polity, 2007), Andrew Davey, 'Faithful Cities: Locating Everyday Faithfulness', *Contact* 152 (2007): pp. 8–20.

[62] The discussion about British urban theology in Part I is restricted to issues that relate to place. A broader investigation would show that the use of liberation theology within a British urban context was not straightforward. R.S. Sugirtharajah, for example, argues that the 1985 Church of England report, *Faith in the City*, failed to connect to the main discourses of liberation theology; and Andrew Davey observes urban theologians failed to fully understand how conditions of post-colonialism were being produced in European cities through changing spatial configurations such as the 'space of flows' (R.S. Sugirtharajah, *Postcolonial Reconfigurations: An Alternative Way of Reading the Bible and Doing Theology* [London: SCM Press, 2003], pp. 162–75; Davey, *Better Place*, pp. 34–5; *Faith in the City* [1985]).

[63] See, for example, Matthew Sparke, *Introducing Globalization* (Wiley-Blackwell, Chichester, 2013).

[64] Chris Hamnett, 'Urban Form', in *Introducing Human Geographies* (ed. P. Cloke, P. Crang and M. Goodwin; London: Routledge, 2014), pp. 690–705.

[65] See Will Hutton, *How Good We Can Be* (London: Little, Brown, 2015).

[66] Andrew Davey, 'Beyond Intervention and Partnership: Struggling for Space', *Political Theology* 3, no. 1 (2001): pp. 102–8. While Chris Shannahan does not specifically discuss place he does recognize the importance of the movement from 'static definitions of the city as fractured places to the city as fluid and hybrid spaces that are interconnected across the globe' and the challenge that this change in the urban environment brought to British urban theology (Shannahan, *Voices*, pp. 15–30).

[67] Baker, *Hybrid Church*, pp. 27–64; Davey, *Better Place*, pp. 33–46; Tanner, *Spirit*, pp. ix–19; Sheldrake, *Spiritual City*, pp. 115–17. These developments within theories of place and their association with urban studies are explored, for example, in: Massey, *World City*; Doreen Massey, *For Space* (London: Sage, 2005); Edward W. Soja, *Thirdspace: Journeys to Los Angeles and Other Real-and-Imagined-Places* (Malden, MA and Oxford, UK: Blackwell, 1996); Edward J. Soja, *Postmetropolis: Critical Studies of Cities and Regions* (Oxford: Blackwell, 2000); Steve Pile, *City Worlds* (London and New York: Routledge, 1999); Leonie Sandercock,

Cosmopolis II: Mongrel Cities of the 21st Century (London and New York: Continuum, 2003); Tim Hall and Heather Barrett, *Urban Geography* (Abingdon, UK and New York: Routledge, 4th edn, 2012); Henri Lefebvre, *Writings on Cities* (trans. and ed. Eleonre Kofman and Elizabeth Lebas; Oxford: Blackwell, 1996); John Allen, Doreen Massey and Steve Pile, *City Worlds* (London: Routledge, 2005); Loic Wacquant, *Urban Outcasts: A Comparative Sociology of Advanced Marginality* (Cambridge, UK, and Malden, MA: Polity, 2008); Ash Amin and Nigel Thrift, *Cities: Reimagining the Urban* (Cambridge: Polity, 2002).

[68] Although themes associated with place are discussed within texts from the field of urban theology and mission, it is notable that since 2000 only a very small number focus specifically on the subject of place. These include Tim Gorringe, *A Theology of the Built Environment* (Cambridge: Cambridge University Press, 2002); Baker, *Hybrid Church*; Graham and Lowe, *Good*; Davey, *Better*, pp. 33-46; Tanner, *Spirit*.

[69] Baker, *Hybrid*; Graham and Lowe, *What Makes a Good City*, pp. 49–66.

[70] Andrew Davey discusses critical challenges to urban theologians including: the nature of their engagement with the broad field of urban studies; theological engagement with the lived experience of the city; and theological methodologies that can adapt to the rapid changes in the configuration of urban spaces (Davey, *Better Place*, pp. 27–46).

[71] Sheldrake, *Spiritual City*. Other texts that deal with place in the context of cities are: John Atherton, *Marginalisation* (London: SCM, 2003), pp. 113–14; Sedgwick, *God in the City*, pp. 119–38; Shannahan, *Voices*, pp. 47–8, 182–4; Jacobsen, *Sidewalks*; Jacobsen, *Space*; Andrew J. Walker and Aaron Kennedy, *Discovering the Spirit in the City* (London: Continuum, 2010), pp. 1–15; Davey, *Crossover City*, pp. 24–37.

[72] Baker, *Hybrid Church*, pp. 27–46, 111–36.

[73] Graham and Lowe, *What Makes a Good City*, pp. 49–66.

[74] Sheldrake, *Spiritual City*, pp. 115–36.

[75] Baker, *Hybrid Church*, pp. 13–26.

[76] Walsh, 'Here's Hoping', p. 57; Shannahan, *Voices*, p. 106.

Part I

Mission and Marginality: The Word Became Flesh . . .

1

Place and Marginality: The Formation of Redemptive Places

Mike Pears

Introduction

> *Tower Hamlets is smartening up and prices are rock-eting. The local indigenous people are still there – we still have a jellied eel stand – but they're surrounded by shiny glass.*
>
> *People like the edgy feel of east London, the 'real London' feel: rich people living cheek by jowl with poor people. Parts of west London feel so safe and mundane.*
>
> *Most overseas investors are looking for a good yield for renting, or buying apartments for their children. We have wealthy Chinese or Asian families who will put one of their kids in an apartment this size.*
>
> *The Guardian*, June 2015

This comment was recently posted in a national paper by a London-based development company advertising a penthouse suite for sale at £4.25 million. The short statement is loaded with references which ascribe meanings to places both implicitly and explicitly:

a '"real London" feel' has a sense of edginess because the 'poor', 'indigenous' people are 'still' there! It seems that the proximity of the 'poor' is a selling point implying that their presence lends vibrancy and a sense of excitement, or even danger perhaps, to the place. This is apparently in contrast to the 'so safe and mundane' feel of west London. To live in close proximity to the indigenous poor does however come at a price – in this case over £4 million for an apartment. Importantly in this instance, the poor pose no threat to the comfort of the prospective resident as they are surrounded by 'shiny glass' much like, it seems, exotic animals in a zoo, to be observed at leisure while at the same time being kept at a safe distance, so safe in fact that such an apartment would be a desirable residence for Chinese or Asian 'kids'.

I recently had some time to spare in the East End and, carrying this advert in my back pocket, took the opportunity to take a slow wander around Shadwell and the Docklands development, spending time as I went to observe the everyday life of the streets and to be attentive to the 'sense of place'. One striking feature was the appearance of order and the feeling conveyed of a place that is cleansed, even sanitized. In contrast to the unruly sense of place experienced prior to the Docklands development, it seems now that everything is ascribed its proper place: cyclists, cars, pedestrians and trains all tightly regulated and controlled; the boundaries of old council block estates clearly demarcated with signage, fences and security doors; lively local markets, springing seemingly from nowhere, but arranged in a compact section of street underneath the Docklands Light Railway; 'shiny' new apartment blocks secured by high walls and electric gates; and all being watched by multiple surveillance cameras.

These two brief forays into a particular urban space – through the commercial representation in a newspaper advert and an immersive experience of 'hanging out' – illustrate the dynamic and complex nature of places. For example, our attention might be caught by the way the often espoused logic that the 'trickle-down effect' will soften economic and social boundaries seems at odds with the geography of extreme inequality with its juxtaposition of the super-rich and 'indigenous poor'. Doreen Massey identifies the paradox of these apparently contradictory positions coexisting in such a way that the prevailing narrative of wealth production eventually benefitting all seems unaffected by the proximity of extreme inequality. The embodiment of apparently contradictory narratives can be understood in terms of the way that place itself functions and is produced; it illustrates the complex and contested nature of place. Thus in the case of London and the Docklands development in particular, Massey argues that the specific concentration of inequality is a function of place – not in the generalized sense that these patterns of extreme inequality will inevitably be reproduced in a global city, but in a particular sense which accounts for the specificity of London itself where neoliberal capitalism is embedded in a long-established social democratic settlement.[1]

Furthermore, social scientific studies suggest that the growth of inequality is not merely incidental but is 'inscribed in the global city'.[2] From this perspective the proximity of rich and poor in the East End is not simply happenstance but is integral to the production of gentrifying urban spaces. Urban theorists such as Chris Hamnett argue that the process of gentrification itself, which describes the regeneration of a largely derelict postindustrial area, is an active displacement of the poor to other less desirable parts of the city.[3] The forceful, even revengeful, nature of gentrification is also emphasized by Neil Smith in *The New Urban Frontier*. He argues that an 'emerging revanchist urbanism . . . embodies a revengeful and reactionary viciousness against various populations accused of "stealing" the city from the white upper classes' so that gentrification is increasingly emerging as 'an effort to retake the city'.[4]

While 'revenge' may not be the dominant motivation driving development in the East End the process of regeneration and gentrification can certainly be understood as forceful. It is difficult to see the close proximity of the 'greedy and the needy' as anything but a landscape of power and in this context the penthouse advertisement plays to vested interests evoking one particular representation of the place which appeals to the super-rich by projecting a particular image of 'urban living'. It does not, for example, give voice to the sellers of jellied eels, or indeed to the army of low-paid cleaners, nannies, café staff, street cleaners and other workers who are needed to service the city's well-ordered infrastructure. At one level, the vision of the city portrayed in the advert is simply a sales pitch. At a more fundamental level, it can be understood as a part of a powerful and influential discourse that is actually shaping the physical and cultural environment and contesting and changing the actual meanings that are associated with those places in the public imagination.

Because, by definition, we are always surrounded by and immersed in places, these processes and the characteristics of place that enable them normally go unnoticed and undiscussed. If however we pause to take notice, to be attentive to our surroundings and the discourses they present, some important features of place begin to become apparent. First, what becomes clear, as in the example above, is that place itself should not be conceived of as some kind of passive or benign material realm, like the backdrop to a play against which the real action takes place. Rather place is produced through co-constructing processes between cultures and the physical resulting in cultures of place, cultural and spiritual landscapes as well as physicality. Second, places are found to be invested with multiple, complex and contested meanings so that the actual materiality of the place – the bricks and mortar, the arrangements of streets, shops and parks, the designations of private and public places – all hold and convey meaning of some sort. Third, the physical nature of places, including the built environment, gives the impression that the meaning or order of the place is natural or permanent. It is our tendency to interpret these meanings as the proper or 'right' understanding of a place and to act accordingly.[5] Place-based meanings are therefore strongly influential, even conveying a sense of what is morally or ethically appropriate, and indeed the 'appropriate kinds of people' one would expect to find in a given place. Thus it might be held as common sense that: homeless people are not welcome on a suburban street; 'gangs of youths' are not welcome in the shopping mall; and 'foreign migrants' do not belong in this part of town.

These understandings, which start to become apparent as we slow down and seek to be attentive to the places around us, indicate that place itself is deeply complicit in the shaping of everyday life, its values, behaviours, senses of identity and belonging, and even ethical norms. In this chapter I will seek to explain why place is fundamental to the formation and functioning of social, ideological and spiritual power and will talk about the relationship between place and marginalization (an argument that is critical to this book, and indeed the series) and why place is an active player in sustaining patterns of exclusion and marginalization. While drawing on the social geography of place, the issues will primarily be discussed from a theological perspective and include suggestions about how such a view of place might inform our approach to mission.

Place and Marginalization

We have used the term 'marginalization' in this series because it combines the sense of both geographical and social exclusion and can also be associated with physical poverty and multiple forms of deprivation. It suggests that these aspects very often (though not always) go together so that the 'poor' are also frequently both geographically and socially marginalized.

This chapter focuses particularly on the relationship between place and poverty, drawing on insights from both human geography and theology. In human geography there has, since the 1970s, been a 'cultural turn' so that understandings of place are seen as fundamental to conceptions of identity, otherness, difference and marginalization.[6] Surprisingly, these developments are not in general well referenced in the various disciplines of theology, biblical studies and mission studies; an omission which needs urgently to be redressed, especially if the Christian community is to develop a deeper understanding about how to engage in issues of deprivation and marginalization in humanizing, non-coercive ways.

Place in the Social Sciences

While place is a central idea within human geography, it is not one that has an easy definition. Understandings of place are complex, varied and contested.[7] The advertised luxury East End development could be 'placed' by using the abstract idea of a grid reference, in this instance something close to Latitude 51.516504; Longitude 0.072808564.[8] However it clearly involves more than its location on a map. The place has been circumscribed and named (in this case as Tower Hamlets); it has a material component which includes the built environment with its streets, shops, offices and housing estates; it also has a cultural component which comprises a rich and complex arrangement of social relations and includes the way that people of all backgrounds inhabit the place. Place also has a subjective element or 'sense of place' which is more difficult to articulate. It could be thought of as one's experience of the place which is shaped by the sensations conveyed when one is in the place.[9] A particular sense of place is conjured in the advert as a means of enticing potential buyers away from west London which 'feel[s] so safe and mundane' to the 'edgy' feel of east London. The sense of place does of course change according to time and the personal circumstances of the one who is sensing. A place that feels safe on a Monday morning, may not feel so safe late on Friday night; somewhere that feels secure for an 'insider' (in the advert an 'indigenous' person) may feel threatening or un-settling for an outsider or newcomer. The 'representation' of a place also has a powerful effect on the way that people approach it – either negatively or positively. Areas of countryside might be represented as 'restful retreat', urban areas as 'alive' and 'exciting', Paris as a city of romance, housing estates or high-rise flats as 'dangerous', or traveller sites as 'dirty'.

Identifying these spatial components of location – material, cul-tural, sensory and representative – helps us to see that place itself is multifaceted and complex. It shows that the culture–space relationship is not a one-way relationship where culture shapes physical place, but that the materiality of a place (its buildings, streets, landscapes, etc.)

also plays a role in shaping its cultural and social aspects. This is known as a 'co-constituting' relationship where each shapes the other; 'society produces space and space produces society'.[10] Furthermore these co-constituting interactions are not limited by a nominal boundary circumscribing the place but, as has been seen in the case of gentrification, they are affected by wider national and global connections of all kinds. Using Kilburn High Street as an example Doreen Massey has shown how places not only have local cultures, but are also part of other sets of relations that connect them to national and global cultures, so that the high street is constituted through a complex web of local and global cultures.[11]

While in one sense our familiarity with place suggests to us that its meanings are obvious, common sense and open to all, in fact its complex, contested and unfixed nature makes it more difficult to perceive and more challenging to study. Indeed these very qualities of familiarity and taken-for-grantedness tend to hide powerful mechanisms which have profound effects on just about every aspect of daily life. Edward Soja draws attention to this saying that 'we must be insistently aware of how space can be made to hide consequences from us, how relations of power and discipline are inscribed into the apparently innocent spatiality of social life, how human geographies become filled with politics and ideology'.[12]

An important step in the development of understanding about the way in which physical, social and cultural mechanisms have powerful effects on daily life came about through the work of anthropologist Mary Douglas and in particular through her arguments concerning notions of purity and dirt.[13] In her 1966 publication *Purity and Danger*, she proposed that, even when contemporary ideas of hygiene are accounted for, notions of purity and dirt are still primarily about shared social systems. One of her main ideas was that 'dirt is matter out of place' and this gives rise to a systematic ordering of place where, for example, 'shoes are not dirty in themselves, but it is dirty to place them on a dining-table; food is not dirty in itself, but it is dirty to leave cooking utensils in the bedroom, or food bespattered on clothing'.[14] This idea that 'where there is dirt there is a system' thus gave some insight to the way that spatial mechanisms might function in everyday settings and indicates how they might both include and exclude.[15]

Further important developments about place and culture, especially in relation to otherness, have been made by David Sibley who, in *Geographies of Exclusion*, suggested that the simple questions we should be asking about places are 'who are they for?' and 'who do they exclude?'[16] According to Sibley, the primary social arrangements of place are based on exclusion such that 'others' (defined by issues such as gender, age, ethnicity and sexuality) are placed as outsiders.[17] In this view, places which are normally portrayed as secure and safe, such as the home, are 'for those who do not fit' inherently exclusionary.[18] This is seen for example in the off-hand comment of a black friend that if we convened an event in a certain location his black colleagues would not attend because they wouldn't come to such a 'white' place; or the reflection of Lynsey Hanley whose words echo so many that we have heard from the residents of our own housing estate, that when she tried to find acceptance in the world outside of the estate that she had grown up in, she found a 'wall in her head' that prevented her.[19] Hanley, talking about the strong sense of being 'out of place', says:

> The problem with having a wall in the head is that it makes you look thick to people who don't have one, or whose walls were only knee-high and could be jumped over without much effort. Invisible barriers to knowledge, self-awareness and social mobility seem to irritate those who think they don't exist, to the extent that they will happily describe walled-in people as 'scum' or, in the current argot, 'chav scum'.[20]

A key point here is that such exclusionary effects are all-pervasive yet go largely unnoticed. A self-conscious effort to 'see' is required if they are to be understood more deeply and this includes a reflexive willingness to perceive our own place, including an openness to be surprised about our own involvement in these exclusionary geographies. Sibley's place-related questions 'who are they for?' and 'who do they exclude?' provide a helpful framework for such vigilance.

By considering these basic ideas about geographies of exclusion we can understand the various components of place – described earlier as material, cultural, sensory and representative – as acting together in a certain kind of way so that particular 'meanings, practices, and identities' are mapped onto places and furthermore that these are all assumed to be 'normal'.[21]

While this might sound a rather complex explanation for the everyday places we inhabit, the reality of the way all this works together is nevertheless portrayed through familiar phrases such as 'know your place' or 'she was put in her place' or 'he looked really out of place'. Tim Cresswell discusses the way in which these meanings, practices and identities are worked out in everyday life by considering the setting of an office: 'in business it is not the secretary's place to sit at the boss's desk, or the janitor's place to look through the secretary's desk. There is nothing logical about such observations; neither are they necessarily rules or laws. Rather they are *expectations* about behaviour that relate a position in a social structure to actions in space.'[22]

These briefly presented arguments show that place is fundamental for the ways in which things get categorized, either as in-place or out-of-place, and that categorization makes a strong link between the geography of a place itself and the social standing of the people within it – that is the relative power that various people hold within a place. Furthermore, this association of place with power means that places themselves can be understood in terms of ideology in that they are 'laden with meanings that tend to reinforce relations of dominance and subordination', and therefore they are 'fundamental creators of difference' defining who is an 'insider' and who an 'outsider'.[23] Thus an outsider is not just someone from another location, they are a person who is 'not to be trusted', they are 'someone who is existentially removed from the milieu of "our" place—someone who doesn't know the rules'.[24]

The ideological potential of place is further reinforced because, as I have previously noted, the meanings invested in places tend to go unnoticed and undiscussed during the course of everyday life; place itself appears to establish associated meaning as 'natural' or 'simply the way things are'.[25] In turn, these meanings then get interpreted through the 'actions' or 'performances' of the people within them – that is, all people tend to act in places according to the commonly accepted meaning of the place.

This ideological conformity to the meanings of places through actions or 'performances' is perhaps best seen when people 'transgress' the normal meanings of place, or act outside of the generally agreed norms, or when different groups have conflicting ideas about the meaning of a place. A classic example of this occurred when a group of protesters from the Occupy movement camped in flimsy tents on the steps of St Paul's Cathedral, resisting the combined attempts of state and church to have them removed. What drew attention to them (as many officials pointed out) was 'the contrast between the camps of the protesters as places and the places they were located in', namely that the City of London and the steps of St Paul's Cathedral were not a place for camping![26]

Theological Ideas about Place

If, as I have argued, place is fundamental to understanding social and ideological power, establishing and enforcing distinctions between insider and outsider, how then should we understand place in theological terms and how might we think about the relationship of mission to place?[27]

One approach to this question is to consider the characteristics of place which are portrayed within the gospels and the ways in which the gospel writers present Jesus as acting in these places. What is important is that these places are not simply background against which the story is told but place itself is a necessary 'character' in the narrative; as can be seen in the following two examples.

The first is in the string of six consecutive stories that form the narrative section in Luke 18 – 19. These include five brief cameos of Luke's poor: the widow (18:1–8), the tax collector (18:9–14), children (18:15–17), the blind man (18:35–43) and Zacchaeus (19:1–10). In

Luke, the poor are not simply the financially poor; they are unclean, ungodly, social and religious outsiders – so-called 'sinners'.[28] However their stories portray not only a sense of social exclusion but also of spatial exclusion: a widow excluded from justice; a tax collector who stood 'some distance away'; children whose approach was rebuked; and Zacchaeus, small in stature and at the back of the crowd. As Luke tells their stories, social boundaries and taboos of all kinds are broken so that they find free access to the places they seek. In spatial terms as well as social and religious terms they are brought near. These characters stand in stark contrast to the archetypal good man, the rich young ruler, who is presented in the central part of the narrative (18:18–34). He finds access to Jesus without hindrance, but in contrast to the other five characters is unable to remain there.

The second passage exemplifies the way in which the social space of the home is portrayed. In Mark 3 a picture is presented of three expanding concentric circles of people with different social and religious standing and these are arranged in a parallel pattern within the text itself. There are scribes 'from Jerusalem' who come as his accusers; Jesus' own family who are twice mentioned as standing on the 'outside' (3:31); and the multitudes and disciples sitting 'around' him (3:32,34). In this story the normal ideas of the social space of the home and family are turned upside down as Jesus says about those sitting 'around him', 'Here are my mother and my brothers!' (3:34). The narrative portrays not only a radical inversion of people's identity but also a radical rearrangement of the place itself – the shock is that Jesus has declared the marginalized to be *family* by bringing them into the physical place of the home so that those who were on the 'outside' are now 'around' Jesus himself.[29]

In both these cases Jesus is seen to challenge and, by his presence, upset and interrupt the normal arrangement of things, which means that in these stories people are not confined to their 'proper place' but find a freedom to move into places and relationships that would have been utterly unthinkable. Moreover, not only are people made free from their normal socio-spatial incarcerations but their new experience of place is presented either as an example of the coming kingdom (Luke 18:16) or as the place in which Jesus himself is the central presence.[30] Jesus' presence seems to become the essential feature of the place within the narratives so that the places themselves are reconfigured around him personally; those who are normally confined to the margins, such as Zacchaeus or the crowds, are now found to inhabit the new central place, namely the relational proximity around Jesus.

Our understanding as to what the authors of the gospels are actually trying to convey through their use of spatial characteristics can be further developed if we go on to consider how 'place' was conceived within the first-century world of the gospels themselves. As today, the manner in which places were formed and understood then were multiple and complex but there are two particular categories that shed light on the way that place was represented by the gospel writers.

First is that of *oikoumene*, a word that denotes 'civilized place' or the notion of the inhabited world – 'the extent of land in . . . which it was possible for people to live'.[31] Eric Stewart presents convincing evidence that *oikoumene* is used in Mark's Gospel as a scheme for representing place. This idea follows the usual pattern of ancient texts from the Greek and Roman cultures where *oikoumene* is used as a standard way of talking about and mapping the world. Mark's Gospel follows this pattern in embedding within its narrative a series of geographical ideas and 'stock stereotypes' to encode certain types of power relations. The intent of the narrative was to map the world in order for the dominant culture to be seen as inhabiting the geographical centre of the story and did so by virtue of the divine will, symbolized for example by the important position of the temple in many biblical narratives.[32]

In 'reality' this would mean that all places, from the vast sweep of empire to the arrangement of an individual house and the corresponding social relations and behaviours of people within those places, would conform to the cultural and religious patterns of *oikoumene* or 'civilization'. This is of course an ideological mapping of the world. In this way every person had their 'proper place' in the grand scheme of things. People who 'lived different types of lives, deviating from the "civilized" lifestyle' were considered out-of-place; they were socially and geographically marginalized.[33]

It is only when we appreciate how Mark employs place as a major character in his story that we get a full sense of the scale of conflict between the social, political and spiritual powers embedded in the familiar arrangements of society and the radical new reality of the kingdom that Jesus proclaimed and embodied. As the gospel story unfolds, Jesus is constantly turning the meanings of places upside down; his kingdom activity liberates the powerless by inverting the orthodox, settled meanings of place that served the interests of those in power. Such is the upset caused by Jesus within the gospel that it seems that Jesus is ushering in a new way of arranging the entire world, a way in which he stands as the new geographic centre. The new arrangement of place inaugurated by his presence stands in 'opposition to the civilized spaces of cities and the architectural spaces of synagogues and temple' which oppress and exclude.[34]

This opposition can be seen in the parallel accounts of demons which form an important part of the structure of the early part of Mark's narrative (Mark 1:21–8; 5:1–20). In the *oikoumene* arrangement of place demons are used as stereotypical characters to represent the fringes of civilization where society is breaking down and borders are not maintained. Thus demons are a locative category in that their proper place is on the chaotic margins. By locating demons in the synagogue (Mark 1:21–8) – the locus of Jewish institutional order organized around purity and Sabbath rules – and in Decapolis (Mark 5:1–20) – the imposition of Roman order through the extension of civilizing cities – Mark is contesting their claims to purity and order and in so doing exposes the ideological and spiritual foundations of the whole system as false. In casting out the demonic presence Jesus is presented as the authentic geographic centre bringing order out of chaos and offering true purity which is not mediated by the temple but based on his own presence and power to cleanse from unclean demons.[35] Jesus turns the world upside down, or at least the meanings associated with its landscapes of power.

The second category around which those in the first-century context would have conceived of place is that of 'purity', as referenced in the work of Mary Douglas. The purity laws mapped out the whole world based on two categories: the sacred and profane, the pure and impure, with seven main categories to define people and seven corresponding categories for creatures.[36] Fundamental for Israel was the belief that 'this purity system derived directly from the God of Israel who created all that exists'.[37] These categories determined where every person and every community stood in the social hierarchy and exactly in what places they were permitted to be, with the temple as the most holy place occupying the central position. Thus the sacred / profane categorization dominated the spatial imagination of Israel mapping the whole world geographically and socially so as to 'allow everything and everyone a certain meaning-endowing, sense-making situation or place'.[38] The purity system provided everyone and everything its proper place, and all were expected to be in the proper place. The goal of life in Israel was not the gaining of status through wealth accumulation as in much of the contemporary West, rather it was the maintenance (or improvement of) one's inherited position in society, which was culturally determined through notions of sacredness and purity.[39]

Given this 'divinely ordained' mapping of the world, based on purity, which put God, his people and their temple at the centre of all things, it is utterly remarkable that Jesus seems so often to act in flagrant disregard for these laws. Indeed, at the mid-point of Mark's Gospel he seems even to proclaim that the purity laws are redundant as 'Jesus declared all foods clean' (Mark 7:19). This declaration was, as we have seen, not simply a point about Jewish law, although that itself would have been profound. It was a declaration that the whole world was being rearranged: the geographical and social map of the world was being turned upside down; powerful social boundaries that supported oppressive hierarchies were being removed so that those who were kept on the 'outside', away from God and far from flourishing human society, were now being drawn in; conversely those on the 'inside' who used their 'pure' status in self-service and exploitation of others are being brought to account.

Thus, with these paradigms of *oikoumene* and purity there is a definite spatial aspect in the narrative of Mark's Gospel and furthermore the spatial nature of the story asserts that the coming of the kingdom, or the presence of Jesus, is always associated with the formation of new kinds of places.[40] These places, which I suggest we could call 'redemptive places', reflect the characteristics of place in the new creation. They are in effect the kind of place we are seeking when we pray 'your kingdom come . . . on earth as it is in heaven' (Matt. 6:10); our prayer being that the actual material stuff of the new creation, along with its radically new social relationships, might become part of our own earthly experience of the places we inhabit.

In light of all the above, how might the Christian community today understand more deeply and engage with our own contemporary landscapes? And what might be the implications for mission, especially in terms of thinking about how to participate with the Spirit in the formation of redemptive places – radically alternative, open-hearted, hospitable places which offer new ways of being in the world? It is to this that we now turn.

Place and Mission

The study of place has important implications for the theory and practice of mission, especially in the way that mission relates to the issues of marginality and deprivation. The arguments presented here have shown that a range of mechanisms function in society (whether ancient or contemporary society) which maintain a hierarchy of power and privilege. These mechanisms are all place-dependent in that it is the material, cultural and spiritual arrangements – including the spatial arrangements – of these aspects that gives them their power. Place is therefore complicit as an actor in creating and sustaining ways of living that divide people as 'insiders' and 'outsiders', 'haves' and 'have-nots'. In other words, place provides the means by which people become marginalized and excluded.[41]

Therefore if mission is to engage more deeply and radically with issues of poverty, deprivation and marginalization it must take seriously the subject of place. All mission activities happen somewhere and in this sense all mission is placed and engages with places. The question raised here is whether these engagements simply affirm or reinforce unjust and excluding arrangements of place (even if unwittingly) or whether there is a self-conscious attempt to act otherwise. The argument I am proposing is that, as well as the conversion of people, the Christian community must also be concerned with the formation of redemptive places; the two are in fact co-constituting – the conversion of people and the conversion of places must go together. The name 'redemptive place' is used to underline the kind of places that are specifically formed around the presence of Jesus as their centre; where Jesus is by the Spirit, there we may expect the formation of a new kind of place. Our task in mission therefore is one of participation with the Spirit in the creation of new arrangements of place, whether that is at a micro / local level or a macro / city or regional level. What then do they look like and what practices might we pursue in order to participate in their formation?

Given this centrality of Jesus, I will focus on two specific practical issues which are foundational for participation in the formation of redemptive places, namely the questions of the 'space *between* the self and the other' and the 'space *within* the self'.

The first of these, the 'space between the self and the other', relates to the radically inclusive characteristic of redemptive place. In a redemptive place there is room for all, each person is given place, especially the person of difference (the so-called 'impure / unclean / uncivilized'). The formation of redemptive place is most definitely *not* about trying to open up 'my space' so that others are welcome: the danger in this is that I might find myself imposing my own social and cultural norms on the visitor or stranger. I am by default (especially as a white male) largely oblivious to my own cultural norms and unaware of how I impose these on others – especially when I am in my own 'home' place.[42] I may be left wondering about why the guest did not seem to fit or why our relationship does not move beyond a certain point.

This is not to say that we should not offer hospitality by inviting others into our home or community.[43] Rather it is to point out that redemptive places are formed as we learn to step outside of our own comfort zones, or our own constructions of place, which include the places over which we have control. As we do, we find a place occupied by people of 'difference'; others who may well provoke in us a profound sense of discomfort and disorientation. This is much like the situation in Luke 18 – 19 which was discussed earlier. The narrative implies that the rich young ruler found the space around Jesus populated by all kinds of 'disreputable' and 'impure' people – children, widows, tax collectors and blind beggars. The sadness, and indeed the shock, of the story was that he was unwilling, or unable, to stay in that place. Presumably it demanded too much of him.

You might think that focusing on 'the space between the self and other' a strange starting point for re-imagining place as redemptive-place. Why, you might ask, don't we start with something physical like re-arranging the room? We are after all talking about place. This is a fair point. However I am suggesting that our main struggle is to understand how profoundly certain ideas about the arrangement of place have dominated our spatial imaginations and that these affect our seeing-of-the-world in ways of which we are generally unaware. Attentiveness to the 'space between the self and other', and the activity of the Spirit in that place, serves to challenge these settled imaginations of place and to show how, by holding these assumptions, we tend to act as participants in sustaining exclusionary arrangements of place.

Mary McClintock Fulkerson refers to this as 'obliviousness' – a non-seeing that 'comes with dominance'.[44] Obliviousness or 'non-seeing' is a quality which works predominantly in one direction (from the dominant to the marginalized), sustaining patterns of difference so that the organizations, and people who work within them, become complicit (albeit unwittingly) with the very forces that define and sustain difference. A new physical and relational proximity to people of difference, and the consequent struggle (both personal inner struggle and struggle in relationships) signify ruptures or fissures in a person's normal experience of place and social relationship. These fissures are created by a break between the dominant view of a place and the new experience of 'appearance' that arises from the removal of obliviousness.[45]

Thus when people of difference find themselves in close socio-spatial proximity and are able to exercise a reflexive attentiveness within that place, the new rupture or fissure that opens up might be thought of as the creation of 'a shared space of appearance' – that is the creation of a place that is the antithesis of the normal arrangement of things where obliviousness sustains harmful and unequal arrangements of power.[46] The 'shared space of appearance' entails a new sense of seeing in two important ways: a seeing or recognition of the other, not through stereotype or representation but through relational connection as human beings; and also a recognition or seeing in oneself of instincts and responses that have been complicit (whether unintentionally or not) in maintaining strong socio-spatial boundaries which function to exclude others.

The new 'shared space of appearance' which is opened up through the encounter is first a space 'between' the self and the other. The location of this new space that gives rise to new insight and new life is recognize by Terry Veling as being neither in the self nor in the other but *between* the two, and indeed, it is in the *between* that the Spirit is found. Veling states that '[A]ll real living is meeting . . . it is an encounter between the two. [The] Spirit is not in the I but between the I and Thou.'[47]

Second, such encounters also affect the 'space within the self'. This inner space through which one makes sense of the world, how it works and where we fit within it, is disrupted and disturbed by the new 'shared space of appearance'. That a realization of one's own obliviousness is of fundamental importance for participating in the new spatiality of the kingdom is identified in Matthew's Gospel where Jesus points to his followers' complete lack of self-understanding: 'Do you not notice the log in your own eye?' (see Matt. 7:3). Jesus' challenge, which is also in the context of an encounter with the other, is to first pay attention to yourself ('You hypocrite, first take the plank out of your own eye,' v. 5) before offering to help your neighbour ('then you will see clearly to remove the speck from your brother's eye', v. 5). Thus the encounter with the other, the realization of obliviousness and the opening up of new spaces of appearance has significant implications for one's sense of identity and social participation; it calls for an open-hearted reflection and self-judgement. Thus mission, and the formation of redemptive places, is configured not simply as a movement 'out there' but is first and foremost a movement 'in here', that is in the space within the self; that nature of the outward journey of mission will be wholly determined by the quality of the reflective inner journey.

In this way, divisive exclusionary boundaries begin to be removed, judgement is for a while suspended and prejudicial reactions begin to be healed. This new space, no longer fortified by the familiarity of my own cultural home, has about it a liminal quality, opening up the potential to see things differently, to see beyond the stereotypical image of the outsider or person of difference. It is on this basis that we can then begin to participate in the formation of new kinds of places based on radically reconfigured relationships – namely redemptive places.

These kinds of places may be experienced (at least in embryonic form) in all kinds of settings. In our own Christian community they happened as a woman in her mid-sixties took home-made cake and flapjack to share with a large group of restless teenagers who roamed the estate; as a group of men from completely different social backgrounds played cards, drank beer and talked into the early hours of the morning; as a group of us met together, crossing all kinds of social boundaries to bake bread – an event that has developed into a weekly gathering, mainly of men, to make all kinds of bread and often to eat a meal together.

The sense of place that emerges through these encounters is usually unplanned, unpredictable and often transient but results in degrees of transformation for all involved. They were all however accompanied by careful attentive reflection which helped to break down stereotypical impressions, diminish anxiety about 'different kinds of people', open up understanding and nurture reconciliation and friendship. There is, in effect, a new kind of place that is glimpsed through these encounters that have about them a redemptive quality giving rise to new insight and new life.

It seems that there is no formulation or prescription here, but that there is an 'artfulness' in recognizing and making room in the encounter for a 'shared space of appearing' – a liminal quality of space that makes room for the Spirit and opens eyes to what has not previously been discernible.[48] I suggest that we could think of this liminality as the 'spatiality of the Spirit'; it is the redemptive place that comes into being when strangers meet only to find that 'between the two there is a third'.[49]

Conclusion

In this chapter I have drawn on socio-scientific and theological sources to highlight the importance of the relationship between place and experiences of deprivation and marginalization. The ideas presented strongly indicate the need for Christian mission to move towards a deeper understanding of and engagement with place and they show how, without such understanding, mission strategies and practices, even those focused on serving the poor, can result in actually reinforcing the very arrangements that cause poverty and deprivation in the first instance.

There is inevitably much that remains unexplored within the limitations of a single chapter, not least some more developed theological ideas about place and also some practical questions about how to research places or become more attentive to our own particular situations. However the ideas about 'space between the self and the other' and the 'space *within* the self' do represent the first steps towards understanding how we can begin to forge a radical engagement with the places around us and the powers that are invested within them; they help us to understand our own contexts more deeply and especially the way in which these fit within the overall landscapes of exclusion and marginalization; they help us to move towards a re-imagination of place and the formation of redemptive places where the patterns of 'them' and 'us', 'outsider' and 'insider', privileged and excluded no longer dominate relationships.

The study of place and its implications for mission in marginal places will be further explored in the books that follow in this series. Also, many of the chapters in this book pick up on the themes introduced here and, although they do not use the language of redemptive place, they do suggest some important ways in which mission can be understood as convening new imaginations of place such as shalom, hospitality or the cruciform spatiality of the inner-self.

I will conclude the chapter by leaving you with one of the consummate Christian imaginations of place, that of the covenant meal – the eucharistic or heavenly feast. This image of place as a meal around the symbols of bread and wine functions as an unyielding prophetic stance against all formations of place that dehumanize people. At its core is the concept of the redemptive place where those previously alienated from each other as strangers and enemies (Jews and Greeks, slaves and free) are united in embrace around one table as one body. This extraordinary meal is a fulfilment of the many gospel stories that anticipate and point towards the formation of a new humanity in a new kind of place where the categories of 'us' and 'them', 'haves' and 'have-nots' are completely erased.

We may never fully achieve the vision that this meal inspires, but it does give us something to strive towards and a clue about the kinds of faithful practices that we need to participate in to at least glimpse this kind of transformative place in our own experiences. We may see them in such unlikely places as sharing cake with a gang of young people, making bread with a group of men or playing cards late into the night. Critically, this practice makes space for *all* to join as participants in a community of embrace and grace irrespective of social or religious standing.

Such expressions may only be embryonic or short-lived embodiments of the heavenly feast, but they fire the imaginations of all involved showing that, with Jesus at the centre, there is indeed another way to live. Mission in this sense could be conceived of as seeking to emulate the place of the covenant meal or heavenly feast; it is a striving towards a newly imagined kind of place that I have called redemptive place.

Notes

1. Doreen Massey, *World City* (Cambridge: Polity, 2007), pp. 55–8.
2. Chris Hamnett, 'Urban Forms', in *Introducing Human Geographies* (ed. Paul Cloke, Philip Crang and Mark Goodwin; London: Routledge, 3rd edn, 2014), p. 701.
3. Hamnett, 'Urban Forms', pp. 698–704.
4. Neil Smith, *The New Urban Frontier: Gentrification and the Revanchist City* (London and New York: Routledge, 1996), pp. xvii–xviii, 211–18.
5. Tim Cresswell, *In Place / Out of Place: Geography, Ideology and Transgression* (Minneapolis and London: University of Minnesota Press, 1996), pp. 149–62.
6. Paul Cloke, Ian Cook, Philip Crang, Mark Goodwin, Joe Painter and Chris Philo, eds, *Practising Human Geography* (London: Sage, 2004), pp. 180–81.
7. For a good introduction to the subject of place see Tim Cresswell, *Place: A Short Introduction* (Malden, MA, and Oxford, UK: Blackwell, 2004).
8. Obtained from http://www.gridreferencefinder.com/# (accessed 30 Nov. 2015).
9. For senses of place see Steven Feld and Keith H. Basso, *Senses of Place* (Santa Fe: School of American Research Press, 1996); Philip Sheldrake, *The Spiritual City: Theology, Spirituality, and the Urban* (Chichester: Wiley-Blackwell, 2014), pp. 1–33.
10. Cresswell, *In Place*, p. 12.
11. Doreen Massey, *A Global Sense of Place* (Minneapolis: University of Minnesota Press, 1994).
12. Edward Soja, *Postmodern Geographies: Reassertion of Space in Critical Social Theory* (London: Verso, 1989), p. 6.
13. Mary Douglas, *Purity and Danger* (London and New York: Routledge Classics, 2002).
14. Douglas, *Purity*, pp. 44–5.
15. Douglas, *Purity*, p. 44.
16. David Sibley, *Geographies of Exclusion* (London and New York: Routledge, 1995), p. x.
17. Sibley, *Geographies*, p. 99. The term 'outsiders' is not intended to evoke a simple insider / outsider paradigm. Sibley argues for much more complex and nuanced social arrangement of place.
18. Sibley, *Geographies*, p. 99.
19. Lynsey Hanley, *Estates: An Intimate History* (London: Granta, 2007), p. 176.

[20] Hanley, *Estates*, p. 176.

[21] Cresswell, *Place*, p. 174.

[22] Cresswell, *In Place*, p. 3.

[23] Tim Cresswell, 'Place', in *Introducing Human Geographies* (ed. P. Cloke, P. Crang and M. Goodwin; London: Routledge, 3rd edn, 2014), p. 251.

[24] Cresswell, *In Place*, pp. 153–54, 161. The scriptural tradition of the 'stranger' as the person of difference offers a contrasting perspective to Cresswell's understanding that they are 'not to be trusted'. See Chapter 6 in this book: Cathy Ross, 'Hospitality'. In addition Parker Palmer says that 'hospitality to the stranger gives us a chance to see our own lives afresh, through different eyes' (Parker Palmer, *The Company of Strangers: Christians and the Renewal of America's Public Life* [New York: Crossroad, 1986], p. 131).

[25] Cresswell, 'Place', p. 251.

[26] Cresswell, 'Place', pp. 257–9. Don Mitchell argues that this kind of struggle for the right to public space in the city is 'the only way that social justice can be advanced', and that anti-camping by-laws are one of the standard ways of excluding those who would seek to practise those rights (Don Mitchell, *The Right to the City: Social Justice and the Fight for Public Space* [New York: Guilford, 2003], pp. 4, 118–59). For a critical examination between religion and the Occupy movement of 2011 see: Paul Cloke, Callum Sutherland and Andrew Williams, 'Postsecularity, Political Resistance and Protest in the Occupy Movement', *Antipode* (2015) (forthcoming, 'early view' available on-line).

[27] While place has not been a major subject of discussion within theology, there are a number of different approaches that have been taken: Craig G. Bartholomew, *Where Mortals Dwell: A Christian View of Place for Today* (Grand Rapids, MI: Baker Academic, 2011); Tim Gorringe, *A Theology of the Built Environment* (Cambridge: Cambridge University Press, 2002); John Inge, *A Christian Theology of Place* (Aldershot: Ashgate, 2003); Philip Sheldrake, *The Spiritual City: Theology, Spirituality, and the Urban* (Chichester: Wiley-Blackwell, 2014).

[28] For the subject of the poor in Luke see Joel B. Green, *The Gospel of Luke*, New International Commentary on the New Testament Series (Grand Rapids, MI: Eerdmans, 1997), pp. 67–73.

[29] For further commentary on this passage see Halvor Moxnes, *Putting Jesus in His Place: A Radical Vision of Household and Kingdom* (Louisville and London: Westminster John Knox, 2003), pp. 22–71; R.T. France, *Divine Government: God's Kingship in the Gospel of Mark* (Regent: Vancouver, 2003), pp. 8–25.

[30] For the importance of this verse see Chapter 2 of this book: Stuart Christine, 'Incarnation'.

[31] Eric C. Stewart, *Gathered Around Jesus: An Alternative Spatial Practice in the Gospel of Mark* (Cambridge: Clark, 2009), p. 62.

[32] Stewart, *Gathered*, pp. 126–7.

[33] Stewart, *Gathered*, p. 127.

[34] Stewart, *Gathered*, p. 180.

[35] Stewart, *Gathered*, pp. 193, 211.

[36] Bruce J. Malina, *The New Testament World: Insights from Cultural Anthropology* (Kentucky: Westminster John Knox Press, 3rd edn, 2001), pp. 171–7; Jerome H. Neyrey, 'The Idea of Purity in Mark's Gospel', *Semeia* 35 (1986): pp. 94–6, 101.

[37] Malina, *Insights*, p. 171.

[38] Malina, *Insights*, p. 171.

[39] Malina, *Insights*, pp. 27–56, 170; Neyrey, 'Idea', p. 96. Jerome H. Neyrey and Eric C. Stewart, *The Social World of the New Testament: Insights and Models* (Massachusetts: Hendrickson, 2008), pp. 85–102.

[40] These arguments are presented in my doctoral dissertation: Michael Pears, 'Towards a Theological Engagement with an Area of Multiple Deprivation: The Case of the Cornwall Estate' (Amsterdam: Vrije Universiteit, 2015), pp. 233–45. They will also be discussed in Book Six of this series, entitled *Locating the Powers*, to be published in 2018.

[41] For an exploration of these ideas in contempoary human geography see Sibley, *Geographies*.

[42] Cresswell, *In Place*, pp. 149–62; Mary McClintock Fulkerson, *Places of Redemption: Theology for a Worldly Church* (Oxford: Oxford University Press, 2007), pp. 3–42.

[43] For discussion on this see Chapter 6 in this book: Cathy Ross, 'Hospitality'.

[44] Fulkerson, *Places of Redemption*, p. 15.

[45] Fulkerson, *Places of Redemption*, p. 21.

[46] Fulkerson, *Places of Redemption*, p. 21.

[47] Terry A. Veling, *Practical Theology: On Earth as It Is in Heaven* (New York: Orbis, 2005), p. 55.

[48] Veling, *Practical Theology*, p. 55.

[49] Veling, *Practical Theology*, pp. 17–23, 54.

2

Incarnation: Connecting with Marginal Communities

Stuart Christine

Introduction

The key issue that I will explore in this chapter concerns the question of how we can best become available to God and to the economically and socially deprived community around us in such a way as to facilitate the emergence of authentic expressions of the body of Christ.

What follows is a result of reflecting theologically on the personal missionary experience of myself and my wife stretching back over thirty years and particularly upon the last twenty-plus years working alongside deprived communities principally in Brazil and, since 2012, in Wythenshawe, Manchester. It is a process that has taken place in dialogue with a rereading of Luke's narrative of the mission of Jesus as he challenges the reader–disciple to emulate and indeed give continuity to that mission as a commissioned agent of kingdom change.

Beginning in the favela of Jardim Olinda in São Paulo, Brazil, and subsequently in deprived communities across Latin America, my wife Georgie and I experienced how often the genesis and growth of kingdom transformation was focused in and through children – children who are themselves the very embodiment of the weaknesses, vulnerabilities and exploitations that characterized the life of the community as a whole. By considering these child-catalysed experiences in the light of Luke's presentation of Jesus as messianic mediator of the kingdom to the poor, it is my hope to offer a fresh hermeneutical lens through which to explore the challenge of missional connecting with marginal places and communities in Christ's name, in a way that might be described as 'effectively incarnational'.

The Child Motif in Luke's Presentation of the Mission of Jesus

Luke grounds his presentation of Jesus in Mary's prophetic restatement of the God of Israel's commitment to act transformationally on behalf of those who are humble and hungry, thus confronting and reversing the social order imposed by the proud and powerful. Events surrounding the birth of Jesus are recounted and through the authenticating voices of Scripture, angels and the Holy Spirit, Luke establishes for the reader the credentials of Jesus as the 'Messiah for the marginalized'. Born into the margins of society to one of the lowly whom he has committed to 'raise up', the child in Simeon's arms is recognized as the Lord's Christ and proclaimed as the agent of eschatological salvation with all its promise of God-centred, radical social inversion.[1]

As his carefully crafted narrative progresses and presents the outworking of Jesus' mission manifesto, a motif of 'child' as a representative embodiment of the 'poor' becomes apparent. This is expressed in the child-focused examples of messianic intervention which Luke sets at the heart of each section of his cyclical narration of the Galilean ministry: the raising of the son of the widow of Nain (Luke 7:12–15), and of Jairus' daughter (Luke 8:52,54), and the restoration of the demon-possessed child (Luke 9:37–43).

Having taken the reader to the point of recognizing the mission and identity of Jesus, but prior to the account of the final journey to Jerusalem with its inevitable and ultimate confrontation with those wielding socio-religious and political power, Luke recounts a further and pivotal, child-centred event: 'An argument started among the disciples as to which of them would be the greatest. Jesus, knowing their thoughts, took a little child and made him stand beside him. Then he said to them, "Whoever welcomes this little child in my name welcomes me; and whoever welcomes me welcomes the one who sent me"' (Luke 9:46–8).

The disciples, together with the reader, are challenged as to their understanding of, and commitment to, what constitutes true greatness. The call is to emulate the attitude and action signed to them in Jesus' taking of the child, an embodiment of social inconsequentiality,[2] and placing her at his side, the place of ultimate kingdom honour. The child is set at his side in a signal enactment of the self-giving solidarity and kingdom affirmation of the 'lowly, poor and little ones'[3] that is characteristic of Luke's presentation of Jesus and his fulfilment of the mission agenda of the One who sent him.

By this dramatic child–sign–action Jesus calls the reader–disciple to enter into agency with him in carrying forward his mission and underwrites this call with a twofold, enabling commitment. In response to the disciples' receiving the child 'in his name', he commits *to giving himself to be received* side by side with the child. Thus, in this act of receiving not only the child but also Jesus who is both the 'Sent- and Sending-One', the reader–disciple is set together with Jesus as an empowered and authorized agent of the kingdom. The motif of the child as a hermeneutical key to understanding Jesus' kingdom mission to the 'poor' is sublimated by Luke into the child–sign–act of 9:46–8.

As such the event offers a positive and empowering *theological* starting point for considering the relationship between three key dimensions of the missionary process. The critical expression that might characterize this interrelationship is 'connection' or, more pertinently, an 'incarnational connectedness'. Exploring this idea of 'incarnational connectedness' under the following three headings will enable us to engage more fully with the question posed in the opening sentence of this chapter.

- *The ground of incarnational connectedness is in Christ's proactive and gracious self-giving.* Incarnational experience and transformation is something that Christ 'does'. The child–sign–act points to this being expressed through intentional relationality involving Christ, the missionary and the community rather than in the pursuit of social identity between the missionary and the community alone.
- *The goal of incarnational connectedness is the community's experience of the kingdom in revelation and restoration.* The child–sign–act points to the potential for the community to experience both the *revelation* of kingdom realities and the *restoration* of the individual or community as a result of kingdom realities, both as a consequence of empathetic self-giving and solidarity expressed by the mission group.
- *The 'genesis' potential of incarnational connectedness is transformational within the missional group.* The child–sign–act points to a missional posture that offers creative empowerment to the missionary community in its commission to become a co-agent with Christ, the kingdom-creator.

The Ground of Incarnational Connectedness is in Christ's Proactive and Gracious Self-Giving

It is not uncommon for the challenge of 'missional incarnation' to be discussed from a primarily sociological perspective, focusing upon the missionary for whom the prerequisite goal is conceived to be that of achieving an 'incarnational' life*style* identical to that of the 'target' community. The seamless social absorption of the missionary into some subgroup of marginalized people becomes the frustratingly unrealistic goal of missionary endeavour in place of that of becoming available to God and the community as a mediator or catalyst of kingdom experience.

In Luke 9, Jesus takes the initiative to reach across the conventional boundaries of marginality to identify with the child, and describes his action in terms of a welcoming acceptance, an expression of positive mutuality. 'Incarnation' in Luke begins with 'the One who is sent' and goes on to be expressed in proactive, gracious action on his part that is essentially relational in character and intention.[4]

I recall being challenged by a visitor to Brazil as to what right I had to presume to 'do mission' in the favela since I had a privileged background and did not share the living conditions of the community. Acknowledging the social mismatch, I suggested that we redirect the question to a lady from the community standing nearby, who responded, 'We know that you are rich compared to us, but that's how the world is. What makes the difference for us is that you treat us like *gente*' – a Brazilian colloquialism for 'proper folk'. For Maria Lourdes[5] at least, what she experienced as empathetic identification through our interaction with the community, in the name of Jesus, bridged the gap between our differing social identities.[6]

In Luke's account of the opening ministry act of the post-resurrection church described in Acts 3 he employs the word ὑπαρχων (being) to bring together both the life conditions of the crippled beggar and those of Peter: the beggar's life is characterized by dependency born of disability while Peter's is a lack of the silver or gold that could meet the beggar's expectations and needs. Significantly, the term is employed in the summary sentence of Luke 9:46–8 to describe the life-dynamic of 'smaller- or smallest-ness' (μικροτερος) that points towards kingdom greatness, grounded in the humble self-giving example of Jesus, the sine qua non of effective missionary qualification. In the light of the usage in Acts 3, this summary could helpfully be read: 'Whoever adopts an empathetic identification with the state of those who are μικροι (marginalized and weak) – as Peter does (Acts 3:2,6) and as Jesus exemplified in the child–sign–act – qualifies as μεγας (great) in the kingdom.' Such a person, an emulator of Jesus, is enabled to become a mediator of kingdom blessing 'in the name of Jesus', as Peter's experience demonstrated.

Luke's presentation of Jesus' reception of children in 9:46 represents his call to the reader–disciple to a connectedness with the 'small, lowly and poor', that goes beyond an identity of life*style* or social posture on the part of the missionary, but is a *way* of life, in relation to and with the community, 'in the name of Christ'. The encounter becomes 'incarnational' precisely because, as the 'other' is affirmed and welcomed in kingdom solidarity and mutuality in Jesus' name, Jesus commits to give himself to be received. The encounter therefore brings together in relational kingdom experience, or incarnational connectedness, the sender, the sent one and the embraced one.

Whether the experience will be one of transformation or of judgement will depend upon the response to the incarnational initiative experienced. In Luke's following narratives, 9:51–6 and 10:5–16, both eventualities are presented.[7] However, what encourages and empowers the disciple (Luke 10:17) is that, despite socio-cultural dissonances and the persistence of kingdom-denying structures of status and power, they find themselves effectively involved with Christ, 'presencing' or embodying the outworking of his mission mandate with the affirmation of the One who sent him (Luke 10:21).

The Goal of Incarnational Connectedness is the Community's Experience of the Kingdom in Revelation and Restoration

It was in the spirit and hope of becoming part of the Sending-One's kingdom purposes that I made my way down into the favela of Jardim Olinda a little after nine that Saturday morning. By then, the smell from the open sewer that ran along between the wooden shacks was increasing with the rising temperature. Sonia Costa had arrived over an hour earlier and with the enthusiastic help of a swarm of young children had already loaded and carried away two lorry-loads of the dank cardboard boxes and general detritus that had taken over the dark inside space of the wood and corrugated iron lean-to that little Abel and an indeterminate number of younger brothers, sisters and cousins knew as their home. I had come to help. Suddenly a shrill cry went up, 'Here comes Jesus!' Unbidden, a thought sprang into my mind, 'Thank God, an end to all this suffering!' However there was no apocalyptic trumpet blast or rush of archangelic wings; only Sonia, a portly lady in her forties, gingerly descending the narrow alleyway that led from the road above to the sewer-side hovel below. But a child called Abel had seen Jesus and was ready to start loading the lorry again!

Is the child Abel's identification of the Christ in the adult warranted? Is his experience comparable to that of Simeon who perceived the Lord's Christ in the infant Jesus? Or is this merely an outburst of childish imagination, a charming irrelevancy in the grown-up world?[8]

Viewed through the lens of Luke 9:46–8, Sonia had indeed acted to receive the child in the name of this Christ. She had opened her heart to receive the hopes and fears, the pleasures and the pains of the children of the favela of Jardim Olinda. She had opened her business schedule to make time and resources from her commercial woodyard available to remove the adult rubbish from Abel's world. In his name, motivated and empowered by commitment to Jesus, she had welcomed the child suffering from the consequences of adult deprivation into her world. In doing so she had become a bridge across which Jesus might pass to bring kingdom transformation into his world, and Abel had spontaneously announced the presence of Christ.

In Luke 7:16, the verdict of the community at Nain had been equally shocking and unambiguous. In response to an outsider's kingdom intervention, impossibly reaching out across the frontiers of marginality expressed in the coffin of a dead boy, and in a widow's tears of desolation and destitution, the cry had gone up, 'God has come to help his people.'

Had not Jesus also revealed himself in and through Sonia as she reached out across the frontiers of marginality, affirming the life of a child and his family, to lay hands on the real life symbols of that marginality, namely the garbage in his home? Had Jesus not been witnessed by Abel that Saturday morning at around 9.30?

Missional commitment to incarnational connectedness had opened the possibility for the community to experience something of a revelation as to the alternative values at work in the kingdom. Likewise, missional commitment to incarnational connectedness also carries the innate potential for bringing community experiences of restoration. This is well illustrated by the story of Andrea and Neuza.

It was the second morning that five-year-old Andrea hadn't come to class. Neuza, the large, imposing and lovely preschool teacher had asked her friends about her absence, but they seemed unable to say why. So she decided to go to find out for herself. Out she went, accompanied by a small entourage of children and dogs. She was alone however when she clapped her hands to call attention to her arrival outside the chained-up door that marked the entrance to Andrea's shack. A conversation through a neighbour's window finally confirmed what she had begun to suspect: they'd gone – or at least the mother had, leaving a note to the local drug-dealer to take Andrea in payment for her debt. The mother had fled for her life back up to the north-east of Brazil from whence she had come with baby Andrea to start a new life in São Paulo. Neuza tracked down the address of the family, and made contact. She confronted the man who held Andrea and negotiated her return. And in another slum, 1,500 miles away, another local church took the family under its wing and the hope of life was restored.

The social and spiritual dynamics of the world of Andrea's mum had worked upon her in such a way that she could countenance the face of Andrea, her child and daughter, becoming recast into the face upon the coinage of exchange needed to buy her own survival. Objectified by her mother Andrea became merchandise in an economy of deprivation and exploitation. In the favela of Tiquatira that day there was no Jairus and his wife (Luke 8:40–56), or desperate father (Luke 9:37–43) to be galvanized by parental love to plead the cause of their only child, nor even the solidarity of a supportive community as in Nain (Luke 7:11–17). So it was Neuza who had been moved to ask the question, 'Where is Andrea?'; Neuza who had followed the signal example of Jesus when, as a member of the small community of faith, she had reached out to 'receive' and set Andrea at her side as one of her preschool preparation programme (PEPE) children honoured and valued in the kingdom of God. For Neuza, Andrea was not just a statistic on an attendance register whose life could be left in the classroom when the register was closed for the day. The name in the register had a life. Andrea was a person, known and cared for, particular and real, signified in Luke 9:48 by '*this* child'. Having embraced

Andrea and her world, it was 'natural' that Neuza noted her absence, and that she knew the way to her home. And of course, she had felt the pain for Andrea and a disturbing mixture of pity, anger and disgust at the dreadful, self-serving abandonment of her mother, as well as fear for herself, as she confronted the dealer in the 'bodies and souls of men',[9] who had taken Andrea for his other world.

The three instances of Jesus' direct intervention on behalf of 'children' in Luke's Gospel illustrate the same dynamic. The hopeless, pain-filled passivity of the widow of Nain at the death of her only son (7:11–17), the public ridiculing in response to Jesus' declaration of life and hope to Jairus and his wife (8:40–56) and the active aggression of the demonic powers at work in the boy child recounted in Luke 9:37–43 all envisaged and worked towards the taking away of life from the child, family and community. But Jesus acts to restore each 'only son' or daughter. Addressing each child personally even as they are on the edge of death, Jesus places his hand upon the coffin, silences the professional mourners, and rebukes the evil spirit threatening to destroy the life of the child.

But what if Neuza hadn't been there, in such a way as to have welcomed Andrea and to act in the name of Jesus? The question brings into sharp focus the imperative of an incarnational connectedness that potentializes kingdom revelation and restoration. The 'saving of Andrea' is surely an example of the church's commission to continue to live out the narrative of 'all that Jesus began to do and teach'.[10]

The 'Genesis' Potential of Incarnational Connectedness to be Transformational within the Missional Group

Marginality is by definition the consequence of rejection by the majority culture and when the majority culture is a contra-kingdom culture, which Jesus showed is its intrinsic tendency, then committing to 'walking upright in an upside down world'[11] in affirmative solidarity with those on the margins is demanding and can becoming emotionally and physically exhausting.

In the painting, *The Pest House*, Dutch artist Edward Knippers expresses this reality in the way he depicts Christ's incarnational mission.[12] The work presents Christ, naked, striving to respond to a dark and enveloping sea of need, his back to the spectating viewer, torn between his involvement with an agonizing figure on his left and a man whose body is covered with Kaposi's sarcoma, the skin cancer frequently associated with AIDS and symbolic of the destructive and marginalizing twentieth-century western equivalent of leprosy.

Carmelo was to know the pressure of facing overwhelming need. He had felt the call to mission after visiting the slum community in Jardim Olinda. Working during the day and studying theology most evenings, he spent his Saturdays going from shack to shack 'reaching out' to those who had no gas to cook with, no money to buy the medicines they needed, who suffered abuse from their partner, whose children were getting caught up in petty crime to fuel their adolescent addictions. It was not many months before he had a nervous breakdown, weeping because he hadn't enough money to pay for the gas or the medicines, because he could not be there to protect the family when the drunken man came in at 1 a.m., despairing at the sight of so many kids criminalized and sacrificed on the altars of the greed-driven trafficking of addictions.[13] However much he tried and however much he gave of himself, the suffering just wouldn't go away and it finally became too much for him to bear.

Carmelo's experience is sadly not uncommon and is a constant threat to the personal balance, not to say 'wellbeing', of churches and mission workers committed to serve with marginalized communities. For some, the challenges of and barriers to such counter-cultural involvement and its sacrificial nature lead either to focusing on less challenging ministry options or to a dogged but discouraged or defensive pattern of discipleship.

Luke's presentation of the child–sign–act event sets the personal and collective demands made by living out the call to 'incarnational mission' in Jesus' name in the context of Jesus' own commitment to be present with the disciple in and through the missionary action. Critically, the call to incarnational mission practice in the name of

Jesus is not made apart from this commitment to an incarnational experience of the presence of Jesus by the missionary. For Luke, it is in the experience of this complimentary incarnational act that the disciple will find the genesis of the personal empowerment and practical enabling that is necessary to serve with the marginalized as an effective agent of the kingdom.

Pastor Gerson had become dispirited. He had accepted the call to lead a small Baptist church set at the heart of a poor and violent community in the south of São Paulo, in the hope of 'making a difference'. The reality was that his mornings were spent sitting alone in his church office waiting for troubled people who never came to seek his help, and coming and going from the church building through the streets of the community where he went unrecognized and un-greeted. It was as if he was invisible and made no difference at all. Having heard how making the PEPE mission preschool part of the life and mission of the church had enabled similar congregations to make effective connections to the local community, he decided to give it a go.

Barely a month after beginning the programme, he unexpectedly turned up at one of the regular training meetings arranged to develop local church members as educators for the five-and six-year-olds in their PEPE. 'I came along because you all need to hear this', he announced! 'For two years I've been walking to and from the church without a soul saying a word to me. Since beginning the PEPE it takes me twice as long to make my journeys home. It's "Oi pastor!" here and "Oi pastor!" there! Suddenly I've become visible! I've even been invited to explain the Bible to a group of escaped prisoners who are holed up at the bottom of the favela.' After that he was known to everyone as 'Oi pastor!' Identifying a relevant and relational activity that reached out to the least and the most vulnerable in the community and affirming the kingdom value of the community as a whole, he was seeing the kingdom breaking in and was re-energized to live out his calling.

A little later, I had occasion to visit his church and, while Georgie was doing in-class training with the local church educator, I got chatting to an older lady who was preparing the mid-morning snacks for the children. I asked her how she felt about being involved in the programme every morning without any pay. 'Ever since I was a child I wanted to be a missionary', she replied, 'but I never had the opportunity to study and then I got married too young to a man who wasn't a Christian and I thought that was the end of my calling. When Pastor Gerson told us about the PEPE program, I saw my chance. It's wonderful – I really feel that I am serving people in the name of Jesus, getting the children's food ready, taking them to the toilet, and speaking to the mums every day – they've got so many troubles. I really feel that I am a missionary now.'

Both Gerson and Maria had come to recognize and celebrate the 'presencing' of Jesus in their relational engagement with their local favela community and had found personal empowerment as well as effective service in and through an activity in which they affirmed 'this child' in his name.

Similar challenges regarding personal empowerment and the effective practice of mission in the face of daunting social need were tackled by the small mission group gathered around a then theological seminary student, Iolanda Miranda, committed to making a kingdom impact in the huge favela named Heliopolis, City of the Sun.[14]

The size and seemingly impenetrable physical and social favela-world that was Heliopolis could generate a sense of hopelessness as easily in the hearts and minds of the small mission group I was visiting, as it did so often in the lives of its own hundred-thousand-plus inhabitants. With the aim of finding a way to connect personally across these barriers, I was meeting with the PEPE preschool teacher, Iolanda, when Eliane, aged five, popped out from a half-concealed alleyway and with a shout of glee ran up to Iolanda, 'Come and meet Daddy!' Easier said than done, as we weaved through the labyrinth of passages, stepping over slime, avoiding dogs and squeezing past suspicious-looking 'friends of Daddy'. Finally Eliane crashed through a bead-curtained doorway and jumped onto Daddy's knee exclaiming, 'This is Auntie Iolanda from the PEPE.' Daddy was seated behind a wooden table with more of his 'friends' in nervous attendance.

'So it's you who run the PEPE . . . well done, very good . . .' And so we talked with the local drug-trafficker about Eliane and PEPE and Jesus and finally, in that place so distant from 'church', we prayed before leaving. A few weeks later Eliane's father and family also left – it would have been impossible to stay – to find a different life.

The drug-trafficking father, an embodiment of counter-kingdom greatness at the heart of the marginalized favela community itself, had been challenged by the church's missionary affirmation of the embodiment of weakness at the heart of his own life: his five-year-old daughter.[15] In that confrontation made possible by the church's reaching out to his daughter, the kingdom of God had come near, penetrating the physical and social barriers of the second largest favela in Latin America. As if at a doorway having the form of a child, and in the manner of the figure of Revelation 3:20, Christ had made himself present and had invited that father into the kingdom community despite his pariah status in society.

By receiving the child in the name of Jesus, the church had gained 'incarnational' access and acceptance – kingdom connectedness – into a community otherwise barricaded in its marginality against 'outsiders'. Perhaps equally significant, in the face of seemingly overwhelming difficulties, the church had been party to experiencing the transformational presence and power of Christ and had become affirmed and energized in its role as an agent of incarnation and catalyst of the kingdom.[16]

Conclusion: Incarnational Mission and the Missionary Experience

Incarnational connectedness across the frontiers of marginality is grounded in the proactive commitment of Christ who embodies the eschatalogical kingdom-bringing servant of Isaiah 61 and Luke 4. In the child–sign–act of 9:46–8, Luke signals to the would-be disciple the radical nature of the missional commitment that they are called to embrace.

Many great figures in the history of missions have recognized and experienced the challenge of embracing what can be a personally sacrificial, counter-cultural ethos of life in order to pursue a kingdom-culture mission. John Wesley famously described his decision to leave the salons and drawing-rooms of his natural social milieu to address the miners of Kingswood near Bristol from on top of 'a mound', as a process of becoming 'more vile'.[17] In what Charles Elliott, former director of Christian Aid, describes as a 'calling out from a settled life of comfort and ease and security', he reflects upon the discomforting ways in which this 'often turbulent process of growth' might be inspired within us.[18] The Dutch Catholic psychologist and theologian, Henri Nouwen, helpfully writes of his experience of the 'very hard and painful' nature of the renunciation of academic life at Harvard to live in the L'Arche community with people with mental and physical disabilities. He employs words that express the challenging reality that many face when entering into the life experience of a marginalized community: he speaks of taking on a commitment to embrace a 'small, hidden life with people [who have] broken minds and bodies'.[19]

In Luke 9:46–8, the call of Jesus to renounce the 'natural' preference for worldly greatness that the disciples have been talking about among themselves is prefaced with a record of Jesus' second announcement of the personal suffering that will mark the pursuance of his messianic mission journey that the disciples are being challenged to share.[20] However, despite the radically challenging dynamics of a life intentionally directed towards what we have called incarnational connectedness, there is a gracious liveliness in the child–sign–act which lightens the otherwise sombre expectation of sacrificial conflict. In setting ourselves side by side with the child in Jesus' name, we find ourselves side by side with the One sent by the Father, enlivened by his life, and at the very heart of his missionary purpose and activity.[21] The experience of many is that the emotional and spiritual resilience demanded by the radical nature of missionary life is grounded in discovering personally effective ways of celebrating and of appropriating this energizing potential.

In summary, the child–sign–act event calls the reader–disciple to develop a liminal space of incarnational connectedness with the marginalized community at the frontier between their experience of social rejection and kingdom acceptance. It is in this space that transformation becomes possible for both the community and the missionary, because it is in such acts of missional activity that the possibility of kingdom acceptance and honour is expressed, and the self-giving of Christ can be experienced. Whatever the particular political or social expressions such a missional posture might entail for a particular disciple in a particular situation, this call will never demand less than personal commitment to true kingdom greatness expressed in self-giving and self-sacrificial solidarity with Luke's poor, lowly and little ones, embodied symbolically in the motif of 'this child', embraced 'in his name'.

Notes

[1] The reader has been prepared for the Nazareth declaration with its focus upon the 'poor' at Luke 4:18–21, through the Spirit-inspired words of Mary (Luke 1:46–55), her pious priestly relatives Elizabeth and Zechariah (Luke 1:68–79), the devout Simeon (Luke 2:30–35) and the prophetic baptizer John (Luke 3:4–6). Luke employs the ταπεινος, 'humble / lowly', word group three times: at Luke 1:48, in the description of Mary's personal social status in conjunction with δουλη, 'slave'; at Luke 1:52 as a class reference over against the ruling class; and at Luke 3:4–6 where the Isa. 40:3–5 citation employs the metaphorical potential of the word to describe the 'eschatological levelling' that will occur at the coming of the Lord. In Luke's ongoing presentation of Jesus' mission to address and redress the status of the 'poor', ταπεινος is recalled, as Jesus is twice presented as warning the proud and worldly status seekers that their eschatological end is to be brought low, ταπεινωθησεται, while those looked down upon, the ταπεινων, will be raised up (Luke 14:11; 18:14). The use of ταπεινωσει in the Isaiah citation at Acts 8:33 is a further example of the force of the word in Luke, as the Messiah is described as one who, 'in his lowliness (ταπεινωσιν) . . .was deprived of justice and his life was taken away'.

2   For a helpful review and full bibliography of the place of children in the
    Mediterranean world of the first century see Judith Gundry-Volf, 'The
    Least and the Greatest: Children in the New Testament', in *The Child
    in Christian Thought* (ed. M.J. Bunge; Grand Rapids: Eerdmans, 2001).

3   Luke develops his 'child' motif as effectively embodying the condition of
    those who are the particular focus of the messianic mission. He makes
    extensive use of three word groups to describe their experience of life-
    deprivation: ταπεινος – the word of social status and exclusion; πτωχος –
    the word of poverty and dependency; and μικρος – the word of small-
    ness and vulnerability.

4   Identification, variously interpreted, is widely recognized as a key ele-
    ment in the pursuit of missional connectedness. It is listed as one of
    principal values of the Urban Expression movement; see Juliet Kilpin,
    Urban to the Core: Motives for Incarnational Mission (Kibworth Beau-
    champ, Leics., UK: Matador, 2013), p. 160. See also Jenni Craig's over-
    view of the history and principles of the Servants movement founded by
    the New Zealander, Viv Grigg. The appendix sets out the ministry ethos
    of the organization. It cites the 'incarnational model' lived out by Jesus
    and recognizes that full socio-cultural identity is not possible but affirms
    that the effective expression of the gospel is through 'relational commit-
    ment' (Jenni Craig, *Servants among the Poor* [OMF Literature, 1998],
    p. 326). See also the very interesting discussion by Pamela Couture in
    her excellent book, *Seeing Children, Seeing God: A Practical Theology of
    Children and Poverty* (Nashville, TN: Abingdon Press, 2000), where she
    discusses the central importance of relationality in the context of what
    she describes as the 'poverty of tenuous relationships' (p. 14) that is char-
    acteristic of the experience of children in deprived communities.

5   Maria Lourdes was one of the first favela mothers to send her child
    along to the preschool preparation programme (PEPE) that Georgie
    developed in response to what we saw in Jardim Olinda. While it was
    clearly evident that children born into a typical favela community were
    entering the state school system seriously disadvantaged because of the
    poor educational and social background of their parents, a survey con-
    ducted with the help of students from the Baptist Theological Seminary
    where I was teaching helped us to appreciate the extent of the problem.
    We discovered that in Jardim Olinda seven out of every ten households
    had at least one child under seven years of age. A thorough evaluation
    of the socio-educational effectiveness of the PEPE programme formed
    the thesis of an MA in international education completed by Geor-
    gie through Sussex University in 2006. For full details of the PEPE

mission preschool programme for deprived communities see *www.pepe-network.org*.

6 In the context of Latin American liberation theological thinking, Jose Miguel Bonino concludes that it is through relational identification with the 'common people' that the church establishes a 'matrix of authentic identity' as effective representative of Christ: 'The church finds its identity when it "con-forms" to Jesus Christ, that is to say, when it assumes his "spiritual structure", his way of being. And what is his way of being? Here again the writings of the New Testament are unanimous. It is to be found in his identification with humanity, and, in particular with the poor and lowly. The logical conclusion is clear: the greater the churches identification with the common people; the more the church will be driven to an identification with the people, the more it will be in a position to reflect the identity of its Lord. Identity pushes towards identification, and identification is the matrix of authentic identity.' (Jose Miguel Bonino, 'Fundamental Questions in Ecclesiology', *The Challenge of Basic Christian Communities* 147 (Sao Paulo, Brazil, 1980).

7 See especially the correspondence between Luke 9:48 and Luke 10:16. The similarity with John 1:10–12 is also notable.

8 For further theological reflection upon this event see Stuart Christine, 'The Child of the Favela and the Christ of Luke 9:46–48', in *Theology, Mission and the Child: Global Perspectives* (Oxford: Regnum Books International, 2014), pp. 189–200.

9 Rev. 18:11–13 (NKJV).

10 Acts 1:1.

11 A phrase inspired by the opening dedication of John Hayes's stimulating book, *Sub-Merge – Living Deep in a Shallow World: Service, Justice and Contemplation Amongst the World's Poor* (Ventura, CA: Regal Books, 2006).

12 For further information about the artist and his approach see http://theologyforum.wordpress.com/2008/11/03/art-incarnation-%C2%BB-artist-statement-by-edward-knippers/

13 During our time associated with Jardim Olinda, around a half of the twenty or so adolescents with whom we had a relationship ended up killed in crime-related violence or police action.

14 Iolanda continues to live and work with children and young people in Heliopolis.

15 As I wrote today, I came across a simple verse quoted by P.T. Forsyth, the late nineteenth-century Scottish theologian:

I had a little daughter,
And she was given to me,
To lead me gently backward,
To the Heavenly Father's knee.
Religion in Recent Art (London: Hodder &
Stoughton, 1901), p. 121.

Although very much in the style of a bygone era, it echoes the innumerable occasions in the favelas of Brazilian mega cities, or the impoverished communities of the Andean mountains and Amazonian forest, when mothers have acknowledged that all they know about God they have learnt from their little children.

16 Mary Beasley expresses this same conviction, 'There is therefore a "mission-in-reverse", emanating from the "magisterium of the poor". The church does not only enter the world of marginal people in order to change their situation; it enters that area in order to be first changed itself.' (Mary Beasley, *Mission on the Margins* [Cambridge: Lutterworth Press, 1997]), p. 93.

17 John Wesley's *Journal*, 2 April 1739. The words are a reference to 2 Sam. 6, which recounts David's uninhibited response to a God-event in his life, that led him to dance and behave in what was considered to be a socially inappropriate, demeaning, manner.

18 Charles Elliott, *Comfortable Compassion? Poverty, Power and the Church* (London: Hodder & Stoughton, 1987), pp. 143–51.

19 Henri Nouwen, *In the Name of Jesus: Reflections on Christian Leadership* (London: Darton, Longman & Todd, 1989), pp. 11–12.

20 Luke 9:44–5. The narrative presents the beginning of the 'journey to Jerusalem' immediately after the child–sign–act. It is a striking feature of the narrative that the account concludes with the third passion announcement in Luke 18:31–3 and is set in juxtaposition with the account of Jesus's rebuking the disciples' rejection of the children at Luke 18:15–17, the co-text of Luke 9:46–8.

21 Rob O'Callaghan, former staff member of the Word Made Flesh mission group, has helpfully reviewed the challenges of inculturation and identification with the poor and mission in the way of Christ in, 'What do We Mean by "Incarnational Methodology?"' (WMF US & Global, http://wordmadeflesh.org/incarnational/, posted 2006) and writes of his personal experience of the challenges inherent to the pursuit of incarnational mission thus: 'We have found that as we seek to live faithful lives in relationships with the poor, they will teach us how to live with fewer things and less convenience, and to pursue this strange "downward mobility" happily' (p. 2).

3

Community: Marginality and Community Formation

Sian Murray Williams

As with the root of all good theology, my interest in community formation as mission sprang from an experience of church in which both happened at the same time and informed each other. It wasn't planned. It wasn't part of a clearly thought-out strategy. It wasn't a result of any purpose-driven reflection. It just happened as those who gathered together sought to be the church, the living body of Christ, at the same time wounded and glorious, story-bearers and hope-carriers, who struggled with living out faith in the daily plod of life.

The incidents were numerous and often tiny:

- a couple who attended a national gathering of the denomination for the first time coming back fired up with enthusiasm for credit unions, and triggering the church's very small involvement in the setting-up of a local branch;
- a woman with complex mental health issues bringing a tub of ice-cream to church so that everyone could celebrate her birthday, resulting in a shared diving into the tub with a multitude of teaspoons;
- asking the question 'Where have we seen God this week?' in worship services leading to urgent, connected prayers of intercession, thanksgiving and confession – and often a visit to the people mentioned in the week after the service 'just to see how they were';

- recognizing that the church met down the road from the county psychiatric hospital resulting in two members of the community joining in the chapel services at the hospital every week; and so on, and so on, and so on.

Small things, organically grown relationships, bite-sized chunks of the kingdom of God recognized and seized for what they were – a working together with God in God's reconciling work by the rough and ready communities of faith God calls into being.

This amazing experience of church led me to reflect on what it was about this group of people, drawn together week by week, that resulted in both growth in faith and friendship, but also a deeper engagement with the wider community. And how they fed each other. The church was small, human-sized, where anonymity was impossible. The core congregation had known each other for a long time, but welcomed in those who joined it with utter gratitude – and the resulting change in dynamic was embraced. People's experience of life had left a number of scars but had also shaped hearts and minds that understood the human condition. They were well acquainted with the light and shade in which life is lived.

The key reflection from all this is that we learn to follow Jesus by following Jesus. Talking about it is useful – but doing it is transformative. Participation is essential. Suzanne Johnson, arguing that the church is the red hot centre of spiritual formation says:

> When we construe spirituality as participation in God's *oikonomia* (housekeeping) then a spirituality cultivated in the private retreat of self is logically impossible. This theme affirms our interconnectedness and our indwelling with the whole of the created order. We are to look after the well-being of all creation, as well as one another, because it is, just as we are, sacred and inviolable.[1]

As a church we were involved in a rhythm of practices that built up community from within, enabling it to not only look out but walk out into the neighbourhood in confidence that love really does change things. Johnson again: 'Through the spiritual disciplines we remember our baptism, realize our vocation, and fulfil our Christian calling in the world . . . The aim of spiritual discipline is not self-actualization, but rather realization of our baptism throughout a lifetime.'[2]

David Augsburger develops that understanding further: '*Tripolar spirituality* . . . possesses three dimensions: it is inwardly directed, upwardly compliant, and outwardly committed. The spirituality of personal transformation (the inner journey), the experience of divine encounter (the God-ward journey) and the relation of integrity and solidarity with the neighbour (the co-human journey with friend and enemy, with neighbour and persecutor) cannot be divided.'[3]

Since then, a move to a new sphere of ministry and location led to engagement with other communities of faith and the learning continued. So this chapter focuses on how the intentional rhythm of Christian gathering – with a particular community of which I was a part as a reference point – shapes a community able to engage with its locality and (which surprised it) the global community too.

Worship

Christian community finds its cutting edge through being engaged with and attentive to the ordinary experiences of daily living. From my own experience, conversations with workmates, a shared cup of coffee with a neighbour, visiting someone in hospital, a bus-journey chat, the regular holding together of family life, raised questions, released encouragement and sympathy, and deepened an understanding of the human heart; Christ was known. And all this came into even keener focus in the Sunday morning worship event when the laser beam of God's love and life illuminated those little experiences. Through worship, the little stories of faith were held in the big story of salvation, revealing areas of concern, increasing insight, strengthening resolve, as each daily experience found significance and meaning. In worship, the previous week was held by the community before God, and God spoke, galvanizing the people for deeper or new involvement in the coming week. Tearing down the old dualism of 'leaving our week at the door so that worship wouldn't be contaminated', the people offered God whole-of-life worship, held in a special way in a particularly focused time on Sunday morning, connecting them with the eternal worship of the church. Alan and Eleanor Kreider remind us that in worship, 'We encounter God, in trembling and thanksgiving, in the brief present; there we recall what God has done in the past; and we receive God's empowerment to collaborate in the future in what God is passionately committed to – the *missio Dei*, leading to the reconciliation of all things in Christ.'[4]

Exploring the formative power of the congregation, or the gathered community, Craig Dykstra writes:

> A basic reality of congregational life is that we are often engaged in socially acceptable (indeed, socially celebrated) patterns of mutual self-destruction; and . . . in and through congregational life, these patterns are at the same time being redemptively modified, transformed . . . Precisely in the midst of its sinfulness, rather than apart from it, the congregation has power to mediate the gospel in such a way that the 'speaking' of it can restructure and transform human personal and social life.[5]

The 'patterns of mutual self-destruction' are formed early on as we appropriate the values and measures of culture and society to live by. They include the relentless search for identity through consumption, an unyielding drive to achieve, the deep desire to be 'right', the applauding of 'success' and the inability to hold failure – all of which are alive and well in the church, and continue to be alienating factors for those who have nothing, are not productive, think differently and do not match up to any socially accepted understandings of 'success'. These 'patterns' are checked in confession and repentance. 'What the congregation can do is acknowledge its participation in patterns of mutual self-destruction . . . recognise its incapacity to secure itself; and accept, proclaim, and give thanks for the establishing and sustaining power that belongs to God alone. In sum, the congregation may worship.'[6]

This is echoed by James K.A. Smith in his work on how humans are much more creatures driven by desire rather than reason. Arguing that we worship what we most love, he lays bare our vulnerability in adopting the secular liturgies of the shopping mall, workplace or academy, which feed a distorted view of human flourishing. It is in Christian worship that the illusions of these liturgies, together with their damaging impact of human lives, are exposed and subverted: 'Christian worship needs to be intentionally liturgical, formative, and pedagogical in order to counter such mis-informations and misdirections. While the practices of Christian worship are best understood as the restoration of an original, creational desire for God, practically speaking, Christian worship functions as counter-formation to the mis-formation of secular liturgies into which are "thrown" from an early age.'[7] This, he continues, results in us inhabiting our vocation to be image bearers of God. 'When we gather, we are responding to a call to worship; that call is an echo and renewal of the call of creation to be God's image bearers for the world, and we fulfil the *mission* of being God's image bearers by undertaking the work of culture making.'[8]

How our community learned to do that could be construed as 'same old, same old' but the deep tradition of the church in its worshipping practices were life-giving. The commonly held practices of reading the Bible, exploring God's word for that community which sprang from the text, engaging in prayer, confession, praise and intercession, singing songs of praise, lament and proclamation, taking up an offering of money and talents for God's use in the world, hearing testimony, breaking bread, pouring wine, baptizing new (and in some cases, old) believers – all that in its quiet weekly rhythm built up a community that positively anticipated God's presence in worship and the week.

Reading the Bible

Reading the text was part of every gathering, on Sundays and at other times. Following the revised common lectionary was interrupted with other foci as we journeyed with God into some theological questions, or into a season where exploring a book of the Bible beckoned. But the emphasis spoke to people's experiences there and then – and it was our experience that God always had something to say. One of the most vibrant times of exploring the Bible together was initiated by the community itself. Under the banner of 'If I could ask God one question, it would be . . .' people submitted questions that were uppermost in their minds, often shaped by their conversations with people with whom they shared the week. No big surprises – Why does God allow suffering? How do I know what God's purpose is for me? What happens to me when I die? Why do some prayers get answered and others don't?' This type of series ran a number of times, building up a keen sense that the biblical text could speak directly into the living issues facing people. We often didn't come up with clear-cut answers, but we explored the contours of the questions, seeking wisdom and reassurance from the Bible, along with embracing the challenges held in the text.

The Word Discovered Together

I've used the word 'we'. That became an important perspective in discerning what God was saying to us. While as a minister, I enjoyed (and still do) tussling with the text and discerning God's word for the moment, what I hadn't anticipated was that in our weekly gatherings we would be joined by staff and service users from the county psychiatric hospital which was just down the road. Their presence was a huge gift in so many ways, not least because any lofty ideas I might have had about controlling the word of God fled through the window fairly early on. Frequent interruptions and contributions of stories to illustrate a point subverted any 'normal' monologue style. We found ourselves sharing the word together so that the community was engaged, listening, contributing and offering perspectives and insights that I hadn't seen in the text at all. There was a real sense of us creating – or co-creating – something together so that week by week

God came close. The word was living. The word created things, new possibilities, new perspectives, new courage, new vision and, thankfully, lives reborn. There was a dynamic sense of God's action in the community. For the sake of complete accuracy, there were also weeks where the conversation veered into the land of fantasy – and the task of oversight became directive. There was no hard and fast rule, just intuition, reason and faith combining, hopefully, in the moment.

Unearthing the word as a community discipline enlivened our collective imagination. Engaging with the God who makes deserts blossom, enables young virgins and old women to give birth, helps the blind to see and the lame walk, restores ruined places, welcomes home exiles and, supremely, raises the dead to life, leads to astonishing acts of kingdom living. Walter Brueggemann speaks of exploring the biblical text as laying out new possibilities both for individual lives and for creation. The dominant narratives of our lives, which in the West are profoundly influenced by Enlightenment assumptions, are upturned as again we inhabit the story of God's work in the world. He says:

> These three dimensions of the textual process – *formation, interpretation, reception* – are all creative acts in which the text and its meaning are not only an offer made to the community, but are a product generated in the community. Interpretation and listening, as well as formation, are creative acts of construal. This creative aspect of the text is unavoidable and should be welcomed as an arena in which faith is received, discerned, and made pertinent. Some may think such creative possibility in interpretation is an aberration to be avoided. It cannot be avoided. Nor should it be avoided, because it is the way in which God's Word is alive among us.[9]

Ensuring all are involved in this type of discovery together also raises the whole question of power dynamics in faith communities. Who establishes the norm? Who holds the key to participation? Who is included and who is excluded in decision-making? As mentioned, in our community we found ourselves challenged by those who were experiencing mental health issues. This however was only one of the ways we were challenged about who was included and who was excluded. In his excellent book,[10] Laurie Green argues that the church needs to foster a more robust engagement with issues of economic injustice and confront systems which exclude people from a thriving life. He criticizes recent government policy regarding poverty which create short-term projects and schemes aimed at the excluded while leaving the underlying structures and systems untouched. Green argues that it is only by hearing the voices of those who are disenfranchised from real choice, or means of self-determination, that the church is able to be a healthy community. Only in this way is the radical vision of the gospel made clear and the transforming power of faithful living revealed. Green speaks of the trust that grows from this kind of long-term listening, saying that 'it is perhaps this trust against all the odds that I have sensed during my worship on the poor estates. Continuing to keep things together as a congregation week after week and year after year is a minor miracle in itself and speaks volumes about the depth of faith despite the ongoing offensiveness of exclusion.'[11]

Bread, Wine and Sending

Our regular pattern of sharing communion, which was largely done in a stripped-back, simple way, brought us to the defining heart of Christian experience. The bread and wine, and the presence of each other around the table, drew us again to encounter Christ in his broken body and blood poured out for the life of the world. This is the pattern of our discipleship. The way of sacrificial love leaves us vulnerable, stripped back, simple and utterly held by a faithful and merciful God, who nourishes us and beckons us along the way in the company of Jesus. This is the meal that becomes a tangible expression of hope in a hungry world. A measure of that hope was symbolized when, one Sunday, we had a feast of bread rolls. Some were broken during communion itself but immediately following the service, where the world had been brought before God in prayer, we each took some of the plentiful supply of rolls that were left to share with neighbours, friends and strangers as a sign of God's provision and care. Giving the rolls invited a story to be told; 'Where have these come from?' And the encounters found their way back into worship the following week.

We also discovered the power of communion as, in Wesley's term, a 'converting ordinance'. Around the table and hearing the invitation to those who 'love the Lord a little and would like to love him more'[12] led to one person discovering the loving embrace of God in Christ. Some months later, we celebrated her baptism in a borrowed pool followed by a barbecue. It might be easier to experience that in a small church where gathering around the table is a lived reality and not a metaphor. Perhaps the words have a peculiar power when you virtually have a set place at the table and know the rest of the guests by name.

Participating in smaller communities of faith in more marginal situations begs questions of the table. The tradition of the church reserves the right to share in the bread and wine for the baptized. All completely understandable theologically, but when those who are still waiting, like Godot, for the first drops of 'trickle-down' economics to reach them, or those who are literally hungry for bread and hope, or those whose sense of self has been stripped away by abuse in many forms, or those who simply have no stake in a functioning society, stand around the table with hands outstretched, it is so obvious that they are met by the Christ of the outstretched arms on the cross, sharing his life made real in bread and wine with them. Jesus Christ is the host of this meal. The presider, or celebrant, simply gets to wait at the table, making sure there's enough bread to go round, enough wine to satisfy the thirsty and do the washing-up afterwards.[13]

Singing New Songs of Faith

The church sang songs from a range of sources – old hymns, new songs, and ones written by musicians in the church itself, through which church expressed her own words of faith in her own melody.

One Sunday morning the lectionary reading led us to the Song of Miriam in Exodus 15. As our response, the church wrote its own song celebrating God's faithfulness to this particular group of people. It wasn't difficult. A flip chart and the question 'Where have we known God's faithfulness in this community's life?' led to all sorts of stories, phrases and words being offered – all written up in no particular order. But the refrain was clearly going to be 'in dark times, he gave us strength, and he will lead us on'. Fashioning the offerings into stanzas, and employing the great skills of two professional musicians in the community, 'Our Song' become a firm part of the church's canon and significant part of the worship offered. It won't feature in any major Christian summer festival, nor find its way into a songbook, but the song helped that community express its gratitude and faith in God. The community gathered around it. The story of that church has now moved on and there's a new song to sing, so no more verses will be added to the original. As with all good hymns and songs, 'what we sing says something significant about who we are – and *whose* we are'.[14]

This experience has left me with a question for every Christian community – what is the song God would have you sing at the moment? For some it would be a glorious song of praise, for others a quiet, humble song of confession, and for others a profound pouring out of grief, and for yet others a call to renewed commitment and unity. It's a great question to ask through the lens of community formation. Around what song can we gather in this season of our shared life?

Witness and Story-Sharing

A key aspect of our worshipping time revolved around asking the simple question 'Where have I seen God this past week?' Initially this met with a little anxiety in response, not least because there's a residual sense of there having to be a 'right' or 'holy' answer to the question. For those who have acres of Christian experience but might not have read widely, nor been, in their own eyes, worthy to respond, this question can be daunting. But over time it led to a number of contributions – from a significant shared conversation, something beautiful seen in nature, a funny incident that caused good, healthy laughter, an interview on TV, or praying with someone. The responses revealed a God who was utterly present in the daily, often small, dimensions of our lives. The effect on the community was threefold. It enabled the community to understand the daily rhythms of other people's lives – who was in them, what their work or home life was like, what gifts lay in the person. It earthed the prayer of the community; as the responses to the question grew, areas of concern for people, circumstances, the caring services, schools, hospitals, the local council, and so on were all prayed for with intensity. And most significantly, asking the question led to a community actively looking for God's presence in the week. Small attention to where we might have seen God once in the last seven days formed a community that could identify the contours of the kingdom of God, or the presence of deep and systemic need, or injustice, or the profound cry for God's presence – and all that was fed back into the praying life of the whole community. Intercession became a significant part of the church's engagement with and gift to the world. Walter Wink writes: 'Intercession is spiritual defiance of what is, in the name of what God has promised. Intercession visualizes an alternative future to the one apparently fated by the momentum of current contradictory forces. It infuses the air of a time yet to be into the suffocating atmosphere of the present.'[15]

The practice of sharing witness demands interpretation. Where is God? What aspect of God do we see? How does this resonate with the biblical witness? Is there something new here? Is it faithful to the story? Are we invited to respond in some way? The very act of sharing stories about our experience of God becomes an act of dangerous proclamation. In her exploration of *Preaching as Testimony*, Anna Carter Florence writes:

It sounds utterly shocking, like walking right over the edge of a cliff, and indeed it is. When we choose testimony, we throw certainty to the wind and trust to the Spirit; we *have* to! We trust that God will initiate encounters with human beings. We trust that we will have the courage and sensitivity and restlessness to interpret these encounters. We trust that we will find the words to testify to what we have seen and believed about it. And we trust that the community of faith and, ultimately, God will judge our witness as well as our own engagement with it. What we give up . . . is control. But I think the first family secret is that we never had it.[16]

Feasting and Friendship

I have yet to meet a Christian community that doesn't in some way enjoy food. What's interesting is that the table will be set with different food depending on context. Eating together for us was transformational. This particular community didn't have a pattern of 'dinner parties', but every church lunch was a 'Bring and Share' – and people brought food from their own table. We could always depend on one contribution of six hard boiled eggs. This principle also spilled over into communion. The person who had been responsible for preparing the table for some decades always brought bread from her table – which in this case was supermarket Value Bread. Behind the scenes, there were some who yearned that we use a freshly baked loaf in a creative design, as the drama of tearing the bread apart when declaring 'This is my body, broken for you' does admittedly lose some of its impact with sliced bread. But it had come from the home, from the one who served the church by preparing the table. And that needed honouring. A 'Bring and Share' democratizes the feasting table which is wrenched from the hands of one particular class or group. It also resonated with the experience of the early Christians who would take offerings of food to worship which was then distributed among the poor by the church leadership. And it was from these offerings, brought from the homes of the rich and the poor, that the bread and wine for communion would be taken.[17]

The way feasting can impact the dynamics of intentionally being together, was highlighted for me in the unlikely environment of 'the church meeting' – which, in my tradition, is where the church discerns the mind of Christ for its life and witness. At this church, I went fresh-faced into my first few meetings with the chairs laid out in rows, me sat at the front and a fairly long agenda, replicating my experience in previous churches. I decided what should be on the agenda, the important business to be discerned (as I discerned it), and off we went. Only we didn't. People didn't speak. Those first few meetings were tumbleweed moments – and no amount of cajoling people to talk worked.

What to do? Clearly the layout had to change, and what if we introduced food into the equation? And if we did that, what food would work here? It became obvious that the food around which everyone could easily gather was fish and chips. So we started the practice of eating together. We gave our church fixer our orders and he nipped off to the local chippy to pick up the food. In the meantime, we rearranged the room so that we met around a long table – on which had been laid cutlery, salt, vinegar and all manner of sauces. The evening began with us sharing good food, news of what had happened during the day, natural stories of concern or laughter, and then we stayed around the table to talk about church issues which needed decision or wisdom. By the time the 'church business' bit came into play, everyone had talked to their neighbour, relationships reconnected, news shared and everyone was now ready. The solution to participation was not rocket science, but it was utterly transformative to our common life. Food alters things in good ways. The old adage 'no eating, no meeting' is a good principle.

'To eat together is to be equal. To sit at the same table, eye-to-eye and fork-to-fork – or chopstick-to-chopstick is to meet on common ground', says Simon Carey Holt, a former chef now Baptist minister in Melbourne, Australia. He continues:

> The civil rights movement of the 1950s in the southern United States began as a dispute over the rights of 'negroes' to eat at the same lunch counters as the whites. More than that, it was the right to sit there *with* the whites. To share food at the same table is a covenant act. In the Ancient

Near East, the incubator of food culture, the sharing of food carried life-long bonds of obligation for host and guest. Though our table customs today don't carry such tangible commitments, obligations remain, for food still has a covenantal power.[18]

Sharing food says something significant about the present, and opens up a new future. An interesting 'in the moment' opportunity involving food happened on a church anniversary where the community had gathered to give thanks to God. Just down the road, a former primary school had become a Muslim school. On the same day, the school was holding a fete and invited the church to come and share food with the school community – which many did. Along with it came the opportunity to have small conversations, to learn names, and to sow the initial fragile seeds of relationship.

Early on, the church met for a Christmas dinner together. It had been the practice of this small community for everyone to buy Christmas presents for everyone else in the church. As the church slowly began to grow, this became quite a draining expectation. So some suggested that, rather than buying each other presents, how about giving what we collectively would have spent to Christian Aid to buy gifts for people overseas. The community needed no persuasion. People within it understood what living in poverty meant from their own experience. We aimed to buy a goat. We ended up buying fourteen.

Alongside being part of this church community, I was also chaplain for a season at an arts centre in a nearby Baptist church which was effectively the church's mission arm. People could dance, paint, sculpt or draw and young people could develop their musical skills. The church hosted hundreds of people each week that came through its doors. Some involved in the centre would articulate a Christian faith, but many others spoke in terms of their spirituality, rather than adherence to any established form of faith. We had so many excellent conversations which, when mediated in a context of the creative arts, held a particular power. Each week we shared lunch, held in the body of the church, where around a series of fold-up tables we shared home-made soup, bread and cheese. As a framework for the event, we devised a simple form of words. These liturgies were seasonal in flavour and simply allowed time for reflection. They included words from the Bible and other writings. Fundamentally, they created space for the possibility of God in lives which would not naturally articulate such a presence. This wasn't 'hard evangelism' and some may find that tricky, but it created a context where people were held, deeper meaning explored, and the potential for further conversation if people wanted one. Ann Morisy calls this 'apt liturgy', which she goes on to unpack in this way: 'Apt liturgy is about churches doing what only they can do. It is an art that churches are becoming increasingly adept at expressing . . . Apt liturgy is specifically about wide accessibility and (usually) engaging with people who are having to deal with hard emotions.' She continues:

> Part of the art of apt liturgy is to indicate or acknowledge God's involvement in these universal struggles as well as His concern for each individual. This capacity to signify God's incarnation or presence in the world is one of the essential tasks of the foundational domain. It is not sufficient just to encourage recognition of there being more to life than meets the eye: if a foundation is to be prepared for the explicit or essential aspects of our faith then God cannot remain a distant, uninvolved power or force. Apt liturgy therefore has to express or allude to the intimacy or alongsideness of God who is our Heavenly Father.[19]

The lunch-time event ticked that box.

Our current church in inner-city Bristol opened a community café three years ago. Staffed by two part-time paid managers and a host of volunteers, the community café offers good, nutritious food at affordable prices. The area is multicultural with people from different parts of the world living alongside old Bristolians, themselves from different parts of the world too. With a bohemian edge, the neighbourhood is home to the world. One of the key values of the café is that no one will be turned away based on their ability to pay. This means that up to a third of the meals served in the day may be free to the customer. This café has a loyalty card. Subverting the usual rules where a loyalty card gives benefit to the cardholder, producing this card at the till will add an extra £1.00 onto the bill to help cover the costs of those who can't pay. And the radical nature of God's jubilee economic framework is made real. In common with many others, the church hosts a food bank, and very strong relationships with food bank organizers and customers have been built up. Again, stories from the café and food bank find their way into the prayers offered by the wider community on Sunday mornings. The church is also well aware of the devastating effect that a delay or change in benefits can have on a family, so raising political and social awareness is just a natural by-product of this engagement.

Carey Holt again:

> In an age of fast food, microwave ovens and fragmented schedules, the dining room table sits routinely empty in many households, a museum-like tribute to a quaint practice of long ago. Indeed, times have changed and so much of life has improved along the way. But what has been lost? The quest for meaning, intimacy and communion seems ever more urgent. The table beckons. It beckons because at its core, the table is about such fundamentally human things as intimacy and family, identity and communication, reconciliation and romance, covenant and community, redemption and friendship, sustenance and celebration, beginnings and endings. The table beckons because it plays host to so much more than biological necessity.[20]

This was *profoundly* our experience.

Prayer, Attentiveness and Discernment

As we've already explored, discovering the vibrant connection between faith and life is key to community formation and engagement with the world. An area ripe for attention is the call to reinvigorate the praying life of a community. Paying attention to God's activity in lives, the community, neighbourhood and world, and discerning God's purposes for the future is a spiritual discipline that needs practising. We live in a season where there is so much cultural change that many Christian communities experience a corresponding wobble in their confidence in the power of God to transform lives and situations, raising anxiety about whether they can hear God at all. I believe that there is a desperate need to get to grips with the discipline of attentiveness to God, orientating hearts and minds to the one who says, 'I am doing a new thing! Now it springs up; do you not perceive it?' (Isa. 43:19). In too many situations we cannot see because we haven't learned how to look. This disguises the fact that there is a deep yearning for greater connection with God, for practices that help us to abide in Christ (John 15). In a culture which expects quick answers and where pragmatism trumps wisdom, the practice of waiting, abiding and deep listening to God doesn't always come easily or as good news. That weighted waiting, however, is part of how we can be fully present as hope-filled communities of good news to the world.

Often we need some specific help or focus in order to develop these attentive and reflective practices. In one instance, where I was assisting a church to discern the next stage of their journey together, we used a resource created by the Baptist Union of Victoria, Australia.[21] Everyone embarked on a very deliberate two-week period of reading set parts of the Bible each day, of guided prayer, and of paying attention to what they noticed in the text, in themselves and in the neighbourhood in that fortnight. The joy of this was that all could be a part of it, from the very young and very old, the highly educated and those with learning difficulties, men and women, those at the core and those on the margins, and it encompassed the theological spectrum. It was an exercise in deliberate attentiveness to God and, following the two-week period, everyone had the opportunity to share what they had discovered. In some respects the things people noticed were not surprising. What was perhaps more profound was the collective sense in which the community took part, the shared openness towards seeing new things and towards being changed in order to join with what God was doing; and the realization that God had indeed spoken.

Conclusion

What all of this shows is that community formation and mission are inextricably entwined having relationship at their heart – as David Augsburger puts it, a commitment to a tripolar relationship with self, God and the world.[22] Establishing healthy relationships and being committed to formational practices that include every class, creed and colour, these communities of faith are called to embrace all people in order to embody the 'fullness of him who fills all in all' (Eph. 1:23, NRSV). They are God's subversive agencies of grace and reconciling love. Settling for less is not an option.

Furthermore, it is clear that Christian community cannot happen without an intentional, creative and open-hearted commitment to relationship, guided by rhythms of worship, word, sacrament, feasting and prayer. These are not simply matters of tradition, but are well-tested ways of Christian spirituality which facilitate the Christian community in every generation to maintain a visionary, radical and counter-cultural engagement with those in marginal places.

Notes

[1] S. Johnson, *Christian Spiritual Formation in the Church and Classroom* (Nashville, TN: Abingdon Press, 1989), p. 26.

[2] Johnson, *Christian Spiritual Formation*, p. 60.

[3] D. Augsburger, *Dissident Discipleship: A Spirituality of Self-Surrender, Love of God, and Love of Neighbor* (Grand Rapids, MI: Brazos Press, 2006), p. 13.

[4] A. Kreider and E. Kreider, *Worship and Mission After Christendom* (Milton Keynes: Paternoster Press, 2009), p. 47.

[5] C. Dykstra, *Growing in the Life of Faith* (Louisville. KY: Geneva Press, 1999), p. 84.

[6] Dykstra, *Growing*, p. 91.

[7] J.K.A. Smith, *Desiring the Kingdom: Worship, Worldview and Cultural Formation* (Grand Rapids, MI: Baker Academic, 2009), p. 88.

[8] Smith, *Desiring*, p. 165.

[9] W. Brueggemann, *The Word Militant: Preaching the Decentering Word* (Minneapolis, MN: Fortress Press, 2007), p. 85.

10 L. Green, *Blessed are the Poor? Urban Poverty and the Church* (London: SCM Press, 2015).

11 Green, *Blessed*, pp. 138–9.

12 Baptist Union of Great Britain, *Patterns and Prayers for Christian Worship: A Guidebook for Worship Leaders* (Oxford: Oxford University Press, 1991), p. 81.

13 T. Gorringe, *The Sign of Love: Reflections on the Eucharist* (London: SPCK, 1997) has a helpful discussion on this perspective.

14 Smith, *Desiring*, p. 173.

15 W. Wink, *Engaging the Powers: Discernment and Resistance in a World of Domination* (Minneapolis, MN: Augsburg Fortress, 1992), p. 298.

16 A. Carter Florence, *Preaching as Testimony* (Louisville, KY: Westminster/John Knox Press, 2007), p. 65.

17 A. Kreider, *Worship and Evangelism in Pre-Christendom* (Cambridge: Grove Books, 1995), pp. 34–5.

18 S. Carey Holt, *Eating Heaven: Spirituality at the Table* (Brunswick East, Victoria: Acorn Press, 2013), p. 121.

19 A. Morisy, *Journeying Out: A New Approach to Christian Mission* (London: Continuum Books, 2004), pp. 156–7.

20 Carey Holt, *Eating Heaven*, p. 3.

21 Baptist Union of Victoria, *Open to God: Resources for Decision Making in Church Communities* (DVD, 2009).

22 Augsburger, *Dissident Discipleship*, p. 13.

4

Mission and Marginality: Editorial Conversation

Mike Pears and Paul Cloke

The Word became flesh and made his dwelling among us. We have seen his glory, the glory of the One and Only Son, who came from the Father, full of grace and truth (John 1:14).

The three chapters in this first part of *Mission in Marginal Places: The Theory* provide us with a most helpful guide to the complex question of how Christian mission can embrace an intentionally incarnational and context-specific approach. How can we become an embodiment of the message of Jesus as we attempt to dwell among marginal communities? How can we embody the grace and truth of God as we involve ourselves in mission in marginal places? As Christian Scharen[1] has pointed out there are two founding attitudes towards mission: either the church withdraws from the world in order to build and maintain a clear identity over against the world; or the church needs to re-enact how Jesus gave himself away for the sake of the world. Our discussion, then, draws on this second option and points us to a reflection of how exactly we can be involved in this contemporary re-enactment of the Word becoming flesh.

Throughout this discussion, we have to assume that the foundation of mission is an ongoing encounter – a connectedness – with God.

Without a continuing search for and appreciation of such connectedness, mission will run on empty. Equally, we need to assume that the goal is not the renewal of ourselves or our Christian community, but rather to take our encounter with the truth and grace of God beyond our congregations so as to impact others. Self-serving mission is, then, a contradiction in terms, although there is plenty of evidence that in the process of serving others, God will renew us and those with us (but not necessarily in ways that we anticipate or desire!).

How, then, do we start to understand this re-enaction of how Jesus gave himself away for the sake of the world? In Rowan Williams'[2] terms, we have to practise 'dispossession'. Being sent out for mission is not a proclamation of how gifted or faithful or energetic or articulate *we* are; it is a practice in which we attempt to give ourselves away for the sake of others, stripping away our proud and sometimes brash self-assurance in order to be in community with others, and to allow the ways they receive the message of Jesus to influence and deepen our ways of seeing and knowing the gospel. Dispossession is a rather anarchic giving-away of ourselves for the sake of the world, in order to point to Jesus' life of no-holds-barred self-giving for the sake of new kinds of community. Dispossession inherently demands a humble posture that acknowledges our personal incompleteness and engages in reflexive and rigorous critique of ourselves. It is this humility, not our personal self-assurance, which enables an openness to others and a capacity to give ourselves away. And the three chapters in this part point to significant aspects of how such humility becomes contextualized.

The first context is that of place. Mission involves the church in being sent out to every creature and all places, and is especially relevant among those who are disenfranchised by the context in which they live. However, the characteristics and dynamics of mission will need to be different in specific place-contexts. One-size-fits-all mission seems doomed to failure because it inherently seeks to bring generic answers to rather different sets of questions. As Mike Pears writes, people involved in mission need to *slow down* and *be attentive to place*. Humility in this context means eschewing any preconceived notions that we know what is best for people, and that the nature of their places is easily understood. Place is a significant factor in the shaping of everyday life, and such shaping needs to be grasped if mission is to be incarnate where particular people dwell. The problem is that places are complex and contested. As Doreen Massey[3] has shown us, places can both be strongly influenced by the different relations they have to the globalizing world and by the product of implicit local orthodoxies. To present a singular picture of a place will be to underestimate the cultural politics of social relations therein – politics that can set up implicit but powerful expectations about behaviour and performative posture, and can end up excluding certain groups of people who are deemed to be 'out-of-place' by others. While some places themselves can be described as marginalized, the social processes of marginalization are uneven and complex, leading to considerable internal variegation of marginality, including forms that are relatively invisible. Mission, then, involves a slow and reflexive 'getting to know' about place, dealing not only with obvious socio-economic traits but also with less visible cultural and spiritual landscapes.

Mike's chapter shows us how Jesus set about upsetting the normal power relations, turning upside down place-based orthodoxies of what was regarded as traditional, civilized or pure. Rather than affirming and reinforcing unjust and exclusionary arrangements of places, Jesus engaged in a kind of redemptive conversion of those places. How do we go and do likewise? Certainly not by bringing with us a preconceived model of place and inviting local people to join in with our model or vision for their place. Surely redemptive conversion involves finding out what God is already doing, and joining in with that; a participation with the Spirit in the turning upside down and rearranging of place. This suggests that mission should be built strategically around a reflexive attentiveness to any forms of unusual arrangements of relations and things within places – where the work of the Spirit brings about unplanned, unpredictable and transformational impacts. Mike very helpfully points to the 'space between the self and the other' as a crucial arena in which the Spirit does this kind of work; that space where we step out into circumstances that we can't control, where the grip of obvious common sense is loosened, and where humility and dispossession permit new encounters with others. Discernment of such spaces is key to joining in with the redemptive conversion of places.

A second aspect in the contextualization of humility relates to how people involved in mission embody the self-giving character of God in among their communities – that is how they can be effectively *incarnational.* Stuart Christine's chapter discusses how we might become available to God and to the marginal community around us in ways that facilitate the emergence of authentic expressions of the gospel and the kingdom. He notes how Jesus used child-centred events and metaphors in which childlike embodiment of weakness, vulnerability and inconsequentiality came to represent core ideas about what it is to be effectively incarnational. We can conclude from that incarnational mission is not predicated on self-aware personal qualities and gifting but is rather about a giving-away of self-importance in order that the person and character of Jesus can freely emerge; so that the community concerned gets to experience the kingdom in events of revelation and restoration.

To be incarnational is to be so connected with God that proactive self-giving points to Jesus and the breaking out of his kingdom rather than to self-subscribed clever or effective Christianity. Only in this way can incarnational mission achieve affirmative solidarity and empathetic relations with those on the margins. Nevertheless, mission in practice is no Disney-movie; mission narratives of revelation and redemption are typically interspersed with very practical expressions of what it is to be vulnerable, inconsequential and weak in contexts which are beyond our control. Stuart reminds us that marginalized communities are often uncomfortable places to be in among, and that attempting to stand in the redemptive spaces that are swamped by a dark and enveloping sea of need can be a practice that is physically and emotionally exhausting. No wonder that most Christians tend to choose to restrict their embodiment of vulnerability by practising a limited flip-in / flip-out from contact with marginalized people and places. There is less risk here of losing control and changing the self. On the other hand, such a recognition can easily induce a kind of pride among incarnational practitioners based on their credentials of having given themselves away to a greater extent than have other Christians. Incarnational humility is slippery in both of these contexts. At heart, incarnation is about being in among marginalized people while at the same time being in among the transformational presence and power of Jesus – a power that is sufficient to induce childlikeness and to energize and restore incarnational catalytics.

The third context in which being sent out to be in among can be considered refers to the use of intentional practices of dispossession in the area of our own spirituality. In her chapter on developing intentional community, Sian Murray Williams demonstrates the importance of Christian community in the mutually reinforcing development of faith and discipleship. She emphasizes the transformative power of *doing* – that is how we learn to follow Jesus by actually participating with him in our everyday lives. In this context, small personal stories of faith involving organic relationships and bite-sized revelations of God's kingdom can be held in creative partnership with the big story of salvation, leading to a potent combination of divine encounter, development of missional relationships with neighbours, and progressive personal transformation. The message here is of the benefits of participating in an intentional Christian community, and the value of adherence to intentional Christian practices such as reading and understanding the Bible, prayerful discernment, worship, testimony and *koinonia*. It is in these practices that the world's distorted view of human flourishing can be exposed and subverted, and it is from these forms of communal participation and sharing that a mission perspective can emerge.

Sian's chapter helpfully reminds us that these basic practices should not be disregarded, and that there is a risk that some forms of incarnational mission will underestimate the importance of developing a community of faith that embodies an intentional, creative and open-hearted commitment to relationship. In this sense, intentional community formation and mission can be inextricably entwined, but clearly this is not always the case. While it is important not to discard the practices of intentional community development, it seems equally important to ensure that emphasis on intentional community does not negate practices that fuel a going-out beyond that congregation into the wider community. In the chapter Sian illustrates several ways in which intentional practices develop organically into outward-facing relations, but it may be that more specific and intentional *missional practices* will sometimes be necessary to ensure exposure to spaces of risk and difference, and the breaking-down of mutual barriers between self and other. So, for example, specifically intentional practices of reflexive attentiveness to surrounding community, or of hospitality to people beyond the confines of intentional Christian community, could also be useful additions with which to enable more radical and edgy practices of mission.

These discussions of what it is to participate in the 'word becoming flesh' in mission in marginal places can be summarized in terms of the practice of God-connected explorations in that space between the self and the other. It is to the question of 'who is this other' that the book now turns.

Notes

1   C. Scharen, *Fieldwork in Theology* (Grand Rapids, MI: Baker, 2015).
2   R. Williams, *A Ray of Darkness* (Cambridge: Cowley,1995).
3   D. Massey, *For Space* (London: Sage, 2005).

Part II

Mission and Others: And You Shall Love Your Neighbour . . .

5

Embrace: Encountering Others in a 'Postwelfare' Society

Andrew Williams

Introduction

In Luke 10:25–37 Jesus tells a story of the 'Good Samaritan' after being asked, 'Who is my neighbour?' The question was deemed to be self-justifying and seeking to narrow God's love for all people to a particular ethical and political expression. Despite its familiarity the story is worth quoting at length:

> On one occasion an expert in the law stood up to test Jesus. 'Teacher,' he asked, 'what must I do to inherit eternal life?'
>
> 'What is written in the Law?' he replied. 'How do you read it?'
>
> He answered, '"Love the Lord your God with all your heart and with all your soul and with all your strength and with all your mind"; and, "Love your neighbour as yourself."'
>
> 'You have answered correctly,' Jesus replied. 'Do this and you will live.'
>
> But he wanted to justify himself, so he asked Jesus, 'And who is my neighbour?'
>
> In reply Jesus said: 'A man was going down from Jerusalem to Jericho, when he was attacked by robbers. They stripped him of his clothes, beat

him and went away, leaving him half-dead. A priest happened to be going down the same road, and when he saw the man, he passed by on the other side. So too, a Levite, when he came to the place and saw him, passed by on the other side. But a Samaritan, as he travelled, came where the man was; and when he saw him, he took pity on him. He went to him and bandaged his wounds, pouring on oil and wine. Then he put the man on his own donkey, brought him to an inn and took care of him. The next day he took out two denarii and gave them to the innkeeper. "Look after him," he said, "and when I return, I will reimburse you for any extra expense you may have."

'Which of these three do you think was a neighbour to the man who fell into the hands of robbers?'

The expert in the law replied, 'The one who had mercy on him.'

Jesus told him, 'Go and do likewise.'

On reading this, our identification with the characters in the story will vary, and often draw on a combination of different identities: the wounded, the wounder, the passivity of the priest fearful of contagion (thereby making himself unclean and unable to carry out religious duties) or risk-averse in tending to the wounded body, perhaps sensing a trap. Maybe we identify as the inn, a house of hospitality that can be understood as a Third Space[1] where sojourners of different traditions sat, ate and replenished their energies for the road. The focus of this chapter, however, is the figure of the Samaritan – the 'one who had mercy' – who embodied a radical capacity to embrace an 'enemy' despite himself being someone who was 'othered' in Jewish society and deemed socially, politically and religiously 'unclean'. In the parable Jesus both elevates the position of the Samaritan as the key protagonist (rather than one simply to be ostracized or pitied); while at the same time he draws attention to the ministry of reconciliation and justice by challenging the 'righteous' believer who could not alone 'name' the Samaritan (preferring to say 'the one who had mercy') to 'go and do likewise'.

Prejudice, stereotyping and anxiety all play a role in causing separation and fragmentation of community. Put differently, each of us wilfully, or inadvertently, entertains our own 'Samarias' – places and identities whose ethnic, social, political, economic, sexual and religious differences prompt feelings of fear, anxiety, discomfort. Examples of this need little rehearsal, but commonly come into popular consciousness through high-profile events; for instance, the killing of unarmed Michael Brown in Ferguson, USA, where long-standing white prejudice and social constructions of the 'black male' produce an embodied reflex to rationalize the event, defend the actions of the shooter and trash the dead with blatantly racist rhetoric and imagery.[2] Equally, popular responses to 'Islamist' terrorist attacks in Europe and beyond often take the form of swift retaliation, intensified surveillance and suspicion which fail to take the opportunity to reflect on the entanglement of violent relationships – locally and globally – and to seek the pursuit of meaningful democratic spaces that readdress power imbalances and systemic prejudices faced by Muslims.[3] The Good Samaritan story is not simply a charitable manifesto for binding the wounds of the wounded. Such acts of justice, charity and mercy were considered self-evident in the life of Jewish faith, as illustrated by the response of the expert in the law in the story (vv. 27 and 37). More radically, Jesus challenges our 'hatred of the other'[4] – people who are not like us. Questions of 'otherness' have become a core concern for practical theologians in rapidly changing social and political contexts, especially in relation to the challenges and opportunities in post-Christendom to develop more reflexive, place-relevant and participatory theologies *with* and *by* people of difference.

In this chapter, I draw on the work of Miroslav Volf to consider the theologies and sociologies of embrace in what social scientists and theologians have come to call a 'postwelfare' society.[5] For the purposes of this chapter, the term 'postwelfare' docs not signal the end of the welfare state but instead is used as a way of acknowledging the hardening values and attitudes towards welfare and welfare recipients that have helped enable the dismantling of collectivist welfare sensibilities in the UK and elsewhere.[6] Alongside blunt economic and ideological arguments for unprecedented retrenchment of the welfare state, postwelfare denotes the resurgence of a moral underclass discourse that translates imaginations of 'poverty' through the behavioural filters of worklessness, welfare dependency and individual responsibility, resulting in more denigrating and punitive social policies aiming to discipline 'the poor'.[7] In a context where justice is concealed by popular stereotypes of idleness, scroungers and shirkers (cf. Isa. 59:14), what opportunities are there for Christians to learn to reflect and engage with those affected so as to challenge these processes of 'othering' and recognize interdependencies?

This chapter seeks to assess the ground-level possibilities for theologies and sociologies of embrace in such a postwelfare society, with a particular focus on the example of food banking. A theology of embrace, put simply, is the attempt to make space for the 'other' within the self. It entails the creation of 'space in myself for the other to come in . . . [and the] movement out of myself so as to enter the space created by the other'.[8] Predominantly, identities of the self are about gaining self-recognition and domination which become inextricably bound up in the exclusion of otherness. Exclusion, Volf argues, has become the primary sin, skewing our perceptions of reality and causing us to react out of fear and anger to all those who are not within our (ever-narrowing) circle. By contrast, embrace is about 'decentring' the self as to embody the intricate self-giving character of the Triune God in whose image humanity is made. Just as in the Trinity, human beings should be 'constituted by one another in their relations'.[9] Just as God gives the divine self to the godless in order to receive them into divine communion through Christ's atoning sacrifice, so we should give ourselves to others, make space for them, and readjust our identities to do so.[10]

The possibilities for embrace and reconciliation, however, face challenges in overcoming cognitive and embodied prejudices that shape relationships between different identities in society. For this reason, Volf conceives the embrace not as a one-off event but one that requires emotional commitment and relationship in order to break down dominant stereotypes of the 'other'. Theologies of embrace have predominantly been developed in the arena of peace and reconciliation studies, in a large part reflecting the fact that Volf's own writing comes from his first-hand experience as a Croat of the devastating consequences of 'exclusion' as practised between Croatia and Serbia. By exploring the possibilities for cultivating a theology of embrace in the arena of welfare provision, I wish to take this in a different direction and begin to reflect theologically and geographically on the ways we exclude people who are different from ourselves by dehumanizing, judging, labelling and demonizing, thereby perpetuating injustice and victimhood. In doing so, I want to reflect on the possibilities that spaces of welfare might generate new lines of reconciliation and reflexive engagement across markers of social and economic difference. Theologies of embrace in areas of marginality have usually been drawn to the imagery of the inner city, for instance, the radical praxis of 're-neighbouring' where the theology and praxis of the incarnation has revitalized expressions of kenosis – Christ's self-emptying love for others expressed in taking up residence with people 'on the margins'.[11] While motivation for this work has often come from a well-founded dissatisfaction with charitable modes of social action that leave power differentials between giver and receiver intact and can preclude real opportunities for non-hierarchical relationships to emerge between people, this chapter seeks to critically assess the challenges and opportunities for embrace in what has now become an established mode of faith-based social action in the UK: namely, the work of food banks.

Food-banking can be read both as an ethical response to, as well as an embodiment of, postwelfare sensibilities. On the one hand, food-banking represents a broad-based mobilization of churches, community groups and campaigning groups wanting to 'do something' about the realities of poverty in the UK. In this respect, food-banking has been a catalyst for faith-motivated people to engage in welfare, and is indicative of a growing series of Christian-run national franchises that seek to harness the local entrepreneurial spirit of the 'local church' over issues of hunger (Trussell Trust), indebtedness (Christians Against Poverty) and the night-time economy (Street Pastors). Food-banking has increasingly become a device used both by the local church and by a broad spectrum of volunteers not traditionally involved in anti-poverty work, to engage in the wider community.

The rapid growth and very visible presence of food banks have not only helped galvanize public and political attention on the reasons why people are going hungry in twenty-first century Britain,[12] but also have led to a renewed visibility of poverty both in the city and in the rural areas, conventionally seen as far removed from such social problems. On the other hand, however, the creeping institutionalization of food banks as a replacement for previously provided state support (for instance, cash entitlements), alongside the growing acceptability of a system of vouchers used by some food banks to distinguish those in 'genuine need' from those who are 'undeserving' of such support, can be read as bolstering support for the ideologies of paternalism, self-help and individual responsibility.[13] For this reason, food-banking represents a prime arena in which to reflect on the different theological and political frameworks at work in faith-based social action and to assess the different ways Christians represent and engage with 'otherness' more broadly. To what extent, for example, do these spaces contribute to a greater recognition of interdependencies that challenge stigmatizing attitudes surrounding poverty; or inversely, do these spaces of engagement and encounter, inadvertently, harden constructions of 'otherness'?

This chapter proceeds by first situating Volf's work on exclusion in the contemporary 'postwelfare' context, and considers the political significance of the embrace in disrupting dominant processes of 'othering'. I then reflect on the ambivalent dynamics within food banks themselves and assess the more hopeful possibilities that food banks might play in creating spaces of embrace that break down stereotypes of 'poverty' and produce more generous self-other identifications.

Exclusion and Embrace in a Postwelfare Society

Volf's *Exclusion and Embrace* offers an important way of discerning and rethinking constructions of identity, reconciliation and exclusion in contemporary society. Developing an exegesis of Genesis 1, Volf notes God first separates the 'formless void' and binds together certain elements. In this sense, he argues 'persons are constituted by God in the medium of their social relationships. Sociality is essential for personhood'.[14] The creative elements of binding and separating are imploded through two violent acts: first, targeting the process of 'binding', second, omitting the process of 'separating'.[15]

If independence rather than interdependence dominates: 'the other then emerges either as an enemy that must be pushed away from the self and driven out of its space or as a nonentity – a superfluous being – that can be disregarded and abandoned.' On the other hand if relations of interdependence fail to recognize the value and distinctiveness of otherness: 'the other then emerges as an inferior being who must either be assimilated by being made like the self or be subjugated to the self. Exclusion takes place when the violence of expulsion, assimilation, or subjugation and the indifference of abandonment replace the dynamics of taking in and keeping out as well as the mutuality of giving and receiving.'[16]

Volf outlines different types of exclusion, including *elimination* (the intent to exterminate the 'other' exemplified in genocide); *assimilation* (conditional acceptance premised on conformity to a group identity); *domination* (categorization of inferiority that results in a form of conditional acceptance requiring the 'other' to fulfil a set of requirements before they are 'helped' or 'welcomed'); and *abandonment* (calculated or habitual indifference to the 'other' characterized in the story of the Good Samaritan by the priest and Levite crossing over the road to avoid contact). Material and physical manifestations of exclusion contain a symbolic exclusion – representations of otherness as dirty, risky and unsafe – representations that validate and normalize exclusion, even to the extent that not excluding is deemed morally 'risky' or culpable. The process of labelling people 'unclean' and to be avoided for their disruptive influence often takes a physical, social and theological manifestation, ranging from strong visceral revulsion (poor hygiene, moral failures) linked to fear of contamination and disgust, to distancing those perceived to be a threat to the 'purity' of theodoxy and its dominant practices. In this way conventional spaces and practices of church can be equally complicit in practices of assimilation along various lines of difference (class, gender, sexuality, race and age) and extend a conditional arm of embrace premised on the willingness or ability of the 'other' to conform to the values and practices of the existing group. As Claude Levi-Strauss puts it, exclusion by assimilation rests on the deal: we will refrain from vomiting you out if you let us swallow you up.[17]

Volf's anatomy of exclusion is helpful in diagnosing the moral logics underpinning contemporary shifts in welfare policy and offers important avenues to reflect on the intrapersonal relationships constructed, experienced and performed in society. At least two insights can be offered. First, by grounding discussion in the relational nature of the Trinity, one which insists on interdependency in human and non-human relationships, the question of poverty and welfare evades narrow calculation of political-economic or social arrangement, but rather the question is reframed to ask what kinds of selves do we need to be in order to find justice and harmony with others. Second, it focuses attention, by contrast, on what kinds of selves we are becoming and the spaces, practices and processes that leave their mark on our values, habits and ethical dispositions. Here, one significant development, but by no means the only factor, has been the emergence of an ever-increasingly competitive and demanding labour market encouraging an individualistic ethic whereby individuals keep a safe distance and close themselves off from people who do not possess some sort of utility value to secure happiness, relaxation, love or career prospects. Sped-up economic and social rhythms of daily life can lead to the deliberate, or inadvertent, segregation of the self from the (un)known suffering of our neighbours. When combined with economic arguments for welfare retrenchment, our lack of meaningful contact with 'others' makes it easier for narratives of 'welfare dependency' and 'personal responsibility' to dominate political discourse and shape the ways we as individuals engage with and imagine 'poverty'. Volf helps us turn critical attention to the politics of 'othering' in relation to the processes of expulsion, assimilation, domination and abandonment.

Politics of Expulsion

The politics of expulsion is most visibly seen in the entrepreneurial city whose desire for a city-image conducive to capital investment results in particular 'undesirable' identities (homeless people, sex workers, travellers) to be rendered 'out-of-place' in the prime parts of the city. In this respect, the will to purify public space is manifest in and through a number of mechanisms, including:

- *legislative* – criminalization of street lifestyles, for instance, police in Los Angeles confiscate camping gear, alcohol, shopping carts;
- *physical* – defensive architecture and the manipulation of urban space itself to exclude undesirable groups / activities, for instance, outdoor sprinkler systems installed in public parks;
- *surveillance* – private security, CCTV; and
- *discursive representations* – media portrayal, for example, of homeless people as dirty, dangerous or culpable for their own plight.

The will to expel can also manifest itself in more subtle ways and operate through the use of acceptable language of 'fairness' and 'efficiency', best witnessed in the recent impact of the 'bedroom tax' and the lowering of the benefit cap for low-income households in London and elsewhere. Emerging evidence suggests these reforms have been disproportionately felt by, and are beginning to slowly alter, the socio-economic profile of particular neighbourhoods in London, as those affected are forced to move out of London boroughs entirely.[18]

Politics of Assimilation

The politics of assimilation helps us disentangle the moral logics underpinning welfare reform, namely, the behavioural requirements placed on welfare claimants as conditions for benefit receipt, and the even more intensive attempt to restructure welfare payment itself to encourage behavioural change.[19] With little regard to circumstance or reason, those unable or unwilling to conform to certain expectations are denigrated or punished through sanctions designed to encourage compliance.

Politics of Domination

In a similar way the politics of domination refers to the normalization of relationships that assign 'others' inferior status and which help enable a politics of assimilation, requiring the 'other' to do what is expected of them before they are 'helped'; for instance, notions that 'they' must 'help themselves' before 'I' show empathy. Such a politics of domination can be seen in the discourse of 'welfare dependency' and 'strivers / skivers' that garner legitimatization for the poorest in society bearing the biggest burden in austerity-driven public-sector cuts and welfare reforms.[20] The same logic can be equally seen in conditional expressions of charitable care and welfare offered to rough sleepers. Politics of domination are premised on the dissolution or negation of the pattern of interdependency, both in terms of the intrinsic inter-dependencies with 'others' that brings empathetic understanding but also a more uncomfortable recognition that inherited privileges are brought at a cost in the life-worlds of 'others', distant and proximate.

Politics of Abandonment

The politics of abandonment, or indifference, owes much to the combined effect of social and spatial segregation in urban life which breeds suspicion, misunderstanding and tougher judgements that more paternalist or illiberal policies are supposedly needed to 'nudge' those unwilling or unable to exercise responsible self-management. Dominant representations of welfare and welfare recipients through the language of deservingness and dependency produce very real embodied judgements and strongly held outlooks about others.

In a society that privileges paid work as a measure of social status, any notion of 'dependency' is considered unproductive and a drain on resources. Where notions of the good citizen are linked to the ability to financially participate in and contribute to society, people experiencing poverty are deemed 'disaffiliated', their agency, gifts and contributions not recognized, and they are perceived to exist outside the comforts and constrains of 'mainstream society'.[21] These divisive constructions produce excluded subjects not only of those who are oppressed directly in and through these representations but also in terms of the indifference created among those who are captured by these imaginations of poverty and the subsequent less empathetic notions of personhood that dissolve the pattern of social and economic interdependency. Reactionary attitudes of fear and anger are easier to express from within ever-narrowing circles of relationship and sociality with otherness. Yet it is the lack of relationship and proximity to 'otherness', compounded by consumerism and socio-spatial segregation, that has allowed a more insidious form of scapegoating to take hold in society, whereby the spectre of individual responsibility and assumed culpability overrides both rigorous evidence and personal testimony of the lived experiences of poverty. Cutting ourselves off from the pattern of God–self–other interdependencies has crucial impact on spiritual formation, placing the 'self' in the position of sovereign independency or domesticating the gospel of reconciliation to a contractual relationship between self and God.

According to Volf, a key way to challenge such rampant divisiveness in sociality is the embrace:

> The will to give ourselves to others and 'welcome' them, to readjust our identities to make space for them, is prior to any judgment about others, except that of identifying them in their humanity. The will to embrace precedes any 'truth' about others and any construction of their 'justice.' This will is absolutely indiscriminate and strictly immutable; it transcends the moral mapping of the social world into 'good' and 'evil.'[22]

The theology of embrace presents opportunities to cultivate a 'double vision' – allowing the voice of the 'other' to resonate with ourselves and see ourselves from their perspectives. However, our own partiality and historical context inescapably shapes the capacity to embrace and opens up the very real possibility for the embrace to reinforce exclusions rather than uphold a creative sociality that recognizes the interdependency and differentiation between people. Without reflexive engagement with and by the 'other', theologies of welfare, exclusion and poverty that claim the label 'contextual theology' can be tyrannical, speaking on behalf of the 'other' and falling back on dominant discourses and imaginings of 'the poor'. Such an approach risks reproducing a 'top-down' orthodoxy which holds little to no regard for deconstructing personal positions of privilege that shape biblical interpretation and community practice.

In what ways, then, might Christians challenge the exclusionary politics of 'othering' and work towards a practical theology of embrace in contemporary arenas of welfare, care and justice? In the remainder of this chapter I highlight some of the opportunities and challenges for cultivating a theology of embrace in a food bank, concentrating on the experience of food-bank volunteers. The following reflections are based on an eighteen-month-long ethnography in a Trussell Trust food bank in the south of England. Further details and empirical accounts upon which discussion is drawn can be found elsewhere.[23]

Food banks: The Politics of Embrace, Reflexive Engagement and Transformation

As noted previously, a significant barrier to challenging the hardening attitudes and stereotypes of 'welfare dependency' is a general unfamiliarity among middle-class Christians with the everyday experiences of those who suffer from chronic and serious multiple deprivations. Despite extensive statistical evidence used to debunk the myths of 'dependency',[24] it seems they show little sign of shifting. Combined with this are a possessive individualism and work culture that result in a lack of proximity to 'otherness', or meaningful spaces of encounter which allow the self to make space for the other to come in, to venture out of its ever-narrowing social networks and enter the space created by the other.

Food banks and other spaces of welfare and care represent key sites in the city that create 'contact' spaces for (predominantly) middle-class volunteers[25] to reflect on and learn from the voices of those who make use of those services. While there are indeed expressions of Christian social action that deliberately eschew the hierarchical charitable model of 'givers' and 'receivers' and perhaps might be better suited to generating more reciprocal set of self–other identifications,[26] the significance of the growth and scale of food-bank provision makes it an important site in the UK where political and ethical attitudes can potentially be reworked in and through the experience of meeting people – clients and other volunteers – who are not like oneself. There are over 445 foodbanks affiliated to the Trussell Trust Foodbank Network, a Christian-run franchise which has mobilized churches across the UK to develop food-bank projects. Just over half of all food banks are affiliated to the Trussell Trust, and there are many independently run food banks operated by local churches, mosques, temples and secular organizations.[27] Such spaces open up experiences of encounter between people of different backgrounds, ideologies, religious belief, social status and financial wealth. These encounters potentially can facilitate dialogical learning and between groups of volunteers and clients, where practices of embrace refuse to prejudge the identities, histories and experiences of people 'unlike oneself' and instead enter into a reflexive and mutual engagement that allows the voice of the 'other' to speak back.

Making space within the self for the other brings injustice closer to view and exposes the partialities each of us brings to engagement with 'poverty'. Indeed, many food-bank volunteers regularly found that the experience of hearing personal accounts of poverty called into question previous perceptions surrounding representations of welfare dependency and individual responsibility. While for some volunteers, this awareness clearly mapped onto existing political tendencies, for others, the experience of working in the food bank came to disrupt received views on poverty and brought a sharper perception of broader structural issues, including: housing and labour markets, with regard to zero-hour contracts / underemployment; delays and cuts to welfare payments; and the impact of specific welfare reforms, such as the 'bedroom tax'.

This is perhaps a neglected, but deeply significant, phenomenon at work within food banks, and spaces of welfare and care more broadly: that such spaces of encounter might rework existing and generate new political and ethical attitudes. In this way, food banks might be effectively reread not solely as charitable providers of free food but also as a space where volunteers learn to become political. Crucially, this process of politicization is not simply directed through engagement with broader ideological debates surrounding food-bank and welfare reform; but rather it emerges through building relationships with people and hearing first-hand the very human responses of lament, anger, hopefulness and humour in the face of hardship.

Rather than ascribing to a fixed 'client' identity that keeps 'them' at a distance by implicitly making out that their lives, circumstances and passions are so different than that of one's own, some volunteers used a range of strategies to equalize the power dynamics and create a more sociable and less hierarchical atmosphere. This often came from clients themselves who refused the passive role as 'recipient' and wanted to talk as equals, find out about volunteers' backgrounds as well as help out with the tea and coffee. Within the organizational shell of a food bank, with all its rules and procedures, some food bank volunteers and clients came to understand the space itself not simply as a site of charitable distribution, but as a more social space that embodies a common vulnerability and solidarity. For those volunteers, this experience of being in common and the heightened awareness not to relate to 'clients' with fixed preconceptions led to a change in ethical praxis: moving from an uncritical contentment to work within a set of impersonal charitable transactions, towards a desire to take up emotional and physical residence with the other, participating and implicating the self in the lives and spaces of the other. For several volunteers, the experience of working in the food bank and forging relationships with clients led to distinct expressions of generosity that often 'spilled out' beyond the food bank itself; with volunteers taking food back to clients' homes (by hand or by car) if people were unable to carry the food parcels themselves, for example, or – in rare cases – with volunteers purchasing toasters and kettles at their own expense for clients who did not have the means to cook the food provided.

In doing so, volunteers of different political persuasions found that participation in the lives of food-bank clients, and by association the politicized debate surrounding food-banking, led to a deeper emotional connection with the unjust and complex circumstances experienced by those people whose life-worlds are normally caricatures on both sides of the political spectrum. Through this, previously held positions of Christian conservatism that regard the charitable provision of food as having little to do with politics came to be questioned and integrated with a deeper understanding of the lived effects of welfare 'reforms'. Most significantly, some volunteers who had previously identified as conservative or disinterested in politics said that listening to client stories had led to a sharper emotional response to the failings of government policy and a greater willingness to engage in various forms of 'anti-poverty' activism, ranging from lobbying local and national MPs to joining local anti-austerity groups in the city. Crucially, a number of volunteers became catalysts in their wider social networks: engaging and challenging discourses surrounding poverty and deservingness, alongside working to recruit other volunteers and supporters willing to speak about issues of food poverty among their own social networks. One volunteer, Lydia, commented: 'I think I was also quite shocked by some of the attitudes within the church as well, a lot of the language of "their responsibility, they are in this situation, they have created it", and I didn't see that that matched up. What I could see from my reading was being reinforced. I just wanted to help people see that.'

Lydia's observation illustrates how one person's experience in the food bank led to a critique of a particular set of beliefs. This in turn opened up discussion in the church about its responsibility to get involved locally, by supporting the food bank, as well as its involvement, more widely, for example with regard to political campaigning. For Lydia, listening to client voices in the food bank led to a renewed sensitivity over the need to show love unconditionally and accept the 'otherness' of social marginality: giving space to understand rather than prejudge the realities behind the stories she was listening to. These spaces of encounter and embrace helped rework and generate new ethical and political sensibilities that sought to communicate the myths and stereotypes surrounding the ways 'poverty' is understood in the UK. Perhaps one of the more hopeful murmurings found in food banks themselves, therefore, is their role in revitalizing the discernment of (in)justice in congregational and social networks, and energizing communities of believers – especially those that might be more politically and theologically conservative – to act ethically and politically.

Challenges to the practice of embrace

While food-banking can facilitate spaces for encounter and reflexive engagement with 'others', the food-bank setting highlights at least three important challenges to the practice of embrace. First, the theological and political frameworks of volunteers will at times present barriers to practices of embrace and reflexive engagement. In practice an assortment or divergence of political sensibilities and standpoints among volunteers, especially on issues of welfare, poverty and austerity, can function to close down, rather than open up, opportunities for embrace and reflexive engagement. The deliberate 'apolitical' marketing of the Trussell Trust franchise and its predominantly church-based volunteer network unsurprisingly has resulted in a diverse set of values and motivations being brought to play inside food banks. For some volunteers, expressions of charity retained a degree of expectation that 'clients' should conform to a particular set of norms and behaviours (not being fussy, displays of gratitude and so on).

Here, motivation was regularly narrated through a form of Christian conservatism which was susceptible to the condescending language of 'helping the needy' and of offering certain methods and theologies of 'rescuing the poor' – bringing 'them' into the spaces, practices and identities that are more comfortably familiar to 'us'. For other volunteers, addressing food poverty was simply considered the alleged 'non-political' domain of Christian charity which in various guises remained welded to right-leaning discourses of the dangers of 'dependency' and only helping 'those in genuine need'. If this was the only political discourse constructed in food banks then such spaces of welfare can be rightfully criticized as cultivating a 'quiet sense of the ordinary'[28] – a gesture of charity that at best eschews structural questions of economic injustice, and at worst works within particular class-based and racialized imaginations that – far from challenging processes of 'othering' – actually reinforce the very exclusions they seek to alleviate.

Second, relational and physical proximity to 'poverty' is no guarantor for ethical transformation, and there are crucial temporal and spatial limits for those who do seek to engage with practices of embrace and allow the voice of the other to shape one's own ethical and political subjectivity. This concerns the contingent character of the food bank itself. The diverse motivations and political attitudes among volunteers, alongside the manner in which volunteers perform their role, can produce a diverse set of experiences for clients, ranging from care / oppression, generosity / stigma and acceptance / shame. The overt charitable roles of giver and receiver can potentially override and close down opportunities for meaningful engagement. In addition, the manner in which clients narrate their story plays a key role in shaping volunteers' perceptions and attitudes towards issues of 'food poverty'. Clients often worked to navigate the charitable social identities and roles – perhaps inadvertently – ascribed onto them. For instance, some clients explicitly challenged dominant media stereotypes of food-bank users as somehow responsible for their own plight (through bad decisions, behaviours and motivations) or as victims of personal misfortune (benefit sanctions and delays);

and instead sought to give volunteers insight into the very real connections between larger-scale and systemic processes that produce heightened vulnerability and the person using a food bank. Nevertheless, the transient and fast-paced service environment of the food bank, combined with the scripted identities of 'giver' and 'receiver', presented barriers to long-term reflexive engagement and embrace with 'others'. Equally, the short-term character of these spaces of encounters might allow moral distancing to creep in whereby client stories are later retranslated through the dominant lexicon of dependency and assumed responsibility.

Third, the actual practices of embrace in social action settings will be at best partial and contradictory if they do not acknowledge the need to address the complicities of many such projects themselves in buttressing systems of exclusion and politics of 'othering'. One common criticism of Trussell Trust food banks concerns its use of welfare professionals to 'gatekeep' the organization by assessing whether prospective clients are in 'genuine need' prior to provision of a food parcel. Each voucher entitles the recipient to three days' worth of food. Clients can receive a maximum of three vouchers 'per crisis' (although longer-term support is available in exceptional circumstances), and if a client comes to the food bank more than three times in a six-month period, the trust's database automatically flags this with the food-bank manager so that they can notify social service professionals to rectify individual crises, such as benefit delays. Proponents regard vouchers as means of stock control, efficiency, even a device to avoid judgementalism at point of delivery. Yet on the ground, the technology of vouchers establishes a hierarchical stance between the 'giver' and 'receiver', one which sifts the 'deserving' from the 'undeserving' and one which fundamentally must be negotiated and overcome for practices of embrace to emerge. Perhaps, inadvertently, a 'will to purify' finds itself worked out through the system of vouchers which results in abandonment, and negation of responsibility for those who do not have a valid voucher. More broadly, food-banking has been criticized by academics for cementing processes of welfare reform (as food parcels replace hardship funds); helping to legitimate damaging constructions of the dangers of 'welfare dependency' and a paternalistic stance towards 'the poor'; and depoliticizing problems of food poverty (by apparently meeting the need for emergency food without confronting the reasons for that need). The possibilities for embrace will remain inconsistent and contradictory if food-bank organizations, volunteers and clients do not seek to challenge the enrolment of food-bank technologies into dominant discourses of welfare dependency that work to embed the politics of 'othering' in postwelfare societies.

Conclusion

As an attempt to illustrate the value of Volf's conceptualization of exclusion and embrace in contemporary postwelfare contexts, I have used the example of a food bank to consider the ground-level possibilities for generating practices of embrace and to suggest, when thinking about engagement with marginal situations, ways in which spaces of welfare might open out opportunities to cultivate a 'double vision' among those who choose to work or volunteer in these spaces. By engaging the 'other' on their own terms and allowing the voice of the 'other' to speak back, volunteers and staff found that inherited views on welfare dependency came to be negotiated in and through conversations with clients. By focusing predominantly on one partner in the embrace, the volunteer, I have tried to focus attention on the contingent, contradictory and provisional possibilities for practices of embrace and reflexive engagement in food-bank settings. In doing so, this chapter has raised questions of the spatial and temporal limits that may shape the capacity to embrace in welfare organizations, even highlighting instances where the desire to embrace can revert back to particular narratives and organizational practices that reify or reinforce a politics of 'othering'.

Nevertheless, in the example provided it is clear that spaces of food-banking also provide real opportunities for encounter and reflexive engagement that rework and challenge dominant stereotypes of

poverty and potentially set in motion more generous self–other identifications of solidarity and interdependency. Through the building of
relationships that venture across social boundaries, there is a potential
not only for volunteers to obtain a deeper understanding of 'poverty'
but also, more radically, to lead to a greater affirmation that all human
beings are constituted by one another in their relations – a stance that
calls into question our own political, economic and spiritual position.
Food banks and other spaces of welfare therefore might present key
sites for discovering, in the words of Samuel Wells and Marcia Owen,
that 'poverty is a mask we put on a person to cover up his or her real
wealth and that wealth is a disguise we put on a person to hide his or
her profound poverty'.[29] In a postwelfare context where such capaci-
ties seem to be eroding, and dominant representations of welfare label,
divide, stir up suspicion and resentment between neighbours, spaces
of encounter inside food banks represent important sites that give
space to discern and challenge the politics of 'othering' and potentially
generate a more hopeful politics of solidarity and 'in commonness'.[30]

Notes

[1] This term was developed by Ed Soja (*Thirdspace*, Oxford: Blackwell,
1996) to draw attention to the fluid and performative character of particular spaces, and in so doing develops a critique of the dualisms used to
understand relationships in society and space, with regard to, for example: inside / outside, home / work, belonging / excluded, white / black
and private / public (see Jo Little, 'Society and Space', in *Introducing
Human Geographies* [ed. Paul Cloke, Philip Crang and Mark Goodwin;
London, Routledge, 3rd edn, 2014]). More recently, the concept of
Third Space has been used to help theorize the spaces and practice of
'church' in ways that deconstruct some of the unhelpful dualisms (for
instance, 'Christian' / 'non-Christian' or 'liberal' / 'evangelical') that are
understood as clear-cut, oppositional categories and fail to appreciate the
ways in which these spaces and identities are constantly being negotiated
and performed. See Chris Baker, *The Hybrid Church in the City: Third
Space Thinking* (London: SCM Press, 2nd edn, 2009).

2 Tim Wise, *Repetitive Motion Disorder: Black Reality and White Denial in America* http://www.timwise.org/2014/11/repetitive-motion-disorder-black-reality-and-white-denial-in-america/ (accessed 24 Nov. 2014).

3 Bob Ekblad, 'I Am Not Charlie: A Christian Response to the Killings in Paris' http://resistanceandrenewal.net/2015/01/14/i-am-not-charlie-a-christian-response-to-the-killings-in-paris-by-bob-ekblad/ (accessed 24 Jan. 2015).

4 Miroslav Volf, *Exclusion and Embrace: A Theological Exploration of Identity, Otherness, and Reconciliation* (Nashville, TN: Abingdon Press, 1996).

5 For the concept of 'postwelfare' see: Geoffrey DeVerteuil, *Resilience in the Post-Welfare Inner City* (Bristol: Policy Press, 2015); Sanford Schram, *After Welfare: The Culture of Post-Industrial Social Policy* (New York: New York University Press, 2000); Jamie Peck, *Constructions of Neoliberal Reason* (Oxford: Oxford University Press, 2010); Robert Fairbanks, *How It Works: Recovering Citizens in Post-Welfare Philadelphia* (Chicago: University of Chicago Press, 2009); Steve Chalke, 'Building a Politics of Hope', William Temple Foundation Conference (24 Feb. 2015).

6 Specifically, I refer to gradual change in public and political discourse on poverty and welfare which has been identified to have shifted from an inconsistent combination of redistributional and social integration-ist approaches under New Labour towards a dominant moral under-class narrative under the later years of New Labour and the Coalition Government (2010–15). See R. Levitas, *The Inclusive Society? Social Exclusion and New Labour* (Basingstoke: Palgrave MacMillan, 1998); C. Deeming, 'Foundations of the Workfare State: Reflections on the Political Transformation of the Welfare State in Britain', *Social Policy and Administration* (2014).

7 T. Slater 'The Myth of "Broken Britain": Welfare Reform and the Pro-duction of Ignorance', *Antipode* 46 (2014): pp. 948–69.

8 Volf, *Exclusion and Embrace*, p. 141.

9 Miroslav Volf, 'The Trinity Is Our Social Programme: The Doctrine of the Trinity and the Shape of Social Engagement', *Modern Theology* 14 (1998): p. 409.

10 Volf, *Exclusion and Embrace*, p. 71.

11 See Sam Thomas, *Incarnational Geographies? The Faith-Inspired Praxis of 'Living Amongst'*, unpublished PhD thesis, University of Exeter (2012); K. Hankins and A. Walter, 'Gentrification with Justice: An Urban Min-istry Collective and the Practice of Place-Making in Atlanta's Inner-City Neighbourhoods', *Urban Studies* 49 (2012).

[12] All Party Parliamentary Inquiry into Hunger in the United Kingdom, *Feeding Britain* (London: Children's Society, 2014).

[13] Andrew Williams, Paul Cloke, Jon May and Mark Goodwin, 'The Politics of Food Banking in the UK', *Contested Space: The Contradictory Political Dynamics of Food Banking in the UK* (forthcoming).

[14] Miroslav Volf, *After Our Likeness: The Church as the Image of the Trinity* (Grand Rapids, MI: Eerdmans, 1998), p. 279.

[15] Pasquale Ferrara, 'The Concept of Periphery in Pope Francis' Discourse: A Religious Alternative to Globalization?' *Religions* 6 (2015): p. 52.

[16] Volf, *Exclusion and Embrace*, p. 67.

[17] Claude Levi-Strauss, *A World on the Wane* (trans. John Russell; New York: Criterion Books, 1961).

[18] Daniel Douglas, 'Over 50,000 Families Shipped out of London Boroughs in the Past Three Years due to Welfare Cuts and Soaring Rents', *The Independent* (29 April 2015). Available from http://www.independent.co.uk/news/uk/home-news/over-50000-families-shipped-out-of-london-in-the-past-three-years-due-to-welfare-cuts-and-soaring-rents-10213854.html

[19] See the roll-out of food vouchers for supermarkets.

[20] Joint Public Issues Team, *The Lies We Tell Ourselves: Ending Comfortable Myths About Poverty* (Baptist Union of Great Britain, The Methodist Church, The Church of Scotland and The United Reformed Church, 2013) www.jointpublicissues.org.uk/truthandliesaboutpoverty (accessed 2 Apr. 2014). Also see M. O'Hara, *Austerity Bites* (Bristol: Policy Press, 2014).

[21] Jon May, 'Exclusion', in *Introducing Human Geographies* (ed. P. Cloke, P. Crang and M. Goodwin; London: Routledge, 3rd edn, 2014).

[22] Volf, *Exclusion and Embrace*, p. 29.

[23] Williams et al., 'Politics of Food Banking'.

[24] Joint Public Issues Team, *Lies*.

[25] It is important to note that volunteers in food banks more generally often come from a greater mix of backgrounds including people who have formerly been 'clients' and subsequently want to give something back, or those who want to develop skills and experience in charity work.

[26] Thomas, *Incarnational Geographies?*

[27] J. May, P. Cloke and A. Williams, *Emergency Food Provision in the UK: A Preliminary Survey*, Submission to the All-Party Parliamentary Inquiry into Hunger and Food Poverty in Britain (London: Queen Mary University of London and University of Exeter, 2014).

28 P. Ehrkamp and C. Nagel, "'Under the Radar'": Undocumented Migrants, Christian Faith Communities, and the Precarious Spaces of Welcome in the US South', *Annals, American Association of Geographers* 104 (2014): pp. 319–28.

29 Samuel Wells and Marcia A. Owen, *Living Without Enemies: Being Present in the Midst of Violence* (Downers Grove, IL: InterVarsity Press, 2011).

30 This is developed in greater detail by Paul Cloke, Jon May and Andrew Williams, 'The Geographies of Food Banks in the Meantime', *Progress in Human Geography* (forthcoming).

6

Hospitality: It's Surprising What You Hear When You Listen

Cathy Ross

Introduction

'It's surprising what you hear when you listen.' This is the by-line for the BBC Listening Project, the aim of which is to 'capture the nation in conversation to build a unique picture of our lives today and preserve it for future generations'.[1] This is an excellent way into the topic of marginalization and how people experience it. So often, people experience marginalization because they are not heard. They, their stories, their history, their culture and context are neither heard nor preserved. The history of Christian mission is littered with such stories and experiences. I remember with sadness and shame a Ugandan bishop telling me that the early missionaries found nothing of value in the local culture to take with them back to Europe. Two centuries earlier, Robert Moffatt, a nineteenth-century missionary, wrote, 'Satan has employed his agency with fatal success, in erasing every vestige of religious impression from the minds of the Bechuanas, Hottentots and Bushmen; leaving them without a single ray to guide them from the dark and dread futurity, or a single link to unite them with the skies.'[2] Really?

My own country of Aotearoa / New Zealand is still struggling with this legacy of not listening to the local culture and context. Part of this legacy has meant that land was stolen by early settlers and promises to local Māori were not honoured. One Māori bishop recently reminded us that the first missionaries 'were hopelessly outnumbered, and utterly dependent on the gracious hospitality that was being extended to them by Māori'.[3] Yet despite this welcome, a deep listening to the culture did not happen. If it had, the settlers and missionaries would have learned that, for example, land ownership in Māori culture is very different from European understandings of it, that land is sacred, land is family and that the land can speak. The consequences of this have meant that some Māori have been deprived of their ancestral lands and marginalized from what they consider to be their homelands. If the early settlers and missionaries had been able to listen to the culture and context, and begun to appreciate differences in worldview, history might have played out very differently and marginalization of one culture by another might have been avoided, or at least its harmful effects diminished. If we do not listen to the stories of the other, if we do not pay attention, then their voices are not heard and invisibility and marginalization can result.

One way to challenge certain aspects of marginalization is to practise the Christian discipline of hospitality. In this chapter I would like to flesh this out by exploring hospitality as welcome, sharing food and stories, seeing otherwise, listening and attentiveness.

Hospitality as Welcome of the Stranger

Most of the ancient world regarded hospitality as a fundamental virtue and practice, as do many cultures still in our world today. In the ancient Near East there was a sacred bond between guest and host and when guest or host violated their responsibility to each other, the world was shaken. The offering and receiving of hospitality was holy ground. Israel experienced God as a God of hospitality. Stories of hospitality are foundational to their very existence and identity. These stories of hospitality contain themes and tensions which resonate through the centuries – stories of hospitality received and hospitality abused. When Abraham and Sarah welcomed three strangers in the well-known story of their hospitality, the strangers brought them good news and bad. The guests confirmed they would have a son in their old age but they also warned Abraham of the impending destruction of Sodom and Gomorrah. Hospitality was considered an important duty and often we see the hosts becoming beneficiaries of their guests and strangers. So Abraham and Sarah entertained angels in Genesis 18, the widow of Zarephath benefited from Elijah's visit (1 Kgs 17) and Rahab and her family were saved from death by welcoming Joshua's spies (Josh. 2). Christine Pohl remarks in her superb book on hospitality, *Making Room: Recovering Hospitality as a Christian Tradition*, 'The first formative story of the biblical tradition on hospitality is unambiguously positive about welcoming strangers.'[4]

The very etymology of the word 'hospitality' is illuminating. In Latin the word that signifies host is *hospes*, which is formed from the word *hostis*, from which we derive 'hostile'. So this suggests ambiguity and tension around the concept of hospitality. However, the Greek offers us something slightly different. There is an interesting and intriguing conundrum around the Greek word *xenos* which denotes simultaneously guest, host or stranger. The Greek word for hospitality in the New Testament, *philoxenia*, refers not so much to love of strangers but to a delight in the whole guest–host relationship and in the surprises that may occur. Jesus is portrayed as a gracious host, welcoming children, tax collectors, prostitutes and sinners into his presence and therefore offending those who would prefer such guests not to be at his gatherings. But Jesus is also portrayed as vulnerable guest and needy stranger who came to his own but his own did not receive him (John 1:11). Pohl comments that this 'intermingling of guest and host roles in the person of Jesus is part of what makes the story of hospitality so compelling for Christians'.[5] Think of Jesus on the Emmaus Road as travelling pilgrim and stranger, recognized as host and for who he was in the breaking of bread during a meal involving an act of hospitality. Or think of the Peter and Cornelius story (interestingly, another story involving varieties of food) – who is the host and who is the guest? Both offer and receive, both listen and learn, both are challenged and changed by the hospitality of the other. So we can see the importance of not only the ambiguity but also the fluidity of the host / guest conundrum. We offer and receive as both guest or stranger and host. In fact, strangers may actually enhance our wellbeing rather than diminish it. The three major festivals of the church, Christmas, Easter and Pentecost, all have to do with the advent of a divine stranger. In each case this stranger – a baby, a resurrected Christ and the wind of the Holy Spirit – all meet us as mysterious visitors, breaking into our world, challenging our worldviews and systems, and welcoming us to new worlds.[6]

This fluidity and ambiguity of roles with respect to hospitality is important to reflect on. Jesus modelled both powerlessness and vulnerability by becoming human in our time and space. He let go and came to our place. This radically alters the power dynamics. So often, we think we have something to offer to the person who is needy or vulnerable. We need to turn this around and realize that we too are needy, vulnerable and in need of help. This then begins to challenge the concept and understanding of marginalization and the margins:

- Where are the margins and who populates them?
- Is it always negative to be at the margins?
- Where is the centre and who belongs there?
- Who determines this and creates those definitions?
- Are the terms 'centre' and 'margins' even helpful or do they create an unreal bipolarity?
- Are margins just about social and economic deprivation?

Marginalization is complex and operates at many levels. At its simplest, I may feel marginalized as a white middle-class woman entering a pub full of rowdy men or I may feel marginalized as a New Zealand woman among a group of establishment English males. At a deeper level, a migrant to Britain whose mother tongue is not English or who is not able to find work will experience marginalization at a much more profound level. Feelings of marginalization create all sorts of sensitivities and insecurities. Perhaps we, who inhabit the centre (however we define that), need those from the margins to confront our perceptions of reality and our understandings of our place in the world in order to uncover and unmask our own need for transformation. Reciprocally, do people at the margins need those from the centre?

Perhaps if we think of margins in terms of stranger (*étranger*) this may help us. The single French term denotes stranger, outsider and foreigner – all of which point to marginalization, strangeness, otherness. Quaker scholar and educationalist Parker Palmer reminds us, in his intriguing book, *The Company of Strangers: Christians and the Renewal of America's Public Life*, of the importance of the stranger. Our spiritual pilgrimage is a quest, a venture into the unknown, away from safety and security into strange places, for if we remain where we are we have no need of faith. The visitors to Abraham and Sarah, and the stranger on the Emmaus Road brought new truths to the lives they encountered. According to Palmer we need the stranger. In his view: 'The stranger is not simply one who needs us. We need the stranger. We need the stranger if we are to know Christ and serve God, in truth and in love.'[7] For Palmer, hospitality is:

> inviting the stranger into our private space, whether that be the space of our own home or the space of our personal awareness and concern. And when we do, some important transformations occur. Our private space is suddenly enlarged; no longer tight, cramped, restricted, but open and expansive and free. And our space may also be illumined . . . Hospitality to the stranger gives us a chance to see our own lives afresh, through different eyes.[8]

So the stranger, the other becomes a person of promise. The stranger may be unsettling, the stranger may challenge or provoke us, the stranger may provide a wider perspective. Remember the injunction from the book of Hebrews: 'Keep on loving one another as brothers and sisters. Do not forget to entertain strangers, for by so doing some people have entertained angels without knowing it' (see Heb. 13:1,2). Strangers save us from cosy, domesticated hospitality and force us out of our comfort zones. Strangers may transform us and challenge us. 'Hospitality to the stranger gives us a chance to see our own lives afresh, through different eyes.'[9]

Hospitality questions one's way of thinking about oneself and the other as belonging to different spheres; it breaks down categories that isolate. It challenges and confuses margins and centre. Hospitality involves a way of thinking without the presumption of knowing beforehand what is in the mind of the other; dialogue with the other is essential . . . To welcome the other means the willingness to enter the world of the other.[10]

Of course this is the magic of mission and the challenge of the gospel. When we encounter the other, the stranger, the marginalized; when we engage in deep listening, we are transformed and changed. We learn new things about ourselves and about the gospel. We learn that the land can 'speak' and that it is sacred, it is not only for exploitation and endless harvesting. We begin to hear voices from the margins in new ways. Indeed, we begin to question where and what exactly are the margins and where is the centre as 'hospitality challenges and confuses margins and centre'.

Hospitality is subversive because it undermines and challenges existing power structures and restores human dignity and respect. Moreover, the practice of hospitality protects us from the danger of abusing ownership and possession. Hospitality to the stranger is, in fact, a statement about how we perceive ownership and possession. In God's new kingdom, we sit lightly to ownership and possessions because the call to follow Christ means that we are willing to give up everything to belong to his family. Jesus reinforces this in the two great texts of Luke 14 and Matthew 25 where he distinguishes between conventional and Christian hospitality. In Luke 14:12–14 Jesus says:

When you give a luncheon or dinner, do not invite your friends, your brothers or sisters your relatives, or your rich neighbours; if you do, they may invite you back and so you will be repaid. But when you give a banquet, invite the poor, the crippled, the lame, the blind, and you will be blessed. Although they cannot repay you, you will be repaid at the resurrection of the righteous.

This is, of course, the prelude to the parable of the great banquet, a powerful metaphor for the kingdom of God, where all are universally welcomed. When the expected guests (the centre?) turn down the invitation to the banquet, the same four groups are to be invited: 'the poor, the crippled, the lame, the blind' (the margins?) and then everyone else from the highways and byways. And in Matthew 25 Jesus explicitly identifies himself with the stranger. Here, God's invitation into the kingdom of God is clearly linked to Christian hospitality in this life. This has been a key passage in the entire Christian tradition of hospitality. Dorothy Day, one of the founders of the Catholic Worker Movement, explained the significance of this passage for her life of hospitality to destitute people – a good example, perhaps of the marginalized: 'There He was, homeless. Would a church take Him in today – feed Him, clothe Him, offer Him a bed? I hope I ask myself that question on the last day of my life. I once prayed and prayed to God that He never, ever let me forget to ask that question.'[11] It is becoming clear that welcoming the stranger or the marginalized is a fundamental requirement of being a Christian.

Ultimately Israel's obligation to care for the stranger is because of her experience as a stranger and alien. Israel knew exactly what it meant to be a foreigner or an *étranger*. God instructs them to care for the alien and stranger as they themselves were aliens in the land of Egypt. Just as God created them as a nation, delivered them from slavery in Egypt and fed them in the wilderness, so their hospitality in turn serves as a reminder of and witness to God's hospitality towards them. And always they have the stories in their tradition that guests and strangers might be angels, bringing divine promises and provision. In the early church, hospitality was an important discipline. Offering care to strangers was one of the distinctive features of being a Christian.

Hospitality from the Margins

Pohl contends that the 'periods in church history when hospitality has been most vibrantly practised have been times when the hosts were themselves marginal to their larger society'.[12] This may be because they were a persecuted minority, hidden away in convents, or poorer sectors of society such as the early Methodists. So it is important to note that hospitality does not need lavish or elaborate resources to flourish and that marginality may in fact be beneficial to the practice of hospitality. Poverty may be a good place to start with hospitality. Poverty of heart and mind creates space for the other. Poverty makes a good host – poverty of mind, heart and even resources where one is not constrained by one's possessions but is able to give freely. Hospitality from the margins reminds us of the paradoxical power of vulnerability and the importance of compassion. Pohl cites the example of a friend of hers who directs a home for homeless people and who, every year, takes a few days to live on the streets. By doing this, he experiences in a small way what it means to be marginal and invisible. He describes the impact of this: 'What I experience in these journeys is replenishing the reservoir of compassion. I tend not to realise how hardened I've become until I get out there. And when I see someone mistreating the homeless – a professional – it's a prophetic voice. It's the most effective teaching method for me.'[13]

Pope Francis reminds us of the responsibility of the missionary impulse of the whole church. He also reminds us of the indissoluble link between the good news and the poor:

> If the whole Church takes up this missionary impulse, she has to go forth to everyone without exception. But to whom should she go first? When we read the Gospel we find a clear indication: not so much our friends and wealthy neighbours, but above all the poor and the sick, those who are usually despised and overlooked, those who 'cannot repay you' (Luke 14:14). There can be no room for doubt or for explanations which weaken so clear a message. Today and always, 'the poor are the privileged recipients of the Gospel', and the fact that it is freely preached to them is a sign of the kingdom that Jesus came to establish. We have to state, without mincing words, that there is an inseparable bond between our faith and the poor. May we never abandon them.[14]

The Pope also reminds us of the importance of mercy and compassion. He claims uncompromisingly: 'It's not enough to love those who love us. Jesus says that pagans do this. It's not enough to do good to those who do good to us. To change the world for the better it is necessary to do good to those who are not able to return the favour, as the Father has done with us, by giving us Jesus.'[15]

To make oneself vulnerable reminds us that both hospitality and engagement in mission require authentic compassion, mercy and genuine love. Somehow these are more freely expressed and experienced from a context of poverty – poverty both within and without. Poverty of heart and mind reminds us that we are the needy ones; that our hands were empty before God filled them; that we are in need of grace, forgiveness, healing and newness of life. Then genuine hospitality as well as genuine engagement in mission can begin as we realize our own emptiness and our own need for God. As we experience the divine welcome born out of divine compassion, so then we can share this grace and hospitality with others. It also reminds us that we, who are not marginalized (and who are reading this chapter because we can afford the book!) need those on the margins to remind us of our own humanity, of how far we can stray in self-interest, of how much we need to listen in order to uncover our own prejudices and fears.

Hospitality as Food and Drink, Stories and Listening

Pohl reminds us that we need to eat together to sustain our identity. Think how important it is to eat together as a family and the same applies to a faith community. She writes, 'The table is central to the practice of hospitality in home and church – the nourishment we gain there is physical, spiritual and social.'[16] Offering food and drink to guests is central to almost every act of hospitality. This takes time. It requires attention to the other, it requires listening and it requires an effort. It requires us to stop and focus. As a Benedictine monk once observed, 'In a fast food culture, you have to remind yourself that some things cannot be done quickly. Hospitality takes time.'[17] This is a challenge in our time-starved culture. Hospitality emerges from a willingness to create time and space and to engage in deep listening.

The theme of banqueting, of food and drink is central in the ministry of Jesus. Was he not accused of being a glutton and a drunkard and of eating with sinners? Jesus was celebrating the messianic banquet but with all the wrong people! Luke Bretherton even goes so far as to state that 'this table fellowship with sinners, and the reconfiguring of Israel's purity boundaries which this hospitality represents signifies the heart of Jesus' mission'.[18] Jesus and his followers here are also celebrating the abundance of God – think of all the stories of food and drink overflowing, of parties enjoyed, of the feeding of the five thousand. God's household is a household of superabundance, of extravagant hospitality, where food and wine are generously shared and the divine welcome universally offered. Jesus' rejection of social and religious categories of inclusion and exclusion, centre and margins, was offensive to the authorities. As one theologian expressed it, 'Jesus got himself crucified by the way he ate.'[19]

Shared meals are therefore central to hospitality and to mission. Michele Hershberger claims that when we eat together we are 'playing out the drama of life'[20] as we begin to share stories, let down our guard and welcome strangers. Alongside the sharing of food is the sharing of stories. The Reverend Rebecca Nyegenye, chaplain at Uganda Christian University, told me that in Uganda, hospitality goes with both elaborate meals and listening to the visitor. Ugandans believe that for any relationship to be strong, food and intentional listening must be shared. Around the meal table, stories are shared, memories created and renewed, friendships fostered and deepened.

Stories help us to 'attend'. 'And "attending" in a setting of storytelling and story-listening, helps us to *remember*, which means more than just to "recall".'[21] To re-member, in contrast to dis-member, means entering into and being part of a community which is foundational for what it means to be human. So the meal table is a 'storied place' where we can be part of a community, even if only for a short while.[22]

At its best, the meal table can be a place where feelings and negative experiences of marginalization can begin to be healed and transformed. In the communal act of telling, listening and eating together, the sense of belonging can emerge. So listening is an important part of honouring the guest – in both hospitality and mission, listening to the other, and the sharing of stories is the beginning of understanding and of entering into the other's world. Telling stories and being heard are part of what it means to be human. Around the meal table, wherever that may be and it does not just have to be a posh dinner party, stories can be told, many voices can be heard, memories can be created and nurtured. The youngest can be heard and listened to; the voiceless can be given a voice.

Jean Vanier claims that as we eat together we become friends – no longer guest nor stranger, no longer on the margins nor at the centre. Indeed, these categories begin to break down as we were all strangers until God welcomed us into his household by grace to be his friends – the supreme act of God's hospitality. Friendship is a powerful force for good; friendship moves us towards wholeness and takes us beyond categories of marginalization. Jesus offered his disciples friendship rather than servanthood (John 15:15) and this is what the Eucharist, Jesus' sacrificial meal, offers us – an invitation to friendship, community and family.

Eating is something that we all must do, so eating together has a profoundly egalitarian dimension. Jean Vanier, of L'Arche Communities, confessed that when he started to share meals with men with serious mental disabilities, 'Sitting down at the same table meant becoming friends with them, creating a family. It was a way of life absolutely opposed to the values of a competitive, hierarchical society in which the weak are pushed aside.'[23] When we eat together, as we let down our guard and share stories, we begin to create relationship and this is at the heart of mission – our relationship with God and neighbour. In a unique moment in the book of Ephesians, we see Jews and Gentiles coming together. The test of their coming together was the meal table – the institution that once symbolized ethnic and cultural division now became a symbol of Christian living. There is no more marginalization or schism between Jew and Gentile and it is symbolized by that most basic of human activities, eating and drinking together. Eating together truly locates us in the *missio Dei*.[24]

This is perhaps most powerfully expressed in the Eucharist, where this ritualized eating and drinking together re-enacts the crux of the gospel. As we remember what it cost Jesus to welcome us into relationship with God, we remember with sorrow the agony and the pain but at the same time we rejoice and celebrate our reconciliation and this new relationship made possible because of Christ's sacrifice and supreme act of hospitality. We rejoice in our new relationship with God, made possible through the cross, and we rejoice as we partake of this meal together in community. When we share in the Eucharist, we are not only foreshadowing the great heavenly banquet to come but we are also nourished on our journey towards God's banquet table. Jesus is, quite literally, the host as we partake of his body and blood, and we are the guests as we feed on him by faith with thanksgiving. In this way, the Eucharist connects hospitality at a very basic level with God and with the *missio Dei* as it anticipates and reveals God's heavenly table and the coming kingdom.[25] This is beautifully expressed in one of the eucharistic prayers from *A New Zealand Prayer Book*:

Most merciful Lord,
Your love compels us to come in.
Our hands were unclean
Our hearts were unprepared; we were not fit
Even to eat the crumbs from under your table.
But you, Lord, are the God of our salvation,
and share your bread with sinners.
So cleanse and feed us
With the precious body and blood of your Son,
That He may live in us and we in Him;
And that we, with the whole company of Christ,
May sit and eat in your kingdom.[26]

Hospitality as Seeing the Other

To be able to practise hospitality we need the gift of sight. This is a gift of the Holy Spirit as John Taylor reminds us. The Holy Spirit is the Go-Between who opens our inward eyes and makes us aware of the other. 'The Holy Spirit is that power which opens eyes that are closed, hearts that are unaware and minds that shrink from too much reality.'[27]

Just as the scales fell from Saul's eyes and he could see again, in the same way the Holy Spirit helps us 'to see'. The metaphor of 'seeing' is very common in the book of Acts. Stephen saw the glory of God and the Son of Man as he was being stoned; Peter saw a vision which eventuated in Cornelius and his family coming to know Jesus; the crowds saw many miraculous signs; the people 'saw' the crippled beggar from the Temple Beautiful praising God. First, our eyes are opened to see Jesus for who he is – our Saviour, Redeemer and Friend. Our eyes are opened to the reality of Jesus and our eyes are opened to the reality of the other. Our eyes have to be opened to recognize Jesus, just as it was for those first disciples – over the dinner table, in the garden, on the lake, on the Damascus Road. Once we can see Jesus, the Holy Spirit enables us to see the other person. Unless we can see 'the other' we will never be able to be authentically engaged in mission.

The concepts of sight and recognition of the other are clear in the parable in Matthew 25 when the righteous say to Jesus, 'Lord, when did we *see* you hungry and feed you, or thirsty and give you something to drink? When did we *see* you a stranger and invite you in, or needing clothes and clothe you? When did we *see* you ill or in prison and go to visit you?'(Matt. 25:37–9, italics added). And we all know Jesus' answer. Here again we experience the subversive dimension of hospitality. When we do what Jesus commended in Matthew 25 – visit those in prison, feed the hungry, clothe the naked, entertain the stranger (all categories of marginalization) – we are living out a very different set of values and relationships. We are according dignity to others, we are breaking social boundaries, we are including those who are so often excluded or on the margins; we are engaged in transformation. It begins with seeing the other person; the act of recognition – a powerful act indeed.

Looking the other in the eye, the establishment of the 'I–Thou relationship', is a fundamental act of hospitality because it acknowledges people's humanity, accords them dignity and denies their invisibility. As Pohl says, 'Hospitality resists boundaries that endanger persons by denying their humanness. It saves others from the invisibility that comes from social abandonment. Sometimes, by the very act of welcome, a vision for a whole society is offered, a small evidence that transformed relations are possible.'[28] Think of the Good Samaritan who refused to pass by or pretend that he had not *seen* the wounded man. His act of hospitality crossed ethnic boundaries, caused him personal cost and inconvenience and saved a life. When we see the other person, we see the image of God, as well as our common humanity, which establishes a fundamental dignity, respect and common bond. The parable in Matthew 25 reminds us that we can *see* Christ in every guest and stranger.

If we had been able to 'see the other' might the genocides in Rwanda or Cambodia never have happened? If we were able to 'see the other' might the ethnic cleansing in Bosnia-Herzegovina, the civil wars in Northern Ireland and Ukraine, the ignorance and apathy concerning Sudan and Congo, apartheid in South Africa, tribalism, caste and class systems, oppressive colonialism, might all this have been avoided – if only we could see? Who are we blind to in our context that prevents us from seeing the other person and, wittingly or unwittingly, means that we practise a theology of exclusion rather than of embrace and so collude in perpetrating marginalization? Might it be the Dalit, the untouchable, the homeless person selling the *Big Issue* whom we have never noticed before, whom we have never seen before, whom we have always passed by in the street and never looked in the eye nor given a greeting? Might it be the older women in our congregations, who always faithfully provide the food, clean the church, arrange the flowers – have we ever taken the time to 'see' them and to thank them? Might it be the young people whose music is so loud, whose language is incomprehensible, whose body-piercing and head-shaving are so alien? Have we ever stopped to appreciate their music, to consider the pressures they may be under such as the bleak prospect of unemployment, broken homes, student loans, an uncertain future? Have we ever stopped to look them in the eye and tried to understand them in their context? Might it be those migrants who never learn our language, who never even try to integrate, who take over whole streets and suburbs in our cities – have we ever had them in our homes, offered them hospitality and tried to 'see' their culture?

So Christianity is a way of seeing and here we are trying to see or envision a world where hospitality given and received from the stranger becomes a way of life. Offering hospitality to the stranger, without gaining advantage or expecting anything in return is counter-cultural. It goes against the grain. But this is what Jesus offers us, an upside-down kingdom, an alternative reality, a remedial perspective. The parables of the great banquet and of the sheep and the goats do indeed mean a reconstruction of reality. God's universal welcome is displayed and, as we see the other, we are welcoming Jesus. This is indeed a new way of seeing and makes me think of one of the Occupy slogans: 'Another world is possible.'

Hospitality as Attentiveness

The gift of sight, listening, paying attention, eating together are all part of attentiveness. To live attentively to the world in God's name is our human vocation. This is why we have been made in the image of God. God pays attention to God's creation – this is obvious by the fact that God created the world and all that is in it; and because of the infinite variety, depths, creativity and diversity present in creation. God pursues our world in its brokenness. God is not a dispassionate observer or a mechanistic maker of models. God is engaged in, identifies with and participates in the world. God does not just pay attention to part of the world, but God is radically attentive to the whole world, at all times and in all places.

The incarnation is, of course, the most radical expression of God's attentiveness – God's proximity, God's imminence, God's presence. As incarnate beings, made in God's image, we too are called to pay attention to the world; to the particular work of people, relationships, culture, economics, religion, sociology, power, land issues, art, literature and more. Our attentiveness to God's world, to creation and to humanity in all its glorious diversity mirrors the attentiveness of God.

Recently my attention was drawn again to the story of Mary and Martha (Luke 10:38–42). Martha seems such a welcoming hostess – indeed we are told that she 'opened her home to him [Jesus]' (v. 38). Then she busies herself with all that needs to be done to provide a hospitable welcome for the guest. However, the text tells us that 'Martha was distracted by all the preparations that had to be made' (v. 40). I have always felt sorry for Martha that Jesus seems so harsh when she complains that her sister will not help her. Moreover, he praises Mary for sitting at his feet and listening. But Jesus can see into Martha's heart and he knows that she is distracted rather than attentive. Perhaps Martha's heart is focused on the tasks rather than on Jesus. 'Mary's whole-hearted focus on her guest is as much an expression of love and welcome as Martha's practical care. Each needs the other. For hospitality is a matter of the heart as well as of the hearth.'[29]

Hospitality involves paying attention. Paying attention and the gift of attentiveness are worked out so much more easily and fruitfully in community. Community means and fosters a sense of belonging and so lessens the danger of marginalization.

For me, being a part of the Church Mission Society (CMS) community has helped me enormously. CMS has enabled me, over the years, to pay attention to God's world, in all its beauty and pain. And CMS has helped to save me from domesticity and domestication; because the weight of sin pushes us to curve in on ourselves, to self-interest and self-absorption, to consumption, to small and myopic distractions. To be a part of the CMS community has opened up a wider vision of the kingdom of God, a broader and more challenging apprehension of the gospel, a larger understanding of God's world and a renewed vision. It has challenged me to see things differently, to be aware of the many and complex issues around marginalization, to look out for the little ones, to appreciate that God's realm is found in surprising places.

Conclusion

The Christian discipline of hospitality is really a spiritual discipline. When we practise hospitality, as both givers and receivers, our world-view begins to change. Our understanding of centre and margins may shift. As we uncover the vulnerabilities within ourselves, as we practise attentive listening and see with our inward as well as our outer eyes, as we break bread together we discover our common humanity, our need for God and the other (*étranger*) in our lives. Hospitality practised in this way emerges from our own brokenness, our own need for God and our own desire to be in mission in marginal places in order to love our neighbour. It is indeed surprising what you hear when you listen. The discipline of hospitality helps us to listen more deeply and attentively. When we listen to God and the other, we may find that God is found more readily on the margins and that the margins are not only waiting for us but also are found in us.

Notes

[1]   http://www.bbc.co.uk/radio4/features/the-listening-project (accessed 17 Feb. 2015).

[2]   D. Tutu in 'Whither African Theology', in *Christianity in Independent Africa* (ed. E. Fashole-Luke; London: Collins, 1978), pp. 364–69.

[3]   Archbishop Brown Turie, http://www.anglicantaonga.org.nz/Features/ Extra/Reflection (accessed 17 Feb. 2015).

[4]   C. Pohl, *Making Room, Recovering Hospitality as a Christian Tradition* (Grand Rapids, MI: Eerdmans, 1999), p. 24.

[5] Pohl, *Making Room*, p. 17.

[6] See J. Koenig, *New Testament Hospitality: Partnership with Strangers as Promise of Mission* (Eugene, OR: Wipf & Stock, 2001), p. 5.

[7] P. Palmer, *The Company of Strangers: Christians and the Renewal of America's Public Life* (NY: Crossroad, 1986), p. 131.

[8] Palmer, *Company of Strangers*, p. 132.

[9] J. Koenig, *New Testament Hospitality: Partnership with Strangers as Promise and Mission* (Philadelphia: Fortress Press, 1985), p. 6.

[10] L. Richard, *Living the Hospitality of God* (NY: Paulist Press, 2000), p. 12.

[11] Quoted in Pohl, *Making Room*, p. 22. See also Sara Miles, *Take This Bread: A Radical Conversion* (NY: Ballantine, 2007).

[12] Pohl, *Making Room*, p. 106.

[13] Pohl, *Making Room*, p. 123.

[14] Pope Francis, *Apostolic Exhortation Evangelii Gaudium of the Holy Father FRANCIS to the Bishops, Clergy, Consecrated persons and the Lay Faithful on the Proclamation of the Gospel in Today's World* (London: Catholic Truth Society, 2013), p. 48.

[15] Pope Francis, General Audience, St Peter's Square, Rome (Wednesday 10 September 2014) http://w2.vatican.va/content/francesco/en/audiences /2014/documents/papa-francesco_20140910_udienza-generale.html (accessed 17 Feb. 2015).

[16] Pohl, *Making Room*, p. 158.

[17] Pohl, *Making Room*, p. 178.

[18] L. Bretherton, *Hospitality as Holiness: Christian Witness amid Moral Diversity* (Hants: Ashgate, 2006), p. 128.

[19] Robert J. Karris, *Luke: Artist and Theologian* (NY: Paulist Press, 1985), p. 47.

[20] M. Hershberger, *A Christian View of Hospitality: Expecting Surprises* (PA: Herald Press, 1999), p. 104.

[21] E. Kurtz and K. Ketcham, *The Spirituality of Imperfection, Storytelling and the Search for Meaning* (New York: Bantam, 2002), p. 79.

[22] See http://urbanlife.org/project/another-project/ for further reflection on this.

[23] Pohl, *Making Room*, p. 74.

[24] See E. Katangole, 'Mission and the Ephesian Moment of World Christianity: Pilgrimages of Pain and Hope and the Economics of Eating Together', *Mission Studies* 29, no. 2 (2012): pp. 183–201.

[25] See Hershberger, *Christian View*, pp. 228–9 for further discussion on this.

[26] *A New Zealand Prayer Book: He Karakia Mihinare o Aotearoa* (Auckland: William Collins, 1989), p. 425.

[27] J.V. Taylor, *The Go-Between God: The Holy Spirit and the Christian Mission* (London: SCM, 1972), p. 19.

[28] Pohl, *Making Room*, p. 64.

[29] Revd Kevin Franz, Mental Health Chaplain and Member of the Society of Friends, http://www.bbc.co.uk/programmes/b01ph59z (accessed 31 Dec. 2012).

7

Crossover: Working across Religious and Secular Boundaries

Paul Cloke

Introduction

One of the most significant changes taking place in the western world over the last thirty years has been the rise of what social scientists call 'postsecularity' – the increasingly noticeable public involvement and significance of faith-based individuals and organizations in the supposedly secular public arenas such as social care, welfare and justice. Although faith-based organizations have been undertaking this kind of work since Victorian times,[1] and despite the continuing decline in formal allegiance to churches,[2] something visibly new is happening 'out there' because of the involvement of faith-motivated people in serving socially excluded and disadvantaged people: 'If, on any given day, you go into the worst neighbourhoods of the inner cities of most large urban centers, the people you will find there serving the poor and needy, expending their lives and considerable talents attending to the least of us, will almost certainly be religious people . . . They are the better angels of our nature.'[3]

In the UK, the welfare state has become hollowed out by ideology and austerity, and the resultant vacuum is being filled by voluntary organizations of various kinds, but in particular faith-based organizations (FBOs).[4] Such groups have been seen to offer motivational

linkages to their communities, as religious values are variously translated into ethical impulses of love, joy, peace, charity, justice and so
on, which can be harnessed in areas of welfare, community cohesion
and ethical citizenship.[5] They also represent some of the last islands of
social capital – the resourcefulness of networks among people and the
shared values which arise from those networks – which as Putnam[6]
has pointed out has declined dramatically over recent decades. FBOs
offer society a series of resources (buildings, volunteers, social leadership) and a sense of local presence and commitment to local areas, as
well as a kind of 'spiritual capital'[7] – the added value of spiritual belief,
practice and insight to local communities. FBOs are now prominent
providers of care and welfare for people experiencing homelessness,
food poverty, trafficking, addiction, refugee status and many other
aspects of social exclusion. Sometimes they are incorporated into, and
funded by government schemes; at other times they go it alone, relying on their own resources. Some commentators[8] even envisage a
kind of Christian welfare state, with FBOs providing schools, social
housing, health care, social work, prisons and so on in a co-ordinated
attempt to rebuild statutory provision along faith-based lines – a process that is already partially evident in the work of organizations like
the Oasis Trust who have been stepping into gaps opened up by privatization and deregulation of state-provided services.

In this chapter I want to focus on one particular aspect of these
developments, and to draw on the interface between postsecular
thinking and theological reflection to open out questions about how
Christians might approach mission among marginalized people. My
particular focus is on how Christian faith can and should interact
with non-religious individuals and groups as it engages in these activities of care, welfare, justice and community cohesion. It often
seems as though a sincere willingness to take Christian faith out into
difficult public arenas becomes dominated by an overriding concern
to maintain a pristine Christian basis for the social action involved.
According to this approach, activity 'out there' in the beyond-church
world needs at all costs to avoid any dilution of the *Christian* basis
for action, especially in terms of becoming 'unequally yoked' with

other participants who do not share that basis. I want to suggest that there are several significant issues with such an approach. 'Badging' activity as exclusively Christian can lead to a self-centred emphasis on the supposedly noble moral identity of the servers rather than on the perspectives and problems of those being served.[9] It risks a prioritization of the integrity of the institution and its modus operandi for participation, rather than of the crucial importance of establishing equal partnerships and mutually embracing communities of care. In extreme cases it can lead to a perception of the non-Christian other as unworthy of partnership, or indeed as fodder for the cannons of Christian mission and evangelism. In all these ways, exclusivist Christian action tends to run scared of infiltration by others who will make it somehow less Christian, and shies away from meaningful partnership with other individuals and groups in local communities. What can follow is a defensive stance, a pre-categorized posture of us-and-them, a recipe for conflict rather than peace.

Any alternatives to these kinds of approaches are usually dismissed in terms of inherent hazards: the ways in which professionalization of activities inevitably squeezes out the Christian message; the danger that Christian truth will morph into some wishy-washy liberal spirituality when thrown into the secular mixer; and the likelihood of the divisive fracturing of faith interests by somehow inevitable political and ethical disagreement. However, careful consideration needs to be given to the possibility that alternative approaches can more hopefully be understood as an opportunity to infuse Christian theo-ethics in local settings as part of a radical faith-based praxis of peaceful and non-judgemental dwelling together.[10] The problem is that a secular society in which the Christian voice is either hushed up or corralled in exclusive and sometimes fundamentalist bunkers quickly becomes denuded of the hopeful and prophetic traces that Christians in partnership can provide. Philip Blond's analysis of secular Britain reflects just such a process. He highlights the ways in which religion has been allowed to fall into the hands of fundamentalist extremists, how scientific and economic maxims have unsuccessfully been permitted to dominate the politics and ethics of welfare, and how overarching narratives about the inevitability of globalization and prevailing market forces have produced a sense of hopelessness in which endless self-serving acts of negation and denial have become the new weak mysticism of the age.[11]

According to these kinds of accounts, we have ended up with a society shot through with cynicism and a lack of hope, not least in people's profound pessimism in terms of their capacity to relate differently to each other, and to the 'nature-places' they inhabit. There is a broad disavowal of any possibility that social melancholia and desperation might be attended to by a form and shape that could transfigure individuals and their world. Such a picture provides us with some key markers for approaches to mission that go beyond institutional badging, exclusivist relations and us-and-them postures. This analysis points to a postsecular alternative, emphasizing the importance of *a capacity to relate differently to each other*, and of an *emphasis on hopeful, other-serving cohabitation* in which *transfigurative possibilities* outweigh institutionalized priorities. Such qualities point to peaceful processes of partnering with others; of incarnational mixing rather than sporadic forays out from spiritual fortresses.

The primary importance of postsecularity, therefore, is not simply as a surge of Christian activity in welfare, care and justice, important though these actions are. It is about finding a new and progressive balance between being in-but-not-of the world and establishing peaceful, other-serving and theo-ethical co-relations with neighbours even in the most hard-to-reach places. Such an approach requires some careful theological consideration, but will also be sharpened by a clear picture of the conceptual thinking about postsecularity.

Postsecularity: Some Basic Ideas

Postsecularity has over recent years emerged as a key idea that both helps to describe the new social, cultural and political visibility of religion in the public sphere,[12] and aids the understanding of how religious and secular domains are co-produced, that is evolving each in relation to the other.[13] In particular, focus has been given to how what might be thought of as *postsecular rapprochements*[14] have arisen, reflecting particular forms of 'crossing-over' in the public arena between the religious and the secular, and in so doing challenging and breaking down the previously assumed divides between secular (= public) and religious (= private). To be clear about the broad societal context here, I want to refute any grand-scale ideas about there being a shift from a supposedly secular age (or epoch) to a supposedly postsecular age.[15] Rather, the focus of this chapter is on a much less grand, but nevertheless significant set of practices; postsecularity needs to be pictured as a bubbling-up of traces of a different kind of religious / secular mix within the continuing secular setting – traces that demonstrate new kinds of spaces populated by new kinds of reconciliatory and partnership ethics based around rapprochement. Secularization has clearly not resulted in the disappearance of religion; it has merely 'hushed up' religion,[16] relegating it away from many public societal debates and into private spaces. Postsecularity occurs as a vital part of religion finding its voice again; where faith-motivated communities re-emphasize *praxis* (that is, practical application) rather than dogma, and seek new forms of partnership relations with non-religious individuals and groups.

The nitty-gritty workings of such partnership have been explored in some detail by the secular philosopher Jürgen Habermas,[17] who establishes a framework of mutual tolerance as the foundation for postsecular rapprochement, and opens out the possibility of distinct *crossover narratives* between the secular and the religious on which this foundation can be built. This idea of crossover narratives is key for understanding how postsecularity can aid mission in marginal places. It suggests that secular / religious differences can be overcome – not by the secular having to convert to the religious way of doing and seeing things, but by establishing actions and discourses of crossover mutual concern as the starting point for partnership. The implication here is clearly that mission cannot operate with preconceived ideas about what is important to local communities. It involves dwelling among, listening, learning, waiting and discerning, so as to find connections between local life stories and place stories and the ongoing faith narratives of Jesus. It may also mean parking some preconceived moral absolutes for a while, so as to engender trust and rapprochement before trying to connect bigger moralities with the narratives of local people.

Habermas argues that crossovers will emerge from processes of *mutual translation*, in which postsecularity sets in place a complementary learning process where faith-based and secular interests involve each other and learn from each other, setting aside prefigured (and often prejudicial) certainties. A mutual openness towards other ways of thinking, he argues, may well open out commonalities as well as differences, not least because secular thinking has through the years assimilated ideas from Christian religion, meaning that those ideas are more accessible to all citizens than is perhaps assumed. Theoethics then can be reconnected with its roots as a part of a postsecular process in which crossover narratives are able to form the basis of new alliances across the religious / secular divide.

An example helps to give practical expression to these ideas of mutual translation and crossover narratives. Lina Jamoul and Jane Wills[18] provide us with an insightful study of the faith / non-faith relations underpinning London Citizens – a broad-based community organization that has been lobbying, among other things, for the implementation of the living wage[19] across London. In their account they chart the development of crossover narratives between religious and secular parties, despite different priorities and moral stances:

> People from faith backgrounds tend to talk about the lack of a belief in God as being partly to blame for prevailing economic and social injustice. They argue that rearranging the dominant values of the economic and political system around religious belief and principles will make for a much better world. They suggest that the adoption of religious faith and values more widely would right the wrongs of the world . . . By living a religious life and putting your values into action, the faithful aim to demonstrate the value of religion and its positive role in the world . . . Many secular organisations – and academics – have no time for this belief

in the power of religious faith to change lives, institutions and systems. Indeed, they fear religious proselytisers for spreading a new 'opium' that encourages acquiescence or misguided reactionism and even violence in the face of social and economic inequality. Many emphasise the patriarchal and homophobic traditions of all the major religions and argue that there is no scope for working across the secular and religious divide. Yet in practice, many of the secular organisations in membership of London Citizens have come to recognise the strength of the religious organisations and their traditions. Marxist trade unionists have found they have a lot in common with faith leaders in their shared struggle for a living wage and they have been able to put aside their differences over questions like abortion, women's and gay rights.[20]

The success of London Citizens is directly related to its broad-based membership of religious and secular organizations. It is clear from the above that a Christian diagnosis that prevailing injustice has spiritual as well as material roots is not necessarily shared by other member organizations. Equally, issues of equality and diversity would be a problematic focus for the group. However, the processes of complementary learning within London Citizens led to the emergence of agreed foci where crossover narratives could be established around the struggle for a living wage. Postsecular rapprochement was therefore achieved around those narratives. Such crossover narratives are highly significant in the understanding of emerging spaces of postsecularity, as they present potential devices for the assimilation and mutual translation (or even transformation) of both religious and secular mentalities in the search for the relations of partnership.

Habermas' work has sometimes been accused of being anti-religious, seemingly demanding that faith-motivated participants in postsecular rapprochement give up their Christian positioning in order to find a place of compromise. Those who seek to institutionalize and 'badge' their mission as the implementation of unadulterated Christianity in a secular world will certainly share this anxiety. However, looked at another way, Habermas offers some very interesting alternative technologies to those who seek another, more peaceful and incarnational, way of practising their Christian mission among socially marginalized people. To explore this further requires consideration of exactly what a Christian approach is and how it can be practised and performed in mission.

The Embodiment of Christian Postsecularity

Social scientists have been increasingly interested in the performance of faith in different contexts. The idea that fixed registers of dogma and belief are somehow straightforwardly implemented in everyday life, and that Christian practice can therefore simply be read off from Christian belief, literally beggars belief in a number of ways. It is undoubtedly the case that scripturally derived theological notions are a central source of guidance for Christian practice, and that these narratives are enlivened by what Miroslav Volf[21] has described as the constantly iterating processes of ascending to God to receive and discern prophetic messages, and returning to the world to practise the received messages in among mundane daily life. However, the ways in which belief and action are interconnected are far from automatic, and faith-motivated activists will be shaped by how they sieve different aspects of belief through different patterns of discourse, assumptions about orthodoxy and typically implicit and unquestioned patterns of being and becoming. To participate in Christian postsecularity, then, the question is not 'how much of my Christianity do I have to forgo in order to relate to secular others?' Rather it is about how my faith shapes my ethical postures and practices towards others in ways that allow me to be faithful to the idea of bringing the Jesus narrative into my life narrative alongside others.

Research in social science has focused on the ethical values and registers that underpin Christian praxis. The idea of theo-ethics[22] has been used to highlight how key theological ideas variously shape the behaviour of faith-motivated activists. Here, the varying understanding of key principles has been shown to matter in terms of how they are performed. For example, *caritas* is often understood in terms of being charitable, but charitable acts alone can sponsor a posture of praxis that is at least in part self-regarding, serving as a signal of moral uprightness or right-on-ness. On the other hand, a grasp of *caritas* as a gracious love for all, involving a clear identification with justice that is precious and costs a high price, provides different theo-ethical impulses to be sieved into everyday life. Equally, *agape* can indicate a rather woolly expectation about love, but when taken seriously as that love embodied by and revealed in Jesus – a self-sacrificial love that does not pursue its own interests – it has far-reaching theo-ethical implications. The purpose of distinguishing between these motivational frames is not to present a judgemental appraisal of these different levels of understanding. Rather, it is to inform an understanding of the lived embodiment of faith[23] by developing a sensitivity of what *makes sense* to faith-motivated people as they combine both the divine supernatural, personal narratives and often unthinking performances in how faith is lived out.

Andrew Williams[24] draws on a range of social-science scholarship to summarize two practical applications of these ideas about theo-ethics in the pursuit of Christian postsecularity. First, a theo-ethical approach requires a shift from propositional forms of belief and ecclesial practice towards theologies that focus on the performance of faith, and especially on how traditions, implicit understandings and unthinking (and often instinctive) practices combine to form different expressions of Christian virtue ethics.[25] In this way, theo-ethics offers a way of understanding the changing nature of Christian belief and praxis, demonstrating how Christians are adapting to the demands of post-Christendom by exploring different expressions and performances of faith. Second, theo-ethics illustrates the failure of many traditional forms of Christian *caritas* and *agape* to deal appropriately with secular others. Previous approaches presumed relationships with others that directly or indirectly pigeonholed them into a set of preconceived roles and expectations. The instincts prompted by Christian postsecularity, by contrast, point to what Romand Coles[26] calls 'receptive generosity' – a desire to accept others as they are and to be generous in the context of these individual characteristics, rather than in the context of self-interested assumptions about what these others should be like.[27] Many Christian engagements with others still represent an effort to convert the other into a Christian world marked by dogmatic senses of what is rational and respectable. Christian postsecularity urges a more experiential appreciation of what is right in particular circumstances, blending virtue ethics with the unfolding narratives of particular people in particular places, and embodying a 'genuine openness to and outpouring of, unconditional love towards, and acceptance of, the other'.[28] In these times of moralizing distinction by government between the supposedly compliant and deserving poor, and the disobediently undeserving poor, Christian mission that is open to postsecularity will find significant crossover narratives with secular interests seeking to counter these dehumanizing social hierarchies of poverty.

What I want to suggest here is that approaches to mission based on blocks of fundamental truths that are prepackaged and implemented in a universally applicable manner are unlikely to appreciate or realize the potential offered by postsecularity. However, mission that practises rather different theo-ethics of engagement with non-believing others, based on an acknowledgement that faith is lived out in embodied and contextualized practices, and on a desire to practise receptive generosity, will have much to learn from ideas about postsecularity. To understand mission context properly actually seems to imply many of the technologies of postsecular rapprochement discussed above. It requires a working together with all kinds of people, seeking to home in on significant context-specific crossover narratives through very practical processes of listening and learning, building trust and discernment, and actively seeking mutual translation across faith-based and secular boundaries. This kind of mission is in no sense a denial of Christian belief. It is in a very real sense a different, more humble and self-sacrificial expression of that belief that forces us to think differently about both our relationship as Christians with the prevailing cultures of places, and the degree to which God reveals himself in our embodied practice of faith as well as through our preconceived statements of belief. These issues raised in the context of social-science scholarship need also to be cross-referenced with some key theological debates, to which I turn briefly now.

Postsecular Theologies?

For many Christians, the search for theological illumination of what it means to be in-but-not-of the world begins with Richard Niebuhr's book, *Christ and Culture*,[29] in which he produces a categorization of different options with which to understand how the authority of Christ relates to other sources of authority within culture. The options are:

1. *Christ against Culture* – in which Christians uncompromisingly affirm the sole authority of Christ and reject any form of loyalty to their surrounding culture, which is to be withdrawn from and avoided as far as is possible.
2. *The Christ of Culture* – in which Christians view Jesus as the Messiah of their culture who fulfils its pre-eminent hopes and aspirations, and are therefore able to feel at home in and celebrate that culture, even if there is potential for the compromise of faith by culture.
3. *Christ above Culture* – a position which mediates Options 1 and 2, suggesting that cultural expressions are basically positive provided that they are augmented and perfected by the work of the church, and by Christian revelation, both drawing on the supremacy of Christ.
4. *Christ and Culture in Paradox* – culture is part of God's creation that has been corrupted by sin. Christians therefore have a paradoxical relationship with culture, simultaneously embracing aspects which reflect the Christlike, and rejecting that which has become tainted.

5. *Christ the Transformer of Culture* – this option repeats the paradox of Option 4 but relies on the redeeming capacity of Christ to transform culture to the glory of God.

Although helpful as a starting point for a discussion about how to engage with and relate to surrounding culture,[30] Niebuhr's classification actually provides relatively little help to those of us pondering the vexed questions about how to take our Christian theo-ethics out into postsecular partnerships in a way that permeates our faith into wider social situations rather than empties out that faith into some kind of secular or multi-faith pluralism. For a start, it seems rather difficult to reconcile the idea of the *Christ of Culture* with the biblical narrative that indicates the need to be within the world yet to address the issues of the world from a perspective provided from beyond that world. Equally, the notion of *Christ against Culture* also establishes an unhelpful binary, in that it seems to ignore the reality that the church is already deeply embedded in the secularized world. As Graham Ward puts it: 'The church is hardwired into the world; that is where it works out its vision and its mission, however that vision and mission are interpreted. Whatever action the church undertakes, whatever proclamations it makes, is located in the world's times and spaces, its histories, its societies, its cultures, its languages, and its ideologies.'[31] It follows that the practice of Christian discipleship and mission in the world is both embedded within and critical of worldly values, priorities and ideologies.

The remaining options – relating to emphases on *supremacy, paradox* and *transformation* – seem to set in stone an almost canonical framework that overgeneralizes ideas of 'Christian' and 'cultural', and gives no credence to the particular characteristics and power relations of different contexts. One size certainly does not fit all, and yet the one church is presented here with seemingly fixed options about how to respond to the one culture. As Subby Szterszky has indicated:

It is to Scripture itself that we must turn, not for a list of cultural dos and don'ts, but for a clear understanding of God and his plans for the world through the Gospel of His Son. He wants us, by the power of His Spirit, to exercise our minds, train our consciences and develop our discernment as we grow in our role of representing Him in the culture where He's placed us.[32]

Even this kind of 'permission to discern', however, leaves us relatively ill-equipped theologically to tackle the specific issues raised by issues of postsecularity. It is all too easy to revert to basic Niebuhr-esque positions in order to justify deeper-seated emotional prejudices for or against partnering with non-faith and other-faith people and organizations.

One way of moving beyond this kind of impasse has been the pursuit of an appropriate public theology that both examines the interconnections between religion and politics and, more directly, the relationship between Christian theology and public life. The challenge of developing a coherent and systemic public theology in the current age is a tricky one; while the voice of religion is certainly being heard more clearly in the public arena, religious and spiritual belief is at the same time becoming increasingly de-institutionalized and remains subject to vociferous public opposition. Public theology, then, has to deal with: '[A] more uncertain, fragmented culture, in which Christianity appears as a minor pursuit, no longer at the heart of civic unity, instead a media curiosity, inspiring fierce defence among some, open mockery among others. This framework suggests neither inexorable decline on the one hand, nor naïve optimism about Christian vitality and influence on the other.'[33]

Elaine Graham[34] provides an excellent account of what a postsecular public theology might look like. She argues that the church has a public vocation both to express concern for the common good of society and to enable Christians to be faithful citizens as well as faithful disciples. Moreover, this vocation cannot be achieved by separation from the world into any kind of 'self-sufficient counter-community with its own religious language'.[35] It needs to speak a language that the world understands in order to achieve dialogue with the world, and to convey a prophetic God-centred alternative that can bring hope into the secularized vacuum. Graham suggests three strands of how public theology might specifically address strands of postsecularity. First, in solidarity with like-minded secular voices, it should champion issues of welfare and justice and promote a concern for the common good. This task indicates, at least in part, the need to 'nurture a pluralist, deliberative space of civil discourse in the interests of a healthy body politic'.[36] Second, public theology needs to speak truth to power, intervening as prophetic ambassadors of Christ into evaluations of unjust institutions and structures. This strand also clearly involves public engagement at a variety of scales. Third, public theology requires the institutional church to educate its laity, such that the day-to-day discipleship of care, citizenship and activism is embedded in a more extensive theological literacy that allows Christians to speak with conviction into their local public arenas.

There is insufficient space here to discuss public theology in more detail. Suffice it to say that there is a clear role here for using theo-ethics to shape national-level discourses in such a way as to establish broad crossover narratives, and perhaps even partnerships between Christian and like-minded non-religious interests. This national-scale public engagement can also be connected to events in more local places. Recent research[37] has demonstrated that religious citizens in the UK are more likely to be engaged in the public arena and its politics than their non-religious counterparts; faithful citizens are in these terms more active citizens, volunteering more of their time than others to improve their communities. These partnerships can, of course, assume radically different shapes. Faith in civil engagement has traditionally been associated with alliances of support for highly conservative causes, but increasingly significant links are being recognized between faith-motivated activity and more progressive, left-leaning modes of social and civic activism. Public theology, then, has certainly played a role in galvanizing parts of the Christian church to become involved with care, welfare and activism in opposition to social injustice, and to take that involvement out into public arenas – sometimes in partnership with like-minded non-religious interests.

However, a theology of postsecularity that relies on the institutional church alone as the vehicle for radical partnerships with society and culture is at best limited and at worst negligent in its failure to recognize the value and potential of mission occurring beyond the church. Michael Frost[38] points to the increasing numbers of Christians who fall into the cracks between contemporary secular culture and a church that is characterized by old-fashioned respectability and conservatism. Such Christians, then, find themselves at home in neither the world or that (still very significant) part of the church that seems to be hoping and praying that society will somehow revert to Christendom and embrace traditional Christian values once again. As we continue to build churches on the basis of an era that has already disappeared, we will discover that these churches become decreasingly suitable as vehicles for public service and citizenship. The contemporary Christian experience of dislocation from past Christendom is one of *exile*;[39] the old familiar ground has slipped out from under the church, which like the Jewish exiles in Babylon is grieving its loss and is often so preoccupied with itself that it struggles to re-imagine new ways of being a radical, subversive and compassionate community of Jesus-followers. In this kind of context, large-scale public theologies inevitably struggle to galvanize the kinds of radical partnerships envisaged by postsecularity.

Part of the problem here is that much contemporary western theology in this area is what Chris Baker has termed *arborescent*.[40] Using Gilles Deleuze and Félix Guatarri's metaphor of a tree trunk that mediates information and meaning from its roots out to its branches, arborescent theology represents hierarchical systems of knowledge with centrally derived delivery of what is significant through pre-existing channels of transmission and communication. It pictures the institutional power of the church over the individual who in this kind of theology is attributed an already allotted place or posture. Operating on the assumption that the world functions in an essentially predictable manner, this kind of theology 'will be primarily interested in how the institution of the church relates (as institution) to other institutions: other churches and the government; large (anchor) institutions in civil society such as charities, NGOs, public sector and the academic sector'.[41] While this kind of arborescent theology is not necessarily erroneous, its emphasis is on stability, predictability and a one-size-fits-all solution to mission and social action. Its focus on the role of the institutional church in a supposedly predictably functioning world often blinds it to the reality that the institutional church has largely lost interest in urban mission, preferring at best to hive off its responsibilities in this sector to so-called 'fresh expressions' of church which are granted licence to experiment in ways that would be anathema to much of the mainstream.

Baker contrasts this arborescent model of theology with its *rhizomatic* alternative. The metaphor here pictures a horizontal underground plant stem (such as found in ginger, bamboo and some species of iris) that can send out both roots and shoots from the same stem, with the possibility of connecting indefinitely at every point. 'Rhizomatic' describes a kind of theology that emerges in cracks and crevices outside of a focus on the institutional church. Rather than assuming that one size fits all, it starts with the specific characteristics of local places, thus recognizing the complexity of different localities. And rather than working with prefigured notions of common social problems, and of the common good, it uses localized understandings and discernments as prompts for tailored and prophetic Christian activity. Rhizomatic theology encourages experimental ways of narrating and practising faith, and is thereby more open to form partnerships with others with whom to assemble new allegiances and events in the liminal spaces between the sacred and the secular. There are strong parallels here with what is labelled elsewhere as 'practical theology'.[42]

In Baker's view, this kind of theology best expresses the potential for Christian postsecular partnerships. In effect, it informs many of the 'fresh expressions' that arise out of the limitations of arborescent frameworks, and provokes a series of new theological themes in urban mission. First, it underpins a series of complex engagements by faith-based individuals and organizations in the social and political fabric of the city, motivated by a theologically inspired vision for change. These are the kinds of postsecular rapprochements described at the beginning of the chapter, where faith-based and non-religious partners engage together in a performative outworking of *agape* and *caritas* on behalf of socially marginalized or excluded people. What is crucial here is that faith-motivated people are willing to take their Christian theo-ethics out beyond the institutional church into wider partnerships, enabling new spaces of hope and new lines of flight that can be released into the politics and poetics of postsecular resistance in marginal places.

Second, rhizomatic theology has led to new and significant use of the visual and the performative to connect the ordinary lived experience of an urban community with the life of its local Christian community. Mission increasingly involves artistic devices as part of an intentional witnessing of and to marginalizing powers and relations that are influential in the ongoing development of local places. Visual and performative narration helps to identify and gain agreement for key crossover narratives in local places, as well as emphasizing the revelatory and prophetic power that is invested in forms of communication that transcend words.

Third, rhizomatic forms of theology provoke more overt forms of political awareness within intentional Christian communities that are leading to engagement in local political affairs that contrasts strongly with the previous fragmentation and disconnection from politics that has for many years characterized the institutional church. Here, Baker quotes research by Andy Wier,[43] who analyses the new forms of urban mission and ethics that have emerged from charismatic-evangelical communities in Sheffield. Weir's account recognizes that God's mission is larger than the mission of the church, and that a richer and more holistic understanding of the kingdom of God is required in order to ground the transcendent dynamics of the Jesus-narrative into the everyday ordinariness of local places. This involves:

A belief that lives need to be changed with a growing recognition of the ethical imperatives to work with others for that change; the idea of 'faithful improvisation' which highlights growing use of reflexive techniques within the evangelical charismatic community including the use of scriptural reflection on crucial incidents; a spirit-infused virtue ethic which reflects the growing tension between the heroic and mundane languages of mission and encounter; the church as *oikos and polis* – namely the tension between the church as service-provider and as an intentional community.[44]

Here, there is a strong sense of how an authentic Jesus-narrative (incarnational, practically relational, sacrificial, resurrectional, present and becoming) can be instilled into the flexible everyday pragmatics of emerging postsecularity in local places and communities. From those places, there are further possibilities of reconnecting to the grander scale of the legitimate debates of public theology about wider and more structural issues relating to justice, welfare and sustainability. These local pragmatics seem to provide a far more helpful starting place for discovering what it is to be in-but-not-of the world, and to envision the amazing possibility of taking faith out into unbelieving communities in a way that regards people as partners rather than some kind of convertible other.

Conclusion: The Subjectivities and Spaces of Postsecularity

In this chapter I have offered encouragement to use ideas about postsecularity in order to think differently about how mission can involve partnership with non-religious others. The recent surge of faith-based involvement has been highly significant as a response to an austere and retreating welfare state, but it has opened up important issues about how to protect or extend the Christian basis of action. Using some of the ideas from the philosopher Jürgen Habermas, I have emphasized the need in mission for dialogue and partnership rather than defensive Christianity, such that the costly process of mutual understanding can reap dividends in terms of arriving at crossover narratives in which our Spirit-infused Jesus-narratives can become relevant to the mundane everyday and contextualized lives of others.

This will involve an embodied performance of faith in place rather than cerebral acceptance of dogma; a lived-out theo-ethics of receptive generosity that mixes service provision with intentional gathering, and a faithful improvisation so as to engage in life-changing community. From those places, there are further possibilities of reconnecting to the grander scale of the legitimate debates of public theology about wider and more structural issues relating to justice, welfare and sustainability.

These ideas need to be envisioned in particular places – your places. However, in conclusion I'd like to suggest two goals that can be worked into your picture of postsecularity in your place. First, there will be a need to engender a *postsecular subjectivity* in your mission. Subjectivity is an academic term that describes the very essence of a person's thoughts, ideas, emotions and consciousness. It is the essential truth of personhood, understood neither in terms of facts about that person, nor in terms of how society might categorize them (although the political peddling of imposed subjectivities – such as that of the so-called undeserving poor – is rife), but as the underlying basis for a person's capacity to act in particular ways. The discussion in this chapter of a theo-ethical prompts towards receptive generosity, relating to others as they are rather than how we think they should be, poses significant questions about subjectivity. Unless Christian mission is founded on an ethical disposition of receptive generosity towards others it will be mired in a subjectivity that is significantly shaped by less-than-receptive generosity based more on self-interest or church-interest.

Second, mission will need to work towards *spaces of postsecularity*. Here, it will be important to find suitable contexts in which ethical subjectivities of receptive generosity can be grounded (lest they remain as a theoretical approach that struggles to find its way into the embodied practice of faith). In some contexts, these spaces will take the form of specific *oikos*-services such as advice centres, food banks, drop-ins, shelters, job clubs and the like. Elsewhere other spaces will emerge that relate more to *polis*-community – community food projects, artistic collaborations, environmental initiatives, local political engagement and the like. In all cases, however, these emergent spaces will result from listening, learning and dialogue, from struggles to achieve mutual understanding, and from the identification of crossover narratives in which the embodiment of Jesus-narratives chimes with the practical and spiritual landscapes of your place. These are the challenges of postsecularity for mission in marginal places. They may not be flashy, innovation-oriented or geared towards short-term victories and successes. However, they may just provide a sounder basis by which transcendent dynamics of the Jesus-narrative, empowered by the living presence and power of God, can be embedded into the everyday ordinariness of local places.

Notes

1   See, for example, F. Prochaska, *Christianity and Social Service in Modern Britain* (Oxford: Oxford University Press, 2006).
2   G. Davie, *The Sociology of Religion: A Critical Agenda* (London: Sage, 2013).
3   J. Caputo, *On Religion* (London: Routledge, 2001), p. 92.
4   For readable accounts of the impacts of austerity and ideology on the welfare state, see J. Hills, *Good Times, Bad Times* (Bristol: Policy Press, 2014); M. O'Hara, *Austerity Bites* (Bristol: Policy Press, 2014). For recent accounts of FBO activity in welfare and care, see J. Beaumont and P. Cloke, eds, *Faith-Based Organisations and Exclusion in European Cities* (Bristol: Policy Press, 2012); P. Cloke, J. Beaumont and A. Williams, eds, *Working Faith* (Milton Keynes: Paternoster, 2013).
5   The seminal source of discussion for these issues is V. Lowndes and R. Chapman, *Faith, Hope and Clarity: Developing a Model of Faith Group Involvement in Civil Renewal* (Leicester, De Montfort University, 2005). See also A. Dinham, R. Furbey and V. Lowndes, *Faith in the Public Realm* (Bristol: Policy Press, 2009).
6   R.D. Putnam, *Bowling Alone: The Collapse and Revival of American Community* (New York: Simon & Schuster, 2001).
7   C. Baker and H. Skinner, *Faith in Action: The Dynamic Connection between Spiritual and Religious Capital* (Manchester: William Temple Foundation, 2006).

8   See for example, C. Baker, 'The Welfare State, Like Christendom, Is Over' (2014) http://williamtemplefoundation.org.uk/the-welfare-state-like-christendom-is-over/ (accessed 22 June 2015).

9   See the discussion of 'moral selving' in R. Allahyari, *Visions of Charity: Volunteer Workers and Moral Community* (Berkeley CA: University of California Press, 2000).

10   P. Cloke, 'Theo-Ethics and Radical Faith-Based Praxis in the Postsecular City', in *Exploring the Postsecular: The Religious, the Political and the Urban* (ed. A. Molendijk, J. Beaumont and C. Jedan; Leiden: Brill, 2010), pp. 223–41. The notion of theo-ethics is discussed in more detail in the third section of this chapter ('The Embodiment of Christian Postsecularity').

11   P. Blond, 'Introduction: Theology before Philosophy', in *Post-secular Philosophy* (ed. P. Blond; London: Routledge, 1998), pp. 1–66.

12   See, for example, J. Beaumont and C. Baker, eds, *Postsecular Cities: Space, Theory and Practice* (London: Continuum, 2011).

13   E. Olson, P. Hopkins, R. Pain and G. Vincett, 'Retheorizing the Postsecular Present: Embodiment, Spatial Transcendence, and Challenges to Authenticity among Young Christians in Glasgow, Scotland', *Annals of the Association of American Geographers* 103 (2013): pp. 1421–36.

14   P. Cloke and J. Beaumont, 'Geographies of Postsecular Rapprochement in the City', *Progress in Human Geography* 37 (2013): pp. 27–51.

15   For closer discussion of this point see: P. Cloke, 'Postsecular Stirrings? Geographies of Rapprochement and Crossover Narratives in the Contemporary City', in *The Changing World Religion Map* (ed. S. Brunn; New York: Springer, 2015), pp. 2251–64.

16   K. Eder, 'Post-Secularism: A Return to the Public Sphere', *Eurozine* (17 August 2006).

17   J. Habermas, *An Awareness of What Is Missing: Faith and Reason in a Post-Secular Age* (Cambridge: Polity Press, 2010).

18   L. Jamoul and J. Wills, 'Faith and Politics', *Urban Studies* 45 (2008): pp. 2035–56.

19   'Living wage' here refers to the authentic use of the term as established by the Living Wage Foundation to describe wage levels that are possible to live on in different areas. This is not to be confused with George Osbourne's 2015 budgetary ruse of renaming the statutory minimum wage as a 'national living wage'.

20   Jamoul and Wills, 'Faith', p. 2248.

21   M. Volf, *A Public Faith* (Grand Rapids, Michigan: Brazos Press, 2011).

22   Cloke, 'Theo-Ethics'.

[23] Olsen et al., 'Retheorising the Postsecular Present'.

[24] A. Williams, 'Postsecular Geographies: Theo-Ethics, Rapprochement and Neoliberal Governance in a Faith-based Drug Programme', *Transactions, Institute of British Geographers* 40 (2015): pp. 192–208. The idea of virtue ethics suggests an ethical focus on the virtuous or moral character of the person concerned, rather than on the particular responsibilities, rules or consequences of particular activities.

[25] Putting virtue ethics into praxis is discussed in detail in: P. Cloke, S. Thomas and A. Williams, 'Radical Faith Praxis? Exploring the Changing Theological Landscape of Christian Faith Motivation', in *Faith-Based Organisations and Exclusion in European Cities* (ed. J. Beaumont and P. Cloke; Bristol: Policy Press, 2012), pp. 105–26.

[26] R. Coles, *Rethinking Generosity: Critical Theory and the Politics of Caritas* (Ithaca NY: Cornell University Press, 1997).

[27] Coles talks of a desire to accept the 'specificity' of the other. Self–other relations in postsecularity are discussed in more detail in the context of homelessness in Cloke et al., *Swept Up Lives?*

[28] Cloke et al., *Swept Up Lives?*, p. 15.

[29] R. Niebuhr, *Christ and Culture* (New York: Harper, 1951).

[30] And the subject of further and rather more nuanced discussion. See, for example, D. Carson, *Christ and Culture Revisited* (Grand Rapids, MI: Eerdmans, 2008); J. Stackhouse, 'In the World, but . . . Review of Christ and Culture by E. Richard Niebuhr', *Christianity Today* (22 April 2002).

[31] G. Ward, *The Politics of Discipleship* (London: SCM, 2009), p. 24.

[32] S. Szerszky, 'Christ and Culture: Five Views', *Focus Insights* (30 April 2003) http://www.focusinsights.org/article/faith-and-religion/christ-and-culture (accessed 15 July 2015).

[33] M. Guest, E. Olson and J. Wolffe, 'Christianity', in *Religion and Change in Modern Britain* (ed. L. Woodhead and R. Catto; London: Routledge, 2012), p. 60.

[34] E. Graham, *Between a Rock and a Hard Place: Public Theology in a Post-Secular Age* (London: SCM, 2013).

[35] H. Bedford-Strohm, 'Nurturing Reason: The Public Role of Religion in the Liberal State', *Nederduitse Gereformeerde Teologiese Tydskrif* 48 (2007): p. 36.

[36] Graham, *Rock*, p. 213.

[37] J. Birdwell and M. Littler, *Why Those Who Do God, Do Good . . .* (London: Demos, 2012).

[38] M. Frost, *Exiles: Living Missionally in a Post-Christian Culture* (Peabody MA: Hendrickson, 2006).

39 W. Brueggemann, *Cadences of Home: Preaching among Exiles* (Louisville: Westminster John Knox, 1997).

40 C. Baker, 'Current Themes and Challenges in Urban Theology', *Expository Times* 125 (2013): pp. 2–12. The ideas of arborescent and rhizomatic are drawn from G. Deleuze and F. Guattari, *A Thousand Plateaus* (London: Continuum, 1987). Examples of alternative non-white / Western theological focus can be found in R. Beckford, *Jesus Is Dread: Black Theology and Black Culture in Britain* (London: Darton, Longman & Todd, 1998); C. Keller, M. Nausner and M. Rivera, eds, *Postcolonial Theologies: Divinity and Empire* (St Louis: Christian Board of Publication, 2004); A. Reddie, *Working against the Grain: Re-Imaging Black Theology in the 21st Century* (London: Routledge, 2008).

41 Baker, 'Current Themes', p. 4.

42 See, for example, B. Miller-McLemore, ed., *The Wiley-Blackwell Companion to Practical Theology* (Oxford: Wiley-Blackwell, 2011).

43 A. Weir, *The Motivations and Practice of the Charismatic-Evangelical Urban Church in Engaging with Disadvantaged Neighbourhoods* (PhD thesis, University of Chester, 2013).

44 Baker, 'Current Themes', using quoted phrases from D. Bebbington, *Evangelicalism and Fundamentalism in the United Kingdom during the Twentieth Century* (Oxford: Oxford University Press, 1989).

8

Mission and Others: Editorial Conversation

Mike Pears and Paul Cloke

Our intention in this second part of the book is to engage in a conversation about difference or 'otherness' and present some conceptual frameworks for mission that engage with the multifaceted social and cultural expressions of difference that are profoundly influential in shaping the geography of our urban and rural neighbourhoods. By discussing three distinct contexts, missional responses to 'difference' are imagined and explored from various perspectives: 'embrace' in a postwelfare context; 'radical hospitality' in the face of complex patterns of marginality; and finding 'crossover narratives' between secular and faith worlds.

These chapters argue that theological ideas such as hospitality and embrace convey the very essence of Christian mission and should be fundamental in determining the manner of the Christian community's involvement in society. At root, mission seeks to expose deeply entrenched socio-spatial patterns of exclusion and the prevailing practices of 'othering' people of difference. It does this not simply as a protest movement, or by offering moral commentary from the sidelines, but by being grounded in marginal places and present to disadvantaged communities; an approach which entails a practical and costly 'living out' of convictions and values that give shape to newly imagined and radically different patterns of relating to others and ways of 'being' in society. Such a vision for living can be summed up by the simple phrase 'love your neighbour as yourself'. We are, of course, not saying that this is the only theological model for mission. What we are arguing is that it should be impossible to conceive of mission that does not include loving neighbours, showing vulnerable hospitality to strangers, building relational bridges across hard cultural boundaries, and seeking to open up spaces of embrace.

The tension between the existence of such deeply embedded arrangements of social and spatial exclusion in society and the contrasting imperative to 'love your neighbour' raises critical questions for the Christian community. The first is about how the church facilitates and nurtures the spaces of embrace, hospitality and crossover narratives between groups in society who are separated, alienated and even hostile to each other. The second is about how the Christian community nurtures within itself relationships that embrace difference and cultivates open-hearted and hospitable characteristics within its own community. The second question is much closer to home in the sense that it challenges congregations and other expressions of Christian community to reflect on whether the divisions, prejudices and hostilities of wider society are replicated within the relationships of the church; this is especially important where the church has a public reputation of being less tolerant of people of difference. In effect these two questions are simply different sides of the same coin so that the call to 'love the neighbour' applies equally to the inner life of the church as it does to the wider neighbourhood; it evokes the ethical imperative expressed in Matthew 7:5: 'First take the plank out of your own eye, and then you will see clearly to remove the speck from your brother's eye.' It is only as Jesus-followers (personified by the Samaritan of Luke 10) are involved through their own daily lives and immediate circumstances to build bridges with others that they can also participate in wider society to convene spaces in which those who are otherwise alienated can participate and encounter each other.

The challenges of mission are therefore very considerable. They involve the deepest places of the self and at the same time engage with the most troubling aspects of society. Such demands might seem daunting, even overwhelming. A critical contribution of the chapters in Part II is that, while not shying away from this radical vision, they offer manageable and practical strategies, tactics and practices for mission in everyday life. In this short commentary we want to observe a particular common theme that is central in all three chapters, namely that of 'vulnerability', and reflect on its intriguing resonance with a central theme from the passage quoted in the title of this section (Luke 10), namely that of 'seeing'.

Vulnerability is variously presented as a relational characteristic, a spiritual value and as representing a sense of place in each of the three chapters. It is seen for example in the hospitality of receiving a stranger, serving a vulnerable person at a food bank, or taking steps to collaborate with other agencies by building bridges across faith and secular divides. In these instances vulnerability is not imagined as a weakness of character or negative attribute, but as the basic condition from which co-equal relationships might begin to form. It describes a posture of open-heartedness which, in seeking to follow Jesus, risks a costly and life-changing encounter with another.

This expression of vulnerability finds a close association with the idea of 'seeing' in the parable of Luke 10. This is apparent in the way that the narrative draws attention to the particular quality of 'seeing' as the defining experience which separates the priest and Levite from the Samaritan – a quality which is described in the verses that lead up to the parable in terms of both 'seeing' and 'perceiving' (Luke 8:10; 10:21–4). This somewhat ironic juxtaposition of two words for seeing is deeply rooted in Israel's prophetic tradition and is central to Jesus' own prophetic critique of those around him (Isa. 6:9–11; Luke 8:10).

While the recurrent use of the verb 'to see' gives rhythm and structure to the story (Luke 10:31,32,33), it also draws attention to the particular quality of 'seeing' which caused the Samaritan to be open to the compassion of God and then to draw near to and embrace the stranger. On the one hand the priest and the Levite both 'saw' and subsequently 'passed by on the other side' (10:31–2); they both maintained a safe physical distance between themselves and the stranger. The repeated pattern in the narrative 'saw' and 'other side' suggests that by maintaining a physical and social separation between themselves and the man on the road they did not in fact actually see; in their seeing, they neither saw nor perceived (Luke 8:10).

In contrast, the specific arrangement of the verbs that are used to describe the Samaritan in Luke 10:33–4 indicate a fourfold movement from *seeing*, to *compassion*, to physical *encounter* ('went to him', v. 34), to *service*. It all started with seeing, but seeing of a certain quality which might be described as 'perceiving'. It seems that the inner inclination of the Samaritan to 'draw near' rather than 'cross to the other side' is what opens his eyes and enables his heart to be filled with compassion for the stranger. There is, in other words, already a 'predisposition to embrace' or 'hospitable space' within the heart of the Samaritan himself which causes him to perceive the world differently. This inner 'space of embrace' has been presented by Andy Williams who, in his discussion about food banks and a postwelfare society, brings an insightful analysis as to the way Miroslav Volf's theology of embrace presents us with a radical response to the enmity of exclusion and carefully considers both the challenges and opportunities that arise from its practical outworking.

However, as already implied, the inner space is not the only critical new sphere that demands attention. There is a second 'space' that features in this story in addition to the space of embrace within the Samaritan himself, and that is the space between the Samaritan and the stranger on the road. This second space, the relational space between the self and the other, is also one to which the narrative calls our attention. It is not presented as a straightforward functional space in which one gives and the other receives. In other words this is not a story about serving others or meeting needs. In fact the narrative seems designed to upset normal societal ideas about meeting the needs of the poor while at the same time maintaining a safe detachment from them. Rather it conforms to the pattern of radical hospitality presented by Cathy Ross who challenges us to think more deeply about ideas of hospitality and how the guest–host relationship imagined in Scripture is fluid and ambiguous so that the 'normal' power dynamics were radically altered.

This ambiguity – or vulnerability – exists precisely in the space between the self and the other so that the self–other relationship is newly defined. No longer can the old patterns of social and religious hierarchies that give legitimacy to those who wish to keep a sensible distance from the stranger by crossing to the 'other side' hold sway. This is the challenge that Paul Cloke articulates so well for us by arguing that 'postsecularity' opens up the opportunity to think differently about secular / religious differences and presents the possibility of forming 'peaceful processes of partnering' rather than occupying – in the terms of the Samaritan story – opposite sides of the road. Paul connects these notions of vulnerable or open-hearted hospitality with specific missional practices that come about through careful reflective engagement with the emerging postsecular landscape where rapprochement – or 'crossing the road' – entails the development of 'a capacity to relate differently to each other' founded on receptive generosity and faithful improvisation.

Through vulnerability a new sense of space comes into play, one in which the self–other relationship is freshly convened by the Holy Spirit. This sense in which the Spirit convenes a new kind of redemptive place in which previously insurmountable socio-spatial barriers are removed is, it seems, imagined by the apostle Paul. Having discussed arrangements for the Lord's Supper in which he exhorts those in attendance to 'examine' themselves (1 Cor. 11:17–34) he then presents the work of the Spirit as opening up a new kind of radically inclusive space: 'For we were all baptised by one Spirit so as to form one body – whether Jews or Gentiles, slave or free – and we were all given the one Spirit to drink' (1 Cor. 12:13).

Thus vulnerability and perceptive seeing are, in these narratives, interrelated ideas; one does not exist independently of the other, but each enables and deepens the other. Indeed, taken together they define two distinct arenas in which the Spirit himself is at work – first, the space within the self (that which calls for reflective engagement with the cruciform activity of the Spirit) and the second in the space between the self and the other (that which calls for the reflexive engagement with the hospitable activity of the Spirit).

Finally, the chapters in Part II emphasize the important relationship between this quality of vulnerability and the possibility of transformation. As with the story of the Samaritan and the stranger, the 'good news' is not expressed primarily as meeting the needs of the stranger, but in redefining or transforming the relationship between the two from 'strangers' to 'neighbours'. It is this radical, socio-spatial transformation that is both the point of the parable and also expressed so consistently and eloquently through each of the chapters in Part II. In other words vulnerability and perceptive seeing are necessary preconditions for transformation. Conversely, transformation is not something that can be managed through existing hierarchical social relations, but it is that which the Spirit brings about when through the practices of mutuality and vulnerability of 'loving your neighbour as yourself' new redemptive places are brought into being.

These ideas raise key questions about the way that the Christian community approaches mission – questions which we hope might be of practical help for those exploring mission in a marginal context:

- How does a Christian community go about establishing spaces which will facilitate encounters between people of difference and that open up the potential for fruitful collaboration with others, new hopeful imaginations, and tangible change?
- How does a Christian community affect the spiritual, cultural, social and physical environment to facilitate this kind of encounter? What practices does the community need to learn in order to do this?
- How does the Christian community nurture within itself the qualities of open-heartedness and vulnerability that will help it grow meaningful relationships with others?

Part III

Mission and God: Where Two or Three Gather in My Name . . .

9

Cruciformity: Mission and Living the Cross

David Purves

Cruciform love is hospitable and generous, especially to the poor and weak – those marginalized or rejected by others. If it has worldly status, it becomes downwardly mobile in order to lift others up. It gives of itself and its material possessions. Cruciform love, in a word, continues the story of the cross in new times and places. Cruciform love is imaginative.[1]

Mission in marginal places brings multiple challenges, not least a sacrificial sense of wrestling with key personal, social and cultural issues. Christians, both those entering a new situation and those converting from within, must learn how to 'let go' of their own prejudice, agendas and consumeristic leanings; embrace smallness by setting aside hopes for reputation or success; and enter into troubling and challenging living conditions in a form of downward mobility. They must also learn to deal with difference, diversity and even injustice and sin through 'speaking out'. Mission as *cruciformity* entails embracing the self-giving narrative of the cross that eschews selfishness, instead looking to the interests of others. Beyond merely accepting an ideal, it involves entering into and surrendering, so the pattern of the cross becomes our own story. Only by accepting such a missionary-narrative spirituality can recent tendencies to polarize belief and action, church community and social concern, be overcome and a more rounded, even biblical, vision of faith that empowers mission in marginal places realized.

In this chapter I introduce Michael Gorman's *Cruciformity*,[2] a concept invaluable to my own reflections on mission among people with a background of addiction. Cruciformity enables us to overcome recent trends in understanding mission with respect to the church. First, a *centrifugal* tendency, where mission is a force or movement essentially away from or outside of the worshipping community, and often concerned with issues of justice and social action. Second, a *centripetal* tendency, where mission is a force or movement aimed at integration into the already formed worshipping community, and faith prioritized as belief and belonging. These tendencies, clarified below, typify mission approaches that have emerged with the end of Christendom, namely mission as *missio Dei* and *liberating service of the reign of God* in the case of the former, and mission as *proclamation of Jesus Christ as universal Saviour* related to the latter.[3] Steven Bevans and Roger Schroeder attempt to synthesize these approaches into mission as *Prophetic Dialogue*.[4] I refine their understanding of the Spirit's work in order to redress their own *centrifugal* leanings. Cruciformity enables key aspects of the two tendencies to be held together, enabling effective inculturation by balancing the dialectic of how to be both prophetic and dialogical regarding mission in marginal places.

Cruciformity: Biblical Roots and Core Convictions

Cruciformity originates in an understanding of Paul's writings beginning with the assertion that 'the Cross is the interpretive, or hermeneutical, lens through which God is seen'. The pattern of faith or faithfulness, and self-giving, other-affirming love revealed in the narrative of Christ's obedience to death on the cross is the starting point for Christian faith. Rather than a theology, cruciformity is a 'narrative spirituality', meaning 'a spirituality that tells a story, a dynamic life with God that corresponds in some way to the divine "story"'.[5]

According to Michael Gorman, an integrative narrative pattern is found in the so-called Philippian hymn of Philippians 2:5–11, where verses 6–8 reveal the shape and meaning of Christ's love.[6] This is a master narrative for Paul, following the pattern, 'although x (status) not y (selfishness) but z (selflessness)'.[7] Christ acts this way not only despite the fact he is divine, but also because he is divine. Ultimately Christ's faithfulness to this pattern is what saves people, but it also outlines the suitable response and posture of faith, as Paul urges believers to believe in and follow Christ's example. The pattern demonstrates the two-dimensional character of love, which Gorman traces throughout Paul's letters,[8] and describes as follows: '*Negatively*, it does not seek its own advantage or edification. It is characterized by status- and rights-renunciation. *Positively*, it seeks the good, the advantage, the edification of others. It is characterized by regard for them. Love, according to the apostle, is the dynamic, creative endeavour of finding ways to pursue the welfare of others rather than one's own interests.'[9]

The response of faith or faithfulness is inseparable from, outworked in and characterized by love. These are often coupled in Paul's writing, and 'cruciform faith becomes cruciform love'.[10] This inseparability characterizes Gorman's integrated understanding of salvation. Salvation involves vertical (related to God) and horizontal (related to others) elements. Restoration of humanity involves right covenant relations with God and others, overcoming the problems of 'impiety' and 'injustice' of Romans 1:18, replacing them with faith and love.[11] Cruciformity resonates with David Augsburger's tripolar spirituality, where spiritual health involves correct relationship with self, God and other.[12] Rather than choose between juridical, participationist and apocalyptic interpretations of Pauline theology, Gorman affirms each as aspects of one model, namely justification by co-crucifixion with Christ.[13] This involves an objective element, namely Christ's quintessential covenantal act of faith and love through his death on the cross, in which the vertical and horizontal requirements of the law are fulfilled, and also a necessary subjective response of faith, in which those who participate experience the self-same fulfilment of the law. This entire process involves a participatory and transformative experience of resurrection through death,[14] as Christ's work on the cross takes effect. The believer joins the cruciform ministry of Christ in the Christian community, choosing to emulate Christ, empowered by the Spirit.

The master pattern occurs throughout Paul's writings, and is integral to Paul's self-understanding. Paul writes in 1 Thessalonians 2:6–8: '[A]lthough we (x) might have thrown our weight around as apostles, we did not (y) seek honour from humans, but we (z) were gentle among you and were pleased to share with you, not only the gospel, but our own selves.'[15] This understanding of apostleship, where the wording suggests the action (y) is not a denial but an outworking of true identity, is seen in other contexts and situations. If the pattern is not overt, the language and themes prevail. In 1 Corinthians 9:1–23, the language of slavery from Philippians 2:7 is used, and the pattern identified as though (x) I am free with respect to all, (y) I did not exercise my rights, but (z) I have made myself a slave to all.[16] Paul's self-enslavement takes two forms. First, he adapts himself to people he meets, Jew or Gentile, becoming 'all things to all [people]' (1 Cor. 9:22). Second, he refuses to demand financial support and recognition, instead working as a tentmaker. This was the role of slaves or recently released freedmen, the remit of those of low social status, humiliating and unworthy of respect. The educated Paul practises 'deliberate socioeconomic self-abasement, self-humiliation and status renunciation',[17] accommodating to and reaching others, while avoiding being a burden. This illustrates inculturation, the cruciform way.

The pattern pertains not only to individuals, but also to the faith community, which is self-giving and looks to others' interests, both internally and externally. The pattern's language and themes frequently recur, dealing with community issues. Regarding resources, Paul urges believers in 2 Corinthians 8:9 to be generous, citing the example of the Macedonians, and of Christ who, though he was rich, for their sake became poor. This allusion clarifies that (x) although they are wealthy (y) they shouldn't keep it to themselves, but (z) share generously.[18] Supporting others is a priority. Similarly, Paul condemns biased, socially divisive customs. Roman practice involved the wealthy arriving earlier to public meals, leaving inferior food and seating for less privileged. This had influenced the Lord's Supper. Paul corrects the Corinthians, saying, (x) although your status gives you the right to privilege in meals elsewhere, (y) do not make use of this selfish right, but (z) wait for one another and eat in unity.[19] Paul clarifies that a cruciform community prioritizes the poor. Gorman explains, 'He does this because his experience of the cross tells him that God has taken, and does take, sides with the poor and weak.'[20] The 'downward mobility' of both apostle and community is central to this pattern. The call is not simply to be others-focused and community-minded, but to willingness to give up or redistribute status, privilege, power or wealth.[21]

Finally, the Spirit is central to authentic Christian life and community.[22] In Romans 5:1–11 Paul describes how love is poured into the hearts of believers through the Spirit, enabling them to experience, participate in and live out God's love revealed through Christ.[23] The Spirit entering the heart is fundamental, with the heart seen as the seat of the human problem, in need of repair.[24] The Spirit facilitates death to the flesh (Rom. 8:12–13), enabling cruciform love, a fruit of the Spirit.[25] The test for the Spirit's presence is not miracles and wonders, but love, as outlined in 1 Corinthians 13. Living by the Spirit's power, however, is predicated on the believer's active response, as seen by the word 'if' in Romans 8:12–17, where the conditions are, '*if* we put to death the deeds of the body, and *if* we suffer with Christ'.[26] The believer is empowered as they respond to Christ, entering a life of self-giving, into the life, death and resurrection of Christ, continuing the work of the Son in the Christian community.[27] The Spirit is also inextricably connected with and points to resurrection, being the down payment of the coming final resurrection.[28]

It is central to cruciformity that Paul never separates faith as belief and belonging from the related actions of love the Spirit-empowered master pattern requires and entails. We must bear this in mind as we reflect on how this helps redress centrifugal and centripetal tendencies in mission.

Avoiding Centrifugal Tendencies

In one sense all mission is centrifugal, involving a sending out (*missio*) of the Christian message through missionaries or Christian community. I refer to centrifugal in a more particular sense, namely as a type[29] of missional understanding, to be understood in contrast to centripetal. The centrifugal tendency sees mission as a *force or movement essentially away from or outside of the worshipping community*. This could manifest in a number of ways. Missionaries could be sent *out* from the church never to have much contact again, or mission could be seen as an activity that goes on *outside* the church by external agencies. It might entail joining in with secular agencies combating injustice, or simply be the worthy work or vocation each member goes *out* from the church to partake in. Crucially, the church itself does not have an ostensible role to play in pursuing such ideals. Mission somehow becomes divorced from church life and even from Christ himself. This is seen in the way many recent social initiatives or forms of aid work started by churches eventually become separate charities or entities, rather than reshaping and redefining the church community itself as cruciformity would require.

In my home city one pastor felt so convicted by needy homeless people visiting the church that he quit his job to start a homeless hostel across the road. The work boomed, and other levels of care such as supported housing and a rehabilitation centre were established, but in time became increasingly secular. Why could the church community not have reshaped itself, with every member in some way involved in the outreach so that the pastor did not feel this incongruity between congregational life and Spirit-inspired mission? That would have been cruciformity.

The seeds for the centrifugal tendency are found in the idea of foreign missions and the voluntarism of mission societies in the age of progress, which introduced the idea of mission as something extra or outwith normal church life. It was, however, the idea of God's work in other cultures and religions, a notion that gathered momentum from the mid-nineteenth century among liberal thinkers, and was augmented by twentieth-century processes of globalization, that led to two recognizably centrifugal approaches.

The first of these, *missio Dei*, became prominent among Protestants in the work of the World Council of Churches (WCC) and also among Catholics during Vatican II. Mission is intrinsic to the very Trinitarian nature of God, as the Father sends forth the Son and Spirit into the world as part of the redemptive plan. The church's role is to join this mission, becoming missionary by its very nature. At one level this resonates with cruciformity, where the church is called to continue Jesus' mission in the Spirit's power, sharing the story of God reconciling humanity to himself, and living out the implications. Paul had no developed Trinitarian theology, but experienced the transformative power of a narrative Trinity while ministering. *Missio Dei*, however, evolved out of attempts to engage with both culture and doctrines of creation and a universal spirit. A central early idea was the pattern of God's acting in history, termed 'the strategy of God's contemporaneity'. God's act in Christ demonstrated a missionary pattern whereby 'God acts in judgment and redemption in the revolutionary movements of the period, especially within communism'.[30] Although somewhat reflecting cruciformity's master pattern, this approach minimized the saving centrality of Christ, and was opposed in the early twentieth century by those with a Christ-centred emphasis.

In the 1960s, however, WCC circles demonstrated increasing desire to be graciously inclusivist, recognizing goodness in other religious and social movements. The 'sending' of God became a universal category[31] seen in social movements, revolution and any locus of liberation, even among atheists or other faiths. This is the Spirit's remit and manifests wherever one sees the advancement of shalom: wholeness characterized by 'peace, integrity, community, harmony and justice'.[32] Although attractive for mission in marginal places, this interpretation of *missio Dei* can be extremely centrifugal, even suggesting that the church, when failing to adapt from Christendom forms, actually hinders the *missio Dei* and might better cease operations.[33] This effectively disconnects horizontal and vertical aspects of salvation. Although a form of *missio Dei* emerged from the 1980s onwards showing greater openness to the church's role within God's broader mission,[34] it still marginalized the particular act of God in Christ, with the church one group among many pursuing God's kingdom.

The church's task is to move outwards from itself and join God's mission in the world. It becomes a place of preparation where Christians learn to recognize the *missio Dei* before joining in through secular or charity work. Such sentiments fall short of mission as cruciformity, where the objective basis of salvation is Christ's faith, around which the community of the Spirit forms. The community's response through a cruciform lifestyle becomes a present outworking of Jesus' ministry. Churches are not simply preaching stations encouraging people to do mission, but cross-shaped communities of mutual commitment, creatively embodying the master narrative through shared action and objectives. Although Paul's practice of tent-making shows how the community's cruciform character spills into the workplace. The idea that mission is something to partake in outside the church, rather than fundamental to the community, is alien to cruciformity's integrated approach.

A second, centrifugal approach is the idea of mission as *liberating service of the reign of God.*[35] Mission continues Jesus' mission in the world,[36] in particular his ministry to the marginalized and poor. This approach emerged from early twentieth-century reflections. E. Stanley Jones rued the church-centred trajectory of the 1938 International Missionary Council meeting, arguing that the priority should instead be the kingdom,[37] while F. Braun and F. Holmström suggested the church exists to orient the world to the future kingdom, being an instrument of, but not itself the kingdom.[38] Rudolf Schnackenburg advocated using 'reign' instead of 'kingdom', emphasizing Christ's and God's reign as relationship, not a place. This relationship is growing yet incomplete, and the church incompletely partakes in it.[39] Such reflections contributed to Vatican II teaching, with the church, 'a kind of sacrament – a sign, an instrument, that is, of communion with God', tasked to preach the kingdom and become 'the initial budding forth of that Kingdom'.[40]

Reflections like these were augmented by growing ethical concerns in the face of social ferment and upheaval. Liberation theologies built on awareness of an incredible 'irruption' of the poor. Large numbers of politically oppressed and landless people required support in their struggle for justice. Renouncing the church's previous association with the rich and powerful, God's 'preferential option for the poor' was recognized, continuing the earthly teaching and ministry of Jesus.[41] Following the methodology of *Catholic Action* the Christian community was to 'see' or analyse the current context, 'judge' or reflect on this theologically, then 'act' in promoting change on various levels, including personal, societal and structural.[42] Humanization and development work were goals of Christian faith. Conciliar Protestantism demonstrated this same desire to pursue issues of peace, justice and economic equality aside from the theology of secularization,[43] assuming that God's mission is outworked wherever people are freed from oppression or injustice. This idea of continuing Christ's cruciform work is also foundational to cruciformity, where there is a commitment to the weak and vulnerable and to missional accommodation through downward mobility. Gorman shares emphasis on God's bias for the poor and siding with the marginalized, picking up Jon Sobrino's language of the oppressed as 'crucified people', emphasizing that 'Cruciform love seeks mercy and justice for crucified people'.[44] Gorman even suggests that the term 'liberationist' is interchangeable with cruciform.[45]

This mission approach, however, contains a degree of internal diversity with respect to the relationship between church, Christ and mission. Catholic reflections like *Evangelii Nuntiandi* attempt to maintain the centrality of both church and Christian Faith, while also incorporating a kingdom orientation. The centrifugal emerges, however, with the idea that the church is merely a sign or sacrament of the kingdom, which exists independently of the church and is not specifically connected to Christian salvation and community as in cruciformity. This is reflected in openness to aspects of salvation among people or religions not knowing Christ. This separation of the kingdom from individual salvation and the church is seen in some liberationist reflections and WCC documents, where the focus is on humanization and progress. The roles of the church and Christ are marginalized, even overlooked in favour of the idea that God brings about his kingdom through liberation movements and other religions.

In cruciformity the Spirit draws people to Christ, but there is need for response to the Christian story. The Spirit entering the heart in response to Christ is the beginning of salvation, which leads to participation in the kingdom through cruciform love. As shown above, mission theology marginalizing response to Christ and the church's role lacks credibility. The centrality of the church to cruciformity is seen when Gorman equates liberation and cruciformity, reflecting on how the church community is sent to interact with crucified people.[46] It is not simply that individuals go out from the church to join in kingdom work. Rather the church itself is mandated to imaginatively re-enact the master story of self-renunciation and seek the good of others, as a form of 'living exegesis',[47] displaying hospitality and generosity. The liberationist Latin American Base Ecclesial Communities are exemplary of Christian community enacting cruciform mission. In the face of the repression of civil society by antagonistic governments, whole faith communities were mobilized to pursue issues of justice, and this shaped the style and frequency of their meetings and social engagement. They involved themselves in court cases, community mobilization and demonstrations, without compromising their personal faith and reflections. Instead they would actually reflect on their actions in the light of Scripture through so-called biblical circles. The result was mutually enriching belief and action.

Avoiding Centripetal Tendencies

In contrast to centrifugal, the centripetal tendency views twentieth-century forces of change more negatively. As a type, rather than openness to God's liberating work in the world or other religions, the focus of mission is bringing people into communities of faith, and it views salvation as unashamedly Christ-centred and church-related. The centripetal tendency views mission as *a force or movement essentially aimed at integration into the already formed worshipping community*, often characterized by emphasis on proclamation. Although superficially this might involve sending missionaries out, the primary purpose is always getting converts *in*. This is demonstrated in contemporary missional initiatives like Alpha or Christianity Explored, groups that exist temporarily as a way to 'bring people in'. As a pastor, however, I have also seen a centripetal mindset cast doubt on the success of any missional venture unless it sufficiently adds to congregational numbers in a traditional form. Even if there are continued positive relationships or small-group contact or significant social transformation apparent, unless traditional expectations are served the mission is incomplete.

Bevans and Schroeder describe mission characterized by this tendency as *proclamation of Jesus Christ as universal Saviour*. The missional focus is, as the name suggests, Christ-centred, emphasizing personal salvation, with a corresponding drive to bring people into church. Within this tendency there is diversity, yet each strand shares the conviction that Christ is universal Saviour. Conservatives, evangelicals and Pentecostals strongly emphasize conversion and explicit confession of faith, continuing the focus of nineteenth-century mission societies and faith missions. Catholics, who maintain openness to 'seeds of truth' in other faiths, see everything as brought to completion in Christ, with documents like *Redemptoris Missio* arguably combatting perceived pluralism of the later twentieth century.[48] For all, proclamation is vital. This shared focus on Christ is affirmed by cruciformity, where the objective basis of salvation is the faith or faithfulness of Christ. Cruciformity, however, demonstrates greater consonance with conservatives, evangelicals and Pentecostals in affirmation of an explicit confession of faith. It sits uncomfortably with the more inclusivist Catholic approach. It is through response to Christ's faith or faithfulness that believers are filled with the Spirit and taken into a new way of life as Christian community. There is, however, need to recognize an important nuance. For cruciformity, proclamation is not simply of Christ, but the Christ of the master pattern. This implies a cruciform response.

Also central to this tendency is Christian community, a resolve strengthened by reaction against secularizing trends of the 1960s and 1970s that marginalized the church. It is not simply centripetal with regards to faith in Christ, but also to entering community. Here cruciformity finds greater affinity with the Catholic and perhaps Pentecostal position; not in affirming the Catholic Church as the true church, but in recognizing that Christian community is closely linked to God's reign, as community of the Spirit. While many Protestant groups retain the conversionist idea that the church is simply a free association of believers, in cruciformity the church experiences a deeper reality, carrying on Christ's ministry through the Spirit. Cruciformity has a communal ethic. The community has a responsibility to outwork the master narrative, empowered by the Spirit. The church does not exist to be centripetal in the sense of inviting people into a pre-established cultural commune of belief, but rather invites others to a form of following, as a servant community, emptying itself and seeking the benefit of others.

It is in understanding the believer's response that this tendency diverges from cruciformity. While a confession of faith and, especially from the Catholic side, joining of the community of faith, are core elements, the importance of social action can be minimized. For evangelicals and Pentecostals in particular, the community's success is often measured by numerical growth. At worst, even if significant social transformation is evident, mission is still a failure unless expectation for growth is realized. Catholics are perhaps less guilty of this polarization, keeping in balance horizontal aspects of salvation, although often more connected with the themes of *missio Dei* and reign of God, than intrinsic to participation in Christ. Cruciformity, however, explicitly measures success in conformity to the master-narrative, where cruciform love confirms the Spirit's presence in power. Vertical and horizontal aspects of salvation are inseparable. Granted, the Lausanne Movement brought something of a balance to the evangelical position, as Latin American theologians from liberationist contexts ensured social responsibility was confirmed an aspect of mission. Nevertheless, this falls short of cruciformity, where cruciform love is central to the Christian message and response.

Prophetic Dialogue and Inculturation

Bevans and Schroeder synthesize the above three mission theologies into *prophetic dialogue*, an overarching mission theology for the twenty-first century. They describe it as a missionary spirituality, meaning an underlying attitude or ethos. Openness, respect and willingness to learn from others are combined with the courage to demonstrate and speak out truth, as well as to denounce whatever contradicts the gospel when necessary.[49] Contrastingly cruciformity is a 'narrative spirituality' in the sense of 'a dynamic life with God that corresponds in some way to the divine "story"',[50] referring to the narrative pattern of Christ's self-giving, other-edifying death on the cross and subsequent resurrection. While cruciformity is focused on participation in the story of Christ in particular, prophetic dialogue emphasizes the values intrinsic to its related parts, with Christ more peripheral. The 'dialogue' dimension of prophetic dialogue draws from the *missio Dei* approach, and the 'prophecy' dimension from the other two. According to the needs of different contexts, prophecy or dialogue take precedence, but the other must always be borne in mind. Prophecy is dialogical in approach, and dialogue considers the need for various forms of prophecy.

For Bevans and Schroeder, however, mission is first and foremost dialogue.[51] God is best understood as a relationship or communion, following the Trinitarian theology of *missio Dei*. Mission reflects dialogical Trinitarian life, where God's nature is an eternal movement of 'openness and receiving, a total giving and accepting'. Through the Spirit's gentle and persuading secret presence, along with the concrete manifestation in Jesus, this communion has been, 'spilling over into creation and calling creation back into communion with Godself'.[52] The Spirit of Creation works alongside, or even as an alternative to

God's manifestation in Jesus. This is seen throughout six key elements of mission.[53] Proclamation is done in respectful dialogue, *because* the Spirit has gone before, active among the people or culture long before the missionary's arrival. Good liturgy, prayer and contemplation align believers with God's priorities, opening their eyes to where God's Spirit might already be moving. God is always working in the world by his Spirit to bring justice, peace and integrity through God's reign in a wide variety of forms. Inter-religious dialogue is characterized by openness to the Spirit's previous and even salvific work in other faiths, and inculturation involves attending to where God's Spirit has already been at work in other contexts. They are essentially inclusivist in their approach, following Vatican II teaching. They emphasize Jesus as exemplary, showing what God is like,[54] rather than talking of the objective work of the cross. The master-narrative becomes a paradigmatic example rather than an indivisible narrative experience of vertical and horizontal aspects of salvation in which to participate. The result is yet another centrifugal approach.

Although prophetic dialogue remains ostensibly centrifugal, it offers vital insight into approaching inculturation in marginal places, although I first adapt their understanding of the Spirit's role. Cruciformity views the Spirit's work outside the Christian community in a preparatory sense. God goes before the missionary by his cruciform Spirit – as happened in Acts with Macedonia, or the example of Cornelius, or even the gospel stories of John the Baptist – and draws people to the resurrected Christ. Part of this preparation may well be attraction to values and morals that characterize the faithfulness of Christ. The Spirit prepares hearts to respond to Christ's faith / faithfulness, in turn enabling participation in the kingdom through cruciform faith and love, empowered by the indwelling cruciform Spirit. This understanding facilitates adopting prophetic dialogue's insights on inculturation. Inculturation is an authentic meeting, entailing vulnerability and change for both parties. It involves awareness that the Spirit has gone before the missionary, preparing and transforming the context or people so they are ready to participate in the gospel. The missionary must be attentive and listening, malleable and ready to submit to God's prior preparation, where the Spirit has imparted cruciform values to the pre-missional context. Bevans and Schroeder suggest two postures appropriate to inculturation. First, the outsider, who learns to 'let go' of their own lenses and filters, presenting a gospel free of cultural additions.[55] Second, the insider, who learns to trust in their local culture and tradition, identifying values previously instilled by the Spirit and who must 'speak out' so these are added to the church's understanding.[56] The converse occasionally applies, when the outsider, through their objective position, sees inconsistencies or positives and must 'speak out'. Furthermore the insider, on identifying something unhelpful, must be willing to 'let go'. 'Letting go' is consonant with cruciformity's master narrative of self-emptying and looking to the interests of others. In prophetic dialogue 'letting go' is compared to the idea of *kenosis*, or self-emptying, the 'basic virtue of a missionary's spirituality'.[57]

I suggest, however, that due to their bias to dialogue, centrifugal leanings and oversensitivity to previous missionary imperialism, Bevans and Schroeder's approach is imbalanced. While it is admirable to affirm any new culture or context, it is possible to overemphasize 'letting go' such that the missionary's useful distinctiveness is lost. They even describe missionaries as 'friendly ghosts'.[58] The missionary need not be completely divested of their cultural background. It too has God-given characteristics worth sharing and should not be devalued. As Miroslav Volf contends, embrace of the other does not entail the violence of eradicating differentiation, but may involve readjusting our identities to make space for them.[59] Genuine self-emptying, according to Philippians 2, involves emptying of selfishness, not self. The missionary brings more than just the bare gospel and objectivity of an outsider.

Relatedly, Bevans and Schroeder are also too affirming of the insider, suggesting that occasional 'letting go' of shadow sides of culture should be a last resort.[60] Similarly the idea of 'letting be',[61] where missionaries leave the gospel in the hands of insiders, is admirable, but forgets the concept of different cultures and peoples brought together in unity through Christ. They attempt to redress previous disparagement of local culture, but tread so sensitively that they lose the appropriate balance. So-called 'insiders' and 'outsiders' must be equally open to 'let go' and 'speak out'.

Finally, the labels of 'insiders' and 'outsiders' are also suspect. The gospel breaks down barriers between those who are different and although differentiation remains, identities are readjusted. New contexts birth a fresh form of Christian community, taking positives from incoming missionaries, but also adopting cruciform values already inherent. This was the case when the Jews and Gentiles first learned to follow Christ together.

Inculturation and Marginal Places

My reflections arise in a context of working with people with addictions. Our church started a 'community house', where church members lived with people from a background of addiction, learning from one another, and sharing in mission among those still caught in addiction. This involved 'letting go' and 'speaking out' by all concerned as lifestyle changes were embraced and preconceptions of personal, communal, church and even Christian identity were frequently challenged. Interestingly, other church members often voiced centrifugal voices, such as suggesting the house might develop into a new charity, or centripetal ones, such as encouraging those involved to move on to an individualistic lifestyle with more conventional participation in church life. For those involved it became clear that the house pointed prophetically towards a more cruciform approach, crying out for the whole community to be more radically malleable. Community living is not for all, but creatively facilitating social engagement and committed and costly relationships is not an optional extra for mission as cruciformity.

We found that mission in marginal places involves people who may find themselves alienated in largely middle-class church culture. Inculturation requires adapting styles and modes of rituals used in worship. Generations develop layers of tradition, with some perpetuated only because of their centrality to previous secular culture. For the church to be downwardly mobile and dialogical it must present itself in a way that connects with people, taking the initiative to 'let go' and walk the way of *kenosis*. Superficially this might entail a change in dress sense, musical taste or building fabrics, and the censoring of religious language. The possibility exists, however, of changing times, structures and content of gatherings, responding to questions and concerns. This reflects a form of 'table fellowship', many times quite literally through shared meals, echoing Jesus' boundary-breaking practice of sharing meals with the excluded, which involved transcending comfort zones and cultural barriers.[62]

In terms of events or points of contact, organization must cater for such simple elements as short attention spans, the need for people to go for a smoke, and health and safety issues. 'Letting go', however, may go deeper, to the point of subverting personal goals and ambitions; challenging prejudice, agendas and consumeristic leanings; embracing smallness (like yeast in dough) by setting aside aspirations for reputation or success; and entering into troubling and challenging living conditions in a form of downward mobility, while simultaneously departing from established cultural norms and expectations. Such self-divestment, however, is not one-sided. So-called 'insiders' from marginal places also learn to 'let go'. This includes entertaining openness to new experiences, peoples and world-views, and a similar setting aside of cultural norms and expectations. Marginal places can be hard platforms from which to dissent or stand out as they often manifest a narrower vision of 'acceptable' social norms, sometimes due to lack of exposure to diversity.

The same mutuality pertains to 'speaking out'. Cruciformity resonates with prophetic dialogue's four elements of prophecy. A cruciform community 'speaks out' without words, through the witness of authentic Christian individual and communal life. Eschewing occasional moments of mission, this is a continued lifestyle choice of witness and commitment to justice. The community maintains cruciformity's vertical and horizontal balance by encouraging a shared life of faith and actions. Lesslie Newbigin described authentic Christian community as a 'hermeneutic of the gospel'.[63]

Second, it 'speaks out' with words. This entails proclamation of God's reign, namely the message that God plans a future new creation, tasted in part now through faith in Jesus and in his community. Christians prophesy by telling about Jesus, through whom humanity sees what God is like: a God that is for his creation, loving, forgiving and ostensibly on the side of the poor and suffering.[64]

Third, it 'speaks against' without words. Counter-cultural Christian life, individually and collectively, 'offers a different vision of the world than what is the natural drift of society',[65] characterized by cruciformity's master-narrative of self-giving and looking to the good of others. Finally it 'speaks against' with words, standing against injustice and denouncing anything contrary to God's reign, even speaking truth to power or disempowering systems.[66]

Such proclamation does not always wait for a verbal question. As in my own context, lifestyles often cry out for fulfilment and intervention can be needed. Each of these elements are not simply mission *ad extra* but *ad intra*, as fellowship, worship and shared mission challenge community members to make these elements part of their own lifestyle. Frequent discussion and engagement with issues mean the community educates itself, becoming more aware of how ministry can be effective. For each element, appropriate dialogue is vital so the message is intelligible. The listening stance and inherent vulnerability of cruciformity anticipates a sense of co-constructed knowledge as all involved, including those normally less empowered, learn to 'let go' and 'speak out'. Insights come from those with an outside voice, but also from the experience of those ingrained in the culture. Such people have a reciprocal objective critical voice, recognizing what does not conform to the master-narrative in the mission endeavour.

Conclusion

Cruciformity entails embracing a narrative spirituality that participates in the self-giving narrative of the cross, eschewing selfishness, and instead looking to the interests of others. Beyond merely accepting an ideal, it involves entering into and surrendering to the master pattern, so it becomes our story. Through accepting such an approach, centrifugal and centripetal tendencies that polarize belief and action, church community and social action are overcome. Instead, a missionary church imaginatively forms itself after the pattern of the cross in a way appropriate to mission in marginal places, calling those that would join from outwith and within to pursue cruciform lives of faith and love, thereby fulfilling vertical and horizontal aspects of salvation. Cruciformity as inculturation involves attending to the preparatory work of the cruciform Spirit, and joining what God is doing. The community forms itself in a way that facilitates conformity to the divine story in the new context rather than assuming the imposition of previous cultural patterns and rituals. This almost certainly involves the kenotic selfishness-emptying of 'letting go' and 'speaking out' by all involved. It implies acceptance of downward mobility and the subversion of cultural expectations and aims, as well as the need to readjust identity to make space for the other. Cruciformity leads to renewed spiritual vibrancy as the Spirit of the Lord is indeed on us to preach good news to the poor, set at liberty those who are oppressed, and bind up the broken-hearted. He enters the hearts of those who accept both the objective work of the cross and the call to serve others.

Notes

[1] Michael Gorman, *Cruciformity: Paul's Narrative Spirituality of the Cross* (Grand Rapids, MI: Eerdmans, 2001), p. 390.

[2] Gorman, *Cruciformity*.

[3] Stephen Bevans and Roger Schroeder, *Constants in Context: A Theology of Mission for Today* (Maryknoll: Orbis, 2004), p. 348.

[4] Stephen Bevans and Roger Schroeder, *Prophetic Dialogue: Reflections on Christian Mission Today* (Maryknoll, NY: Orbis, 2011).

[5] Gorman, *Cruciformity*, p. 4.

[6] Gorman, *Cruciformity*, p. 169.

[7] Michael Gorman, *Inhabiting the Cruciform God* (Cambridge: Eerdmans, 2009), p. 16.

[8] Gorman, *Cruciformity*, p. 160.

[9] Gorman, *Cruciformity*, p. 160.

[10] Gorman, *Cruciformity*, p. 154.

[11] Gorman, *Inhabiting*, p. 51.

[12] David Augsburger, *Dissident Discipleship* (Grand Rapids, MI: Brazos, 2006), kindle.loc.169.

[13] Gorman, *Inhabiting*, p. 45.

[14] Gorman, *Inhabiting*, pp. 45, 56–7.

[15] Translation from Gorman, *Inhabiting*, p. 23.

[16] Gorman, *Cruciformity*, p. 186.

[17] Gorman, *Cruciformity*, p. 183.

[18] Gorman, *Cruciformity*, p. 244.

[19] Gorman, *Cruciformity*, p. 235.

[20] Gorman, *Cruciformity*, p. 303.

[21] Gorman, *Cruciformity*, p. 390.

[22] Gorman, *Cruciformity*, p. 52.

[23] Gorman, *Cruciformity*, p. 72.

[24] Gorman, *Cruciformity*, p. 53.

[25] Gorman, *Cruciformity*, p. 58.

[26] Gorman, *Cruciformity*, p. 57.

[27] Gorman, *Cruciformity*, p. 58.

[28] Gorman, *Cruciformity*, p. 55.

[29] See Avery Dulles, *Models of the Church* (Dublin: Gill & Macmillan, 1976), pp. 7–10.

[30] John Flett, *The Witness of God: The Trinity, Missio Dei, Karl Barth, and the Nature of Christian Community* (Grand Rapids, MI: Eerdmans, 2010), p. 139.

[31] Flett, *Witness*, p. 201.

[32] J.C. Hoekendijk, 'The Call to Evangelism', *International Review of Mission* 39 (1950): p. 168.

[33] David Bosch, *Transforming Mission* (Maryknoll, NY: Orbis, 1991), p. 384.

[34] Jacques Matthey, 'Missiology in the World Council of Churches: Update', *International Review of Mission* 90:4 (2001): p. 430.

[35] Bevans and Schroeder, *Constants*, p. 305.

[36] Bevans and Schroeder, *Constants*, p. 305.

[37] Bevans and Schroeder, *Constants*, p. 310.

[38] Bevans and Schroeder, *Constants*, p. 310.

39 Bevans and Schroeder, *Constants*, p. 310.
40 *Lumen Gentium* 1 in Bosch, *Transforming Mission*, p. 374.
41 Gustavo Gutiérrez, *A Theology of Liberation* (London: SCM, 1988), pp. xx–xxviii.
42 Faustino Teixeira, *A gênese das CEB's no Brasil* (São Paulo: Edições Paulinas, 1988), p. 72.
43 Bevans and Schroeder, *Constants*, p. 307.
44 Gorman, *Cruciformity*, p. 393.
45 Gorman, *Cruciformity*, p. 394.
46 Gorman, *Cruciformity*, p. 394.
47 Gorman, *Cruciformity*, p. 400.
48 Bevans and Schroeder, *Constants*, p. 323.
49 Bevans and Schroeder, *Prophetic Dialogue*, p. 2.
50 Gorman, *Cruciformity*, p. 4.
51 Bevans and Schroeder, *Constants*, p. 348.
52 Bevans and Schroeder, *Prophetic Dialogue*, p. 26.
53 Bevans and Schroeder, *Constants*, p. 351.
54 Bevans and Schroeder, *Prophetic Dialogue*, p. 12.
55 Bevans and Schroeder, *Prophetic Dialogue*, pp. 90–92.
56 Bevans and Schroeder, *Prophetic Dialogue*, p. 95.
57 Bevans and Schroeder, *Prophetic Dialogue*, p. 91.
58 Bevans and Schroeder, *Prophetic Dialogue*, p. 94.
59 Miroslav Volf, *Exclusion and Embrace* (Nashville, TN: Abingdon, 1996), p. 28.
60 Bevans and Schroeder, *Prophetic Dialogue*, p. 100.
61 Bevans and Schroeder, *Prophetic Dialogue*, p. 92.
62 Bevans and Schroeder, *Prophetic Dialogue*, p. 108.
63 Bevans and Schroeder, *Prophetic Dialogue*, p. 44.
64 Bevans and Schroeder, *Prophetic Dialogue*, p. 45.
65 Bevans and Schroeder, *Prophetic Dialogue*, p. 46.
66 Bevans and Schroeder, *Prophetic Dialogue*, pp. 47–8.

10

Shalom: Participating in the Deeper Narratives of Peaceful Presence

Juliet Kilpin

Introduction: Exploring Shalom

Shalom has become a popular word among those choosing to seek the welfare of their city or their neighbourhood. For some it denotes a reactive opposition to what they have perceived as repetitive frenetic and dehumanizing evangelistic programmes unleashed on urban communities and marginalized people. For others it denotes a proactive stance taken in unfamiliar, horizon-expanding contexts of a majority urban world. For some it marks the absence of specific practices yet for others it emphasizes the presence of particular actions. For many it explains what they are not. For others it describes what they are choosing to be.

Translated as 'peace', the English does not adequately express the truly multifaceted depth portrayed in the Old Testament which depicts shalom as the world whole, good and complete under the generous and just reign of its Creator. The damage caused by humanity's decision to choose life without God is not deemed irreparable as the prophecies of a sent Saviour promise that once again 'the earth will be full of the knowledge of Lord as the waters cover the sea'. For N.T. Wright this suggests a world 'drenched with God'.[1] In the New Testament this hope is repeated when Paul promises that we are moving towards a time when God will again be 'all in all'.[2] Wright notes that this is 'one of the clearest statements of the very centre of the future-oriented New Testament worldview'.[3] When anticipating this future completeness Jesus frequently talked of the 'kingdom of God' coming near or being present as a result of something he had said or done. Jesus chose ways of being and doing that 'presenced' this anticipated rule of God, which brought something of the promised completeness and healing to the here and now. Through the Great Commission[4] those who choose to follow him are also sent to join in the task of presencing this future here and now. How might we see those kingdom signs in our marginalized communities and to what degree can we 'presence' kingdom qualities through our own lives that might, like a trail of radioactivity, leave a trace that others might notice?[5]

Our understanding of shalom informs the individual priorities that shape how we live. For example, if our primary understanding suggests that a shalom-filled community where the kingdom of God is fully evident is one where everyone is a Christian, goes to church, believes the same and behaves the same way, then we will be seeking to live in ways that we believe might make these characteristics more likely. Anything that suggests our neighbourhood is moving away from these aspirations, such as the opening of a mosque or Sunday Assembly,[6] people of other faiths moving in or schools not delivering 'Christian' assemblies may be deemed threatening to these ideals of God's kingdom on earth.

On the other hand if our primary understanding is that a shalom-filled community is marked by working towards a healthy planet and sustainable communities, then we will live in ways we think might make these characteristics more likely and it might be the opening of another multinational supermarket, petrol station, or unethical farm that concerns us the most.

If our understanding is that a shalom-filled community is marked by the absence of tension, racism, violence, unemployment, illness, loneliness, selfishness, hunger, poverty, war and debt, then how might we live in order to make these attributes more likely? If a shalom-filled community is marked by the presence of peace, diversity, understanding, conflict resolution, dignity, justice, respect and fairness, how do we live in such ways as to ferment these hopes into bubbling reality?

For those concerned about place a vital question is how to discern these signs of shalom and tell if shalom is already present in a neighbourhood or not. An inexperienced shalom-observer may bring all sorts of assumptions to this quest. For example they may assume that in a suburban neighbourhood where there is low visible crime, high employment and quiet streets, shalom is clearly evident. Inadvertently they may miss the high levels of debt, dissatisfaction and isolation which may challenge this. Conversely, when they think of marginalized urban communities they may interpret the perceived chaos, noise and overcrowding as a lack of peace, missing the beautiful shalom of lives shared and needs met and the wonder of life learned through diversity and inclusion.

A key challenge for the urban church is not to confuse shalom with some of the characteristics that might be found in the suburbs or in areas that are being gentrified, where typically the indices of deprivation may be lower. Indices of deprivation are not the same as indices of shalom. Even though there may be elements of deprivation that hinder shalom, there may also be elements of shalom that are more abundant in marginalized areas which are coping with significant challenges of inequality and poverty.

This is an important challenge for the suburban church and indeed the wider Christian community too. In 2013[7] I met Ian Stackhouse, author of *Primitive Piety*.[8] He described the 'suburban mediocrity' that so much of society aspires to, a kind of middle-of-the-road inoffensiveness and orderliness which seeps into many areas of life, including the collective of shalom-seekers, called church. He lamented how 'suburbia lobotomises spirituality' leaving a 'church culture [that] knows neither the soul's deepest despair nor breathless gratitude'. For some churches, shalom has come to mean that peaceful absence of trouble or quarrel, a bland Shoreditchification[9] of culture, an outward veneer of unruffled feathers, masking real-life conflicts and differences, seething frustration against injustices, desperation for an outworking of solidarity and deep gut-wrenching belief that there must be more to following Jesus than being nice to each other.

This is where the English language that translates shalom to peace lets us down in its inability to contain the fullness of this concept in just one word. Inoffensive, bland niceness is not the shalom that Jesus revealed.

More than Peace

Since its inception in 1997 I have been involved in Urban Expression,[10] an urban mission agency committed to pioneering creative and relevant expressions of Christian community in under-churched urban neighbourhoods. One of the things we encourage our self-financing teams of volunteers to do when they move into a neighbourhood is to take a year simply to listen. They are encouraged to resist the dominant paradigm of finding solutions, starting projects and running programmes and instead to discern what God is already doing in that place, among the people who are already there, to see how they might join in and indeed, to see what it may teach them. Al Barrett, in a blog post which summarizes a presentation he made in 2014,[11] calls this 'Hearing to Speech'.[12] This requires listening, attentiveness and research that goes beneath the surface of what presents itself to hear marginalized voices and alternative narratives that challenge the status quo. This kind of attentiveness opens up the possibility of seeing beyond first impressions of a place to realize that what seemed 'obvious' at first sight may not be the reality experienced by many.

It is important in seeking shalom to try and look below the surface and take note of the assumptions and experiences we bring to our understanding of shalom and to be open to the way in which our encounters with others might stretch our perspective so that it is broadened and deepened. As we do so we might allow our imaginations to join with others to explore what might make this place and these people more whole, rather than what will make this place more like we want it to be and these people more like we think they should be. In doing so we may also discover that there are ways we can become more whole too and allow those who cross our paths to help us on that journey of more fully expressing God-characteristics in our lives.

The pursuit of shalom challenges the imagination to resist the urge to reduce the idea of peaceableness to our own vision – a struggle for imagination that is seen around the world. For example on a trip to Cambodia in 2014 I visited the disturbing Tuol Sleng Genocide Museum in Phnom Penh, a former high school which the Khmer Rouge used as a prison and torture chamber during the 1970s. On a top floor of the museum was an exhibition on the theme of peace in which paintings from school children adorned the walls. There were many similarities in their different pictures including the national flag, a dove, a gun with its barrel tied in a knot, and a diversity of Cambodian people – intellectuals and farmers together.[13] But there was also a disconcerting similarity in these dreams of what a peaceful Cambodia might look like with most pictures depicting clean, straight-lined streets, skyscraper offices and shops, banks and cars. In a city which is dominated by tuk-tuks and motorbikes, dust and grit, and in which the more permanent buildings hide the burgeoning slums that are growing behind them, it might be no wonder that the children yearn for the 'developed world' ideal they see portrayed on their televisions. But to what extent does this sanitized, orderly, bank-rolled version of peace express the biblical understanding of shalom, the very presence of God's kingdom on earth as it is in heaven? Is this really what we are yearning for and investing our lives in? Is this our biggest hope? In aspiring to this ideal alone are we suggesting that there is less shalom in the monsoon-flooded slum than in the shiny streets of Los Angeles, Toronto, Paris or Manchester?

Resistance and Narrative

If Jesus on earth embodied the fullness of God's presence, the exuberance of all that is good and the totality of grace, it raises questions not only about the nature and purpose of his death and resurrection, but the nature and purpose of his life. If, through his life, the kingdom of God came near, what were those characteristics of shalom and how were they experienced by those to whom it came near?

A key thing about how Jesus' life is conveyed in the gospels is that he completely re-imagines and re-enacts the idea of shalom. This re-imagining is seen in two particular ways. First, Jesus exhibited resistance to the dominant story and practices and, second, he consistently told and lived by an alternative, peaceable narrative. A later section will explore, under six headings, how Jesus displayed these attributes and help us ask how we, as followers of Jesus, might also become communities of resistance and narrative.

But first, let me tell you the parable of two sofas.

The Parable of the Two Sofas

The Pink Leather Sofa

One day a pink leather sofa, softened and scratched by the years of comfort it had given to its owners, appeared on a street in Glasgow. Sitting at the base of a tenement building it stared across the street at the other items discarded and no longer loved. An inquisitive photographer, on the lookout for shots to illustrate rising poverty in Glasgow, noticed the shabby sofa, took a photo, uploaded it and gave the sofa its fame as it depicted the habits of the urban poor, who irresponsibly dump their unwanted goods and rubbish bags on the streets with no concern for their neighbours.

A shalom-seeking resident of the tenement block, in browsing local political news sites, stumbled upon this interesting article but was concerned to see the pink sofa being used to illustrate rising poverty. You see, he knew the family who used to own the pink sofa and had watched them carry it down to the street, not in an act of mindless, uncaring waste, but as a considered act to ensure the pink sofa was ready to be picked up by the waste management team who came each week to this estate to collect bulky items that non-driving residents could not take to the tip.

In seeking to resist the dominant story which so readily demonizes the undeserving poor[14] he chose to post his own article, telling the truthful narrative and vindicating the socially responsible residents of his functioning community and the services of the local council who responded effectively to the social needs of the non-driving public.

The Orange Velour Sofa

Another day an orange velour sofa, threadbare, squishy and stained, received its fame. Situated outside a house in a Birmingham street with local residents making themselves comfortable on its cushions, a film crew interviewed them about how they coped living on 'benefits'.[15] When aired, many viewers of the documentary series[16] assumed the sofa had been there a long time and that it was frequently used by these recipients of social welfare. Fuelled by the dominant narrative of the lazy poor,[17] people took to social media to criticize the interviewees.

A shalom-seeking friend and visitor of the neighbourhood, in watching the documentary series, noticed the orange velour sofa outside a friend's house and remembered seeing it originally in the next street down, again awaiting collection by the waste management service. As the shalom-seeker spoke with the residents about the impact of the television series on their lives, some told tales of how the sofa might have been placed outside the house solely for the purpose of interviewing residents.

The shalom-seeker chose not to endorse the dominant narrative and negative conclusions that were being drawn by viewers of the television series, but took the time to hear the residents' stories first-hand and tried to provide opportunities for them to share elements of their life stories that had not been picked up by viewers.

Time passed and the orange velour sofa was eventually collected, as originally planned, by the waste management team. Time passed and while some residents took advantage of the opportunities that came their way through the fame of television, for others who had perched on the orange velour sofa, life on the street became unbearable. The constant intrusion, name-calling and unwanted attention from those who toured this now 'famous' street became too much, and they moved away.

The Peaceful Presence of Jesus

My hope is that as we now turn to examine the characteristics of shalom that we see embedded in the life of Jesus we will do so in conversation with the parable so that it might shed light on how his patterns of living shalom connect with our own everyday, contemporary world.

Key to all these attributes of Jesus is his humility and vulnerability. Observing the tenderness of the Living One as he knelt next to the prostrate John in his Revelation vision, Catherine Cowell says: 'There is no difference between the glorious, risen Christ and the carpenter and healer. They are one and the same. He did not leave aside his power as an object lesson only to take up dictatorship again as soon as he could. For Jesus this is the normal way to exercise power and leadership.'[18]

1. Jesus Lives with His Feet on the Ground

Michael Frost, in *Incarnate: The Body of Christ in an Age of Disengagement*, suggests we are increasingly living excarnate lives where we are 'present but not available'.[19] Objectification, depersonalization, rootlessness and disengagement, he suggests, are temptations of our current age which are impacting the expectations and experiences of Jesus-followers in relation to community, worship and mission. Simultaneously, 'incarnational mission' is becoming trendy with a plethora of agencies motivating people to move into 'poor' neighbourhoods to build community, plant churches or play an active role in its regeneration. The extent to which we are becoming more excarnate than previous generations is debatable – before the iPhone was invented people on the train used to bury their heads in the newspapers so as not to engage! However Frost is right to ask how we can marry an excarnate lifestyle with following an incarnate God.

'The incarnation', Frost states, 'is not God's attempt to fix humankind by getting in and out as quickly as he can. It was God's plan for fashioning friendship between himself and us. It is like all true friendship – messy, frustrating, joyful and unending.'[20] He goes on to suggest, 'If God reveals himself most sublimely in the incarnation, then it follows that the journey of discipleship must be learned incarnationally. No mere formulas or simple steps can suffice.'[21]

Indeed, it is only by living among and with those we are called to serve that we see most clearly what God is already doing and have the most opportunities to join in and learn. There are some hugely challenging issues in our complex world that demand urgent attention and solutions, but many humanitarians agree that 'to tackle an issue effectively, you need to understand it – and it's impossible to understand an issue by simply reading about it. You need to see it firsthand, even live in its midst.'[22] Of course mission in marginal places can take place in all sorts of ways, and many programmes which leave me deeply concerned still seem to bring about gracious shalom-impact, but if the nature of Jesus' life is as important as his death and resurrection, then an incarnational posture must be of utmost importance.

This was brought home to me during a visit to a slum community in Phnom Penh in October 2014 where it was arranged that I would stay with a local lady in her home. Being present in her home, on her doorstep, in her alley, meant that I learnt the sounds and smells of her neighbourhood. By the end of just one week I knew the sound of the bread-lady making her early morning deliveries and the man collecting the recycling in his cart; I knew whose clothes rails, used for drying our hand-washed clothes, belonged to who; I smelt the early morning routine of the neighbours' cooking and heard the mopeds being wheeled out of the shacks for work; I knew that when it rained the lady opposite had to bail out buckets-full of water, whatever time of day or night, and that the only way to get their baby to sleep was for the dad to drive her around on their moped; and when I walked out of the neighbourhood in the morning to visit a different team I said goodbye to my temporary neighbours, while an incoming team of visitors made their way into the slum community for their day's 'mission work'. I witnessed neighbours sharing food and cooking for one another, massaging each other's aching backs and concerns. A community that, to the onlooker, might have looked like it lacked peace and needed 'help' exuded evidence of deep shalom rarely seen in the UK. But I only got to see that because for a brief moment I had the privilege of being welcomed and embedded within the community in a way which, to me, embodied a rich sense of incarnation.

As I wash the dust off my feet from a second visit to this slum community I identify with David Bosch who described the church as 'an inseparable union of the divine and the dusty'.[23] The more we follow Jesus' incarnational example, the more dusty our feet become.

Those who are intentionally present for the long term will inevitably encounter, experience and understand so much more. And of course, those who have always lived there have potential to see most clearly the God who already dwells with them and discern where shalom is and is not. Which makes sense of course, because only those who know the neighbourhood can ever know where the sofas originally come from and why they are truly there.

2. Jesus Tells a Truthful Narrative

For the majority of my adult life I have lived in neighbourhoods that I was advised not to live in. The dominant narrative frequently provokes judgements from people who have never lived in those places, who assume that certain characteristics make places 'bad' or 'undesirable' to live in. Assumptions are also readily made with people boxed together in phrases like 'those people are like this', most frequently by those who have never interacted with the very people they are critiquing. The barrier caused by compartmentalizing people heightens the reluctance to even try and find out what the truth is.

Such neighbourhoods often have to overcome a third narrative that dominates many marginalized communities that 'nothing ever changes round here'. People, places and prospects can all be victims of false narratives.

Jesus faced such narratives: Nathaniel wondered if anything good could ever come from Jesus' home town,[24] assumptions were made that certain people should not be socialized with,[25] and doubts about whether freedom and justice would ever come to a people under occupation abounded.[26] Resisting these assumptions, Jesus practised a truth-filled life. Through his very existence he showed that good could come from Nazareth, that people were surprising and should not be put in boxes, and that justice could be sought through non-violent means. Instead of simply protesting and bemoaning the unjust situation, Jesus lived out the truth, embodying an alternative narrative, refusing to be enslaved by the current expectations.

How did Jesus develop such a truthful character? Evidence certainly points to an enthusiasm for learning from a young age, but I am also intrigued by the fact that Jesus heard his host community for thirty years before he began a public proclamation of an alternative way. In fact Jesus blended in so well that when he entered public ministry people queried the legitimacy of Joseph's son to speak out at all.[27] Yet Jesus spoke with authority, but in a way that seemed different to his contemporary rabbis.[28]

Truth is ambiguous and not always easy to discern, but space for truth-telling is nurtured through dialogue. We are often reluctant to engage with people and places that are beyond our life experiences because we are fearful. What a shame that fear can prevent us learning so much about ourselves and about others. It can trap us in a world far smaller than the one God graciously invites us to inhabit. Fear can also be used as a controlling tactic to limit people. Fear reduces our capacity for relationships rather than expanding it, causing us to exclude and decrease our connectivity. This often leads to reluctance to engage with people who seem to be different, places that have a reputation, or scenarios that seem unhopeful. But by creating opportunities for dialogue where voices are heard and differences honestly explored, as opposed to posturing and polarizing rhetoric, we can reduce fear. Truths about people, places and prospects are brought to light. Possibilities are expanded. Whether we explore truth quietly, loudly, creatively, personally, publicly, compassionately or angrily, we follow the peaceful example of Jesus by seeking to be truth-tellers, and we resist the temptation to isolate our own story from others.

Which makes sense of course, because those who seek shalom through telling a truthful narrative won't move sofas to manipulate or exaggerate their own version of a story.

3. Jesus Seeks the Welfare of the Whole Community

A key thing about Jesus's life is how he resists exclusion and coercion. Jesus seems remarkably inclusive, able to look beyond the particular context he was born into, acknowledging that the kingdom of God also comes close to, and at times even manifests itself through, those who are beyond his immediate circle of familiarity.

While Jesus was himself enculturated into his own particular context, he was at the same time opened to having his world-view challenged. Ann Morisy suggests that the Syro-Phoenician woman's challenge to Jesus that 'even the dogs eat the crumbs under the table',[29] was a blatant rebuttal of inculturated racism. Jesus did not respond to this challenge defensively, nor by seeking retaliation as we so often do when feeling humiliated, but with a considered acknowledgment that she spoke truth. Jesus fraternized with a woman he shouldn't have, and as a result was re-neighboured[30] with her. Later he wept over a cosmopolitan Jerusalem, desperate for the city to know peace, and turned over the tables of those in the temple who were making profit from division.

A key step towards creating a peaceful presence and joining in the task of seeking the welfare[31] of the places we are in is to actively live out of the conviction that God originally created all things 'good', and that all people are made in God's image. It is easy to fall into ways of talking and reacting which strengthen walls between people, yet Jesus' radical removal of barriers, and indeed the example of his early followers whose range of inclusion was challenged with a vision of unclean food[32] and a Holy Spirit who gave visions to both men and women,[33] gives us hope that there is another way of responding when our paradigm is called into question.

Those who seek shalom and seek the welfare of the whole community are those who are open to the narratives of others and resist the urge to use people to endorse their own ends. They consider the wider impact of moving or sharing a photograph of a sofa.

4. Jesus Radically Redefines the Use of Power

A peaceful presence depends significantly on how aware we are of the power we each embody. Each of us has power to do good or harm, to influence, to enable or restrict ourselves and others. Yet some of us are less aware of our range of power than others. An urban community might exhibit remarkable powers of durability, solidarity and cohesion, yet it may also have little power over changes wrought by decisions made beyond its control.

While desiring to serve urban communities, missional teams, congregations, church plants and Christian projects have just as much potential to wield power if they do not take time to acknowledge the dangers and choose an alternative approach. Of course most communities do not get to choose who moves in. This can sometimes create fear and tension, particularly when unfamiliar cultures take up residence. But in neighbourhoods that have had projects, plans and schemes 'done to' them for decades, an alternative approach might be more peaceable.

Inner CHANGE[34] teams, when exploring whether to move into a particular neighbourhood, take time to 'court' the community, meeting and listening to potential neighbours and, in effect, asking if they would be welcomed. This is a way of guarding against becoming 'the

Church Condescending'[35] and misusing the power that financially supported outsiders may have at their disposal. It recognizes the potential all people have of imposing their own preferences on others. As Jesus chose not to exploit 'equality with God'[36] so we can take seriously the call to humility and the invitation to coexist and sit in solidarity with our fellow humans, for 'servanthood replaces dominion, forgiveness absorbs hostility'.[37]

The surprising narrative of Jesus discerns the dynamics of power that often go unnoticed. Jesus did not choose the trickle-down approach when seeking to bring a new order to the world, but chose twelve grass-roots people. Jesus must have seen potential in them and on a human level I suspect he must have enjoyed being with them as no one wants to be followed by people they don't get on with! In today's terminology we might call Jesus a community organizer, drawing alongside people and developing the assets they have to form community and galvanize a vision of shalom for society.[38] These were not the usual makers and shakers in positions of control or status, but had more power to think creatively, influence others and mobilize for change than many of their superiors. Jesus exhibited solidarity with these disciples as he drew alongside to mentor and embolden them in a different use of power, correcting them when they failed to resist the dominant narrative of greatness.[39]

As we seek to be a peace-filled presence in our neighbourhoods we will do well to take notice of the power-filled and resist the temptation to always court them. Al Barrett suggests that Jesus, in his forty days in the wilderness[40] renounced temptations to become the provider (look what you could do with this bread), the possessor (look what you could do with this kingdom), and the performer (look what you can do if people see you do this).[41] Jean Vanier also suggests that 'in order to stand by the downtrodden, never to exclude but include them in our lives, we need to be freed from our compulsive needs to succeed, to have power and approbation'.[42]

Those who seek shalom are aware of their ability to overpower, and so they look for peaceful potential in unusual places and resist the temptation to coerce or manipulate for their own agendas.

Which makes sense of course, because those who are conscientious about power will think about the consequences their decisions might have on those who do not choose where the sofas go.

5. Jesus is Calming

Jesus inhabited a place struggling with challenges familiar to the world today. Occupations, prejudices, misogyny, religious extremism, human trafficking and inequalities have existed throughout history and are brought into sharp focus on our screens today. In such situations anxieties run high and the tiniest things can tip the balance from relative calm into all-out chaos. So it is immensely helpful to explore what Jesus modelled in such times.

It is important to note that Jesus was birthed in chaos and that stability is not everyone's normal. Guy Standing introduces the new normality experienced by the 'global "precariat"', consisting of many millions around the word without an 'anchor of stability'.[43] Born in unsettled circumstances Jesus encountered the perpetual movement that much of our planet's population experiences constantly. A refugee for his early years, Jesus shows that wise, thoughtful and peace-filled leadership can develop within such circumstances. Chaos, sometimes regarded by the risk-averse as the antithesis of all that is peaceful, is often the crucible of creativity and character. Ask any artist or ideas person what their desk looks like and it is rarely likely to be tidy! Sometimes it is only out of the disorder that creativity comes. Out of the ability to look at things from an alternative angle comes new perspectives and clarity. A shalom-filled neighbourhood, organization, business or congregation does not necessitate an absence of disruption. Indeed a context which exudes too much order may not provide the very laboratory for new and creative thinking required for a world in perpetual change. This perhaps feels contrary to Old Testament concerns about the chaos that existed before the created order, and the unprincipled, dehumanizing bedlam that has occasionally surfaced since. Yet it is in tune with the Creator God, who brought beauty from chaos, and is akin to Jesus' intentionally disruptive lifestyle that, while serene, surprised, provoked and challenged the existing norms.

Jesus was faced with numerous emergencies that required his attention. People with life-threatening illnesses,[44] women to be imminently stoned to death,[45] soldiers brandishing their weapons,[46] and mob-rule[47] barged in on his life with tumultuous predictability. How did Jesus react in these circumstances? The only situation which appeared to provoke an angry response from Jesus was the divisive money-changing in the temple.[48] Aside from this it seems that he approached each panic-fuelled occasion quite calmly. Not akin to the 'keep calm and carry on' attitude of denial,[49] but a thoughtful, yet active and peaceable response. Jesus chose not to react, but to respond, mining the depths of his wisdom and taking into account the bigger shalom ideal before taking action.

Jesus frequently offered another option, a third way, an unpredicted response which came deep from the kingdom of shalom embodied in his spectacularly extraordinary life. His third way often involved choosing non-violent resistance. Jesus was not passive in the face of injustice, but he never responded in a violent manner. Instead he spoke truth, provoked reflection and encouraged his followers to challenge dehumanizing behaviours through their actions. Walter Wink suggests that 'Jesus is not telling us to submit to evil, but to refuse to oppose it on its own terms. We are not to let the opponent dictate the methods of our opposition. He is urging us to transcend both passivity and violence by finding a third way, one that is at once assertive and yet nonviolent.'[50]

Carrying soldiers' packs an extra mile when this is not permitted by law, demanding to see the face of a hand as an equal as it slaps your cheek, standing naked as you give away your remaining layer of clothing to the one humiliating you by taking your cloak, are all challenging actions of resistance which break the cycle of violence. 'The logic of Jesus' examples in Matthew 5:39b-41', continues Wink, 'goes beyond both inaction and overreaction to a new response, fired in the crucible of love, that promises to liberate the oppressed from evil even as it frees the oppressor from sin.'[51]

Anxiety-filled neighbourhoods or situations need activists who will pour water on fears and petrol on peace; who look beyond winning arguments and toward the bigger hope of shalom; who resist the temptation to shame and blame others in their faults and failings and claim the promises of the final scapegoat who makes reconciliation, forgiveness and restoration possible. Hate has never solved anything. Through Jesus, hate is being phased out.

Those who seek shalom resist the narrative of bewilderment, anxiety and hate and seek to embody the peace of Christ. Which makes sense of course, because those who are peace-filled and calm refuse to demonize those who sit on the sofa.

6. Jesus is Relational

God's strategy for establishing a new shalom-order for the world was to become present and build relationship. Without presence any strategy would have constituted a domination and any invitation to join in, a coercion. 'To not attend is to be absent,' declares Augsburger. 'In absence one flees to the past in memory, or projects into the future in fantasy without inviting the other to come along.'[52]

The gospels show that Jesus spent most of his time in one-to-one or intimate conversations, at meals, on walks, in boats and at parties. He was intensely relational, fully present. Jesus didn't see people as projects to fix. If that was the case, and if being born a human, dying and being raised again was the way to achieve this, then surely he could have done that at any stage of his life, even on day one! Yet Jesus stayed and inhabited the earth.

This relational God who walks with people contrasts with impositional powers that make decisions from a distance and seemingly without much regard particularly for the appropriateness or impact of their projects, plans and schemes on the lived experiences of those in marginalized communities. Many such communities, as in need of investment and involvement as they may be, grow tired of being on the receiving end of things being 'done to' them; grow wise to the fact that funding is often only temporary; and angry that the promises and opportunities offered in the cause of regeneration or 'gentrification' seem to come at their expense as they are the ones often faced with no choice but to move away from their support networks and roots. Many long-standing but lower-income residents are left feeling that their rights count for less than those of others. This 'nonrecognition', says Volf, 'can inflict harm, can be a form of oppression, imprisoning someone in a false, distorted, and reduced mode of being.'[53]

Projects can indeed be helpful, and diversity of people, family shape, wealth and culture can build healthy neighbourhoods, but the cohesion and wellbeing of communities that is formed from reciprocal relationships[54] cannot be imposed on a place. Social engineering is not a magic formula. Social trust needs to be discovered or sown at grass roots, nurtured and fed, given the right environment to flourish. The work of relational-based initiatives such as Near Neighbours,[55] the Poverty Truth Commission[56] and Citizens UK[57] model alternative approaches and emphasize the interdependence of people to one another, the value of each other's stories and the equality of all. They resist the dominant narrative of gentrification and its power dynamics that often result in division, and embrace an appreciation of all cultures. There is an investment in relational depth.

Without relationship we are at risk of making assumptions about and patronizing one another, even dehumanizing. To reiterate, Jesus didn't see people as projects to fix. He took them seriously as persons, making himself available time and time again. There was no formula. Discipleship was encountered through messy, complicated, beautiful relationship. This is a helpful and hopeful perspective to have; after all 'we can't fix everything, but we can all make life more beautiful', said my friend Helen after an evening exploring these themes.

Those who seek shalom resist the dominant narrative that people are projects to be fixed and seek to embody the relationality of Christ. Which makes sense of course, because those who value relationships above results will sit next to the people on the sofa and hear their story.

Conclusion

These sofa stories offer practical examples of shalom-responses that honour people experiencing deeply embedded marginalization and deprivation. This peaceable presencing shows how mission can embody non-violent and non-coercive relationships while still seeking gospel transformation in ourselves and our communities.

A key characteristic of shalom that I have sought to present here is that it gets under the surface of everyday life in a way that opens our eyes and our hearts to a completely different way of seeing things. It is not based on the predominant narratives that are encountered, which work mainly for the benefit of those already in places of power. Rather, the narratives that shalom draws upon are those that only emerge from a deep sense of being embedded in a community so that the voices of the most marginalized are allowed to open us up to things which are otherwise hard to see. It is in these often difficult and discomforting encounters that we find we are also encountering the presence of Jesus in new ways that draw us and challenge us to live more peaceably in the community of which we are a part.

In a society experiencing a monumental rise in instantaneous networking, rapid population growth, overwhelming migration to cities, huge increase in the numbers of urban poor and an increasing narrative of mistrust and fear, the pressure along the social fault lines of our globe is steadily increasing, suggests Miroslav Volf. This is 'creating ripe conditions for imbalances of power and profound disagreements over truth and justice perpetuated'. In such a world the peaceful reign of God is acutely needed and deeply yearned for. The church, as 'first fruits of the reign of God . . . anticipates that reign in the here and now. It is the knowledge of this that gives [the church] confidence to work for the advance of God's reign in the world, even if it does so with modesty and without claiming to have all the answers.'[58]

Our small Spirit-filled steps towards imitating the peaceful presence of Jesus lead us ever closer to this reality. Those who seek this way of peace are likely to resist the narrative that only the strong can have impact and fully express God's character. They will seek to embody the humility and fragility of Christ. Which makes sense of course, because those who are fragile are less likely to coerce people to sit on the sofa because it will serve their purposes and will find joy in discovering a different way to join in with the story of peace that started before us, appears beside us, and will continue after us.

Notes

[1] N.T. Wright, *Surprised by Hope* (London: SPCK, 2007), p. 113.

[2] 1 Cor. 15:28.

[3] Wright, *Hope*, p. 112.

[4] Matt. 28:19.

[5] N. Moules, *Fingerprints of Fire . . . Footprints of Peace: A Spiritual Manifesto from a Jesus Perspective* (Arlesford, Hants: Circle Books/John Hunt Publishing, 2012).

[6] Sunday Assembly is 'a global movement for wonder and good' frequently referred to by some as the Atheist Church (www.sundayassembly.com).

[7] East Midlands Baptist Association Minister's Conference, September 2013.

[8] Ian Stackhouse, *Primitive Piety: A Journey from Suburban Mediocrity to Passionate Christianity* (Milton Keynes: Paternoster, 2012).

[9] For more on Shoreditchification see http://www.telegraph.co.uk/men/thinking-man/10561607/Why-this-Shoreditchification-of-London-must-stop.html (accessed 12 Aug. 2015).

[10] Urban Expression (www.urbanexpression.org.uk).

[11] The presentation was made at the UK 'Inhabit' conference October 2014 (www.inhabitconference.com).

[12] http://journalofmissionalpractice.com/community-building-as-spiritual-practice/ (accessed 12 Aug. 2015).

[13] The Khmer Rouge wanted to 'transform Cambodia into a rural, classless society in which there were no rich people, no poor people, and no exploitation' and looked to achieve this by eradicating intellectuals and civil servants (http://www.cambodiatribunal.org/history/cambodian-history/khmer-rouge-history/).

[14] The 'undeserving poor' is a phrase popularized by Owen Jones, author of *CHAVS: The Demonization of the Working Class* (London: Verso, 2012).

[15] 'Benefits' is a crude reference to income support, an income-related benefit for those on a low income in the UK.

[16] *Benefits Street* was produced by Love Productions (www.loveproductions. co.uk/node/172).

[17] The 'lazy poor', is another phrase popularized by Owen Jones to denote the perception many have of the poor in contrast to the hard-working rich.

[18] S. Cowell and S. Kennedy, *Church Uncorked* (Instant Apostle, 2015), p. 57.

[19] Michael Frost, *Incarnate: The Body of Christ in an Age of Disengagement* (Downers Grove, IL: InterVarsity Press, 2014), p. 20.

[20] Frost, *Incarnate*, p. 84.

[21] Frost, *Incarnate*, p. 88.

[22] N.D. Kristof and S. Wudunn, *Half the Sky: How to Change the World* (London: Virago, 2009), p. 98.

[23] David Bosch, *Transforming Mission* (Maryknoll, NY: Orbis, 1993), p. 389.

[24] John 1:46.

[25] Matt. 9:11.

[26] John 11:48.

[27] John 6:42.

[28] Matt. 7:29; Mark 1:22; Luke 4:32.

[29] Ann Morisy, *Journeying Out: A New Approach to Christian Mission* (London: Morehouse, 2014), pp. 132–5.

[30] Morisy, *Journeying Out*, p. 59.

[31] 'Also seek the peace and prosperity of the city to which I have carried you into exile' (Jer. 29:7).

[32] Acts 10.

[33] Acts 2:17–18.

[34] www.innerchange.org

[35] A phrase coined by Stanley Evans and referred to by Ken Leech in *Doing Theology in Altab Ali Park* (London: Darton, Longman & Todd, 2006), p. 50.

[36] Phil. 2:6.

[37] David Augsburger, *Dissident Discipleship* (Grand Rapids, MI: Brazos, 2006), p. 34. For further reading: Samuel Wells and Marcia Owen, *Living without Enemies: Being Present in the Midst of Violence* (Downers Grove, IL: InterVarsity Press, 2011); Stanley Hauerwas and John Vanier, *Living Gently in a Violent World: The Prophetic Witness of Weakness* (Downers Grove, IL: InterVarsity Press, 2008).

[38] For more on Asset Based Community Development see http://www.ab-cdinstitute.org or www.citizensuk.org

[39] Mark 9:33–7.

[40] Matt. 4:1–11.

41 http://www.journalofmissionalpractice.com/community-building-as-spiritual-practice/

42 Jean Vanier, *Becoming Human* (London: Darton, Longman & Todd, 1999), p. 103.

43 Guy Standing, *The Precariat* (London: Bloomsbury, 2011).

44 Mark 5:22–43.

45 John 8:1–11.

46 John 18:3.

47 Luke 4:28–30.

48 John 2:13–16.

49 Designed in preparation for the Second World War to motivate and 're-assure the public by stressing the certainty of ultimate victory and emphasizing that the whole community was committed to the war effort' https://history.blog.gov.uk/2014/06/27/keep-calm-and-carry-on-the-compromise-behind-the-slogan/ (accessed 22 July 2015).

50 Walter Wink, *The Powers That Be: Theology for a New Millennium* (New York: Doubleday, 1999), pp. 98–111.

51 Wink, *Powers*, pp. 98–111.

52 Augsburger, *Dissident*, p. 48.

53 Mirslav Volf, *Exclusion and Embrace* (Nashville, TN: Abingdon, 1996), p. 19, quoting from *Multiculturalism and The Politics of Recognition* by Charles Taylor (Princeton, NJ: Princeton University Press, 1992).

54 For more see the chapter on 'Social Capital' in Morisy, *Journeying Out*, pp. 45–65.

55 http://www.cuf.org.uk/how-we-help/near-neighbours

56 http://www.povertytruthcommission.blogspot.co.uk

57 www.citizensuk.org

58 Volf, *Exclusion*, p. 277.

11

Hope: Prophetic Vision and the Lie of the Land

Stephen Finamore

Introduction

The purpose of this chapter is to offer some thoughts on a troubling phenomenon. As other contributions to this book have pointed out, many of Britain's poorer communities appear to be both desolate and desperate; they are without comfort and without hope. In some cases huge efforts have been made and considerable resources invested without any apparent lasting impact having been made. One of the questions this raises concerns the sources of such intractability. What are the roots of this profound malaise and can anything realistically be done to address them?

The intention is that the reflections below will offer some prophetic insight into the issues around this. That is to say, because the reflections are rooted in the Scriptures, they will help us to understand what is at stake from a perspective that is outside of the system which drives and nurtures those issues; that ultimately, it may be possible to glimpse these things from the perspective of transcendence. Or to put this in faith terms; the goal is to discover what God might have to say about these things.

What follows takes the form of an extended theological reflection. It draws on two main resources: the Bible and the mimetic theories of René Girard.[1] The principal ideas to be explored concern human creatureliness, purpose and desire. The goal is to consider what the Scriptures might teach about these things and then to discuss how they are treated in our contemporary market economy and how such treatment might impact poorer communities. It is the market economy's implicit doctrine on these issues that I call 'the lie of the land'. If part of prophetic activity is to expose the 'lie of the land', what then might be the kinds of ethical practices demanded in order to act upon this analysis and where might seeds of hope for an alternative way of living be found?

Human Creatureliness, Purpose and Desire

Genesis

The Bible begins with an account of creation[2] and here my interest lies in the theological and anthropological ideas it contains. The first thing to note is that the Bible's chapter divisions can sometimes mislead us. They are not a part of the original text. Genesis 1 ends with the creation and commissioning of humanity and this can suggest that humans are to be considered as the goal and principal purpose of creation. In other words, it suggests an anthropocentric or human-centred understanding of the world. However, while humans are clearly very significant in the narrative, they are not its culmination. The account continues in the opening verses of Genesis 2 where we hear about the seventh day and reach the true climax of the story. It becomes clear that humans are not an end in themselves but have a particular purpose within the larger whole. It turns out that the story is not anthropocentric but theocentric, that is God-centred; it starts and ends with statements about God.[3]

It is within this wider, theocentric account of creation that humans are given their primary mandate to fill and to subdue the earth.[4] The story of human hubris found in the succeeding chapters has yet to be told. The mandate is therefore primal. It is given, in the pattern of the wider narrative of Genesis, before the event we have learned to call 'the Fall'. This suggests that we should be wary of considering the world as it was originally created as having been perfect or complete. It was certainly good,[5] even very good,[6] but it needed humans to work within it to subdue it. And the humans were to carry out this task as an integral part of creation. The world did not exist for the sake of humanity; humanity existed for the good of the world. In other words, the Bible invites humans to understand themselves within a theological framework. They are created, they are a significant part of the creation as a whole, they have a purpose within that creation, and their role is a participative and creative one.

If humans are intended to be participative, this is true in relation to one another (the mandate is shared between male and female), to the rest of the created order and, most significantly, to God, their Creator, and to God's wider purposes. Human fulfilment and wellbeing will therefore necessarily depend on these things.

The Bible says nothing, within this creation account, about human desire as such. Nevertheless, it may be fair to assume that this would find expression in terms of the mandate humans had been given. Humans would be conscious of their creatureliness and would have wanted to participate with one another and with God in their role within the creation as a whole. The stories in the succeeding chapters of Genesis can be read in terms of the distortion of these understandings and of the corresponding desires. The result would not so much be that humans would fail to carry out their mandate, as that they would seek to accomplish it in distorted ways. One result of this will be that they seek to subdue creation for their own sake rather than for the sake of the creation as a whole; relationships with God, between humans, and with the rest of creation, are all adversely affected. Human health and wellbeing will ultimately lie in the healing of those relationships, the restoration of the capacity to participate fully in activities associated with the primal mandate, and the carrying out of these for the sake of creation as a whole. These things require that human desire be directed accordingly. This is the Bible's anthropology, its understanding of what it means to be human.

René Girard

One of the significant thinkers of the twentieth century, René Girard spans many disciplinary perspectives, but the focus of his work concerns philosophical anthropology – or questions around what is it to be human. As a central theme, Girard takes up the idea of desire and demonstrates that every human culture inevitably shapes the desires of the people within it. Desires do not spring from within the individual but are mediated to him or her by models. Desire is imitated or, as Girard insists, *mimetic.*[7] Different cultures do these things in different ways and with different consequences. However they all, when considered in the light of the Bible's anthropology, distort human desire in some way. Our own culture is no exception to this and the following addresses more specifically the distortions associated with the UK and, in particular, their impact on marginal, poor, urban communities.

Shaping Desire and Aspiration in the UK

Much of what follows may read to some as though it is purely about economics and the market economy and they may wonder what any of it has to do with questions of mission. My intention is to show what the market, in its present manifestations, does to human desire – and desire is, I believe, a profoundly spiritual issue. This is true whether my longing is for God, for a commodity, or for a particular lifestyle. As Jesus insists, 'Where your treasure is, there your heart will be also.'[8] When he teaches us that our first desire should be God's reign,[9] Jesus is reminding us of our primal mandate; our creatureliness and the call upon us to actively participate in God's purposes. So, if cultures shape and distort desire, then this is something that needs to be explored within missiology. Issues of desire cannot be ignored if we want to understand the dynamics at work within our society and the part they are playing in helping to generate the crises that many perceive to be confronting our marginal urban communities.

There is a case for arguing that the way in which desire is shaped has changed profoundly in the last seventy-five years and that the changes have accelerated greatly in the last couple of decades. This has happened in a number of ways.

First, there has been a change in the way in which desire is mediated. Intermediary figures within local communities are becoming redundant and desires are being mediated to individuals directly by corporations. For example, a shopkeeper may once have maintained a limited stock and have advised customers about their proposed purchases. Now, we shop by self-service, making our own selections directly from the shelves or on-line from a website. There is no human intermediary in the process. Something similar applies in other areas of life. Trusted representatives of significant civil society institutions might once have played a part in advising people about their desires. This would have been an accepted role of ministers of religion and other community leaders. Now, those who seek to provoke desire for their product do so through advertising and branding mediated directly to the consumer.

Second, the sheer number of images intended to provoke desire to which we are all subjected has increased exponentially, carried by media such as television and the internet; which for most users has seemed to become dominated by commercial interests. Moreover, the amount of public space where advertising is permitted has grown. We are subjected to advertising in the toilets of motorway service stations, on the sides of major buildings, on vast placards on farmland beside major roads and so on.

All this amounts to what one might call 'representation saturation' where our senses are dominated by people and images who stand for something else, whom we do not know personally, and that seek to shape our desires in particular ways. Of course, all human societies have representation in this sense, but our use of television, the internet and public space means that on most days most of us may spend more time interacting with the 'represented' than we do with the 'real'.

Finally, we need to consider the nature of most advertising. There was a time when most commercial notices sought to accomplish their goal by providing prospective purchasers with information. Of course, the content was often slanted or misleading, if not actually false, but the idea was that the advertisement invited the consumer to engage their rational faculties and think for themselves about a product and its purported usefulness. Surprisingly little contemporary advertising works in this way though some purports to do so. Its main goal is to associate the product or service it is seeking to promote with a particular model. In terms of Girard's thought, the model is depicted as having a *being* (a sense of being fully alive and of bearing meaning and significance) that is desirable. The audience is encouraged to desire that *being* and hence the product that is associated with it. Essentially, the advertisement functions by telling the audience that they should be dissatisfied; they lack *being* and this lack can be remedied through the acquisition of a commodity or the purchase of an experience. This is a strategy that encourages people to be discontent with their own lives, their own bodies, their own possessions, and the long-term consequences of a culture's exposure to such a practice needs to be carefully considered.

Symbols are powerful things. In every human culture they help both shape and articulate the way in which we understand ourselves. They therefore affect the way in which we interpret reality and they inevitably impact our desires. It is probably true that most of us spend most of our time oblivious to the fact that we are being influenced or persuaded. We may even think that, as adults, we are not affected by these things. We believe we are somehow complete and have charge of our own desires which we see as a reflection of our own identity. In these circumstances we may insist that children might be inappropriately affected by images and by advertising but resist the idea that our own desires may be being mediated to us by others. While it is conceivable that some of us have never been persuaded by advertising to buy a particular product, this need not mean that we have not been influenced. The influence lies in consequences that may be unintended or secondary. We are affected by the values implicit in the advertisements and their cumulative effect is to make us understand ourselves in particular ways. Michael Northcott, basing his argument on Girard's ideas, refers to the cult of consumerism and insists that it 'is essentially driven by mimetic desire, which the advertising, marketing, and public-relations industries clearly indicate, since they so frequently link the sale of products to mimetic desires and to rivalry for material status objects and sexual attraction'.[10]

Unlike images associated with areas such as art and architecture for example, advertising images are effectively non-discretionary; it is virtually impossible to refuse to see them. Furthermore, the values and language associated with the discretionary images such as transcendence, loyalty, identity and passion have been co-opted and so subverted by promotional materials. Very often we see the vocabulary of devotion, sacrifice and enduring significance applied to what is essentially ephemeral and so is deprived of meaning, while hyperbole has become our mode of discussing the mundane.

The Lie of the Land and the Erosion of Hope

Taken together, these factors are producing within the UK's population a functional anthropology, a way of understanding ourselves as human, a kind of *myth* (a means of promoting a world-view through narrative). This anthropology is profoundly at odds with the biblical version discussed earlier. If the Bible's understanding of humanity is true then this new myth is a lie. It is a lie which has impacted the whole of society in the UK. It is a form of false consciousness which affects the way all our interactions get shaped. It is the lie of the land.

I think it is important to stress that the issue does not lie with the commodities or experiences that people are competing to sell, nor is there any suggestion that malice is involved. The point is that the issue is systemic; the system as a whole produces a particular way of understanding ourselves. Commercial interests, consciously or otherwise, promote the dominant anthropology. There are several issues to consider.

The first part is that, as a result of advertising, we are increasingly convinced that we lack *being* and that this lack can be remedied by acquisition of things modelled by those who appear to possess *being*.

One result of this is that we perceive ourselves primarily as consumers rather than as participants. Another is that, since consumption is our main goal, human wellbeing should be understood in terms of our being free to consume in whatever way we might choose. The consequence of this is that freedom is understood in terms of unrestricted choice which is best served by a market that is allowed to operate with as few constraints as possible. Choice is seen as the most important value and the free market as its guarantor. The act of choosing then becomes the essence of our understanding of *being*. This may be why people refer to shopping as 'retail therapy'.

The next significant thing is that advertising is targeted, for understandable reasons, at individuals and, to an extent, at households. No external sources of authority or influence in these areas are acknowledged. One consequence of this is that we see ourselves as sole actors rather than persons in relationship and our experience of *being* arrives unmediated by other relationships. We understand the world and ourselves in terms of our consumption choices and we learn to distrust all intermediary institutions. The outcome of all this is that we understand ourselves in terms of a story in which we shape ourselves and our identity through our acquisition of commodities and experiences and on this basis we feel that we have the potential to become anything that we choose to be. And so we imagine ourselves to be our own creations. This is, of course, wholly at odds with the biblical anthropology that stresses our creatureliness and our relationality. The lie is a powerful one and we are inclined to think that it represents our natural state. However, it is in fact wholly dependent on our particular political and economic circumstances. It is, as I have claimed, the lie of the land.

The lie may be promoted at the macro-level but the symptoms associated with its internalization are visible at the micro-level and will be assimilated differently between classes, ethnicities, age-groups and regions. Because the symptoms vary, different communities perceive themselves as being faced by different sets of issues and so fail to make common cause. Indeed, they will often presume that their interests are actually opposed to one another's. Furthermore, even if the source of the symptoms is correctly identified, the fact that the issue is systemic means that no single local community or group can imagine that it has the capacity to accomplish real change. The symptoms of the false anthropology are experienced locally but the forces at work are structural and to some extent global.

Impacts of the 'Lie' Among the Relatively Wealthy

The lie is, of course, an extremely seductive thing and its effects are very powerful. Among the relatively wealthy it is possible, to varying degrees, to embrace the lie. Everybody is aware of the sense of *being* associated with the making of purchase, especially a significant and discretionary one; a luxury commodity or a holiday for instance. We also all know that this sense of *being* is a transitory phenomenon. However, among the wealthy, resources either are or soon will be available for a further purchase to be made and so the illusion of *being* can be sustained. As a result, for those within this group, the system can appear to offer both hope and purpose. Of course, it does nothing of the kind and, at some level, most people recognize this. The dissonance inherent in these attitudes to the prevailing *myth* finds itself manifested in all kinds of ways, especially among the young. Sometimes, these appear to be voluntary: there are the quests for alternate states of consciousness pursued through hallucinogenic drugs; the desire for the *being* associated with particular models that results in an unhealthy perception of one's own body;[11] the need to wrest back some control over one's life and experience leads to experimentation with self-harm; and the world of representation, such as a video game, is actively preferred to the real world. On other occasions, the manifestations of this dissonance are apparently involuntary: people experience depression, lack of self-esteem or stress-related disorders.[12]

My point here is not that these things never have their origins in other factors but they have become far more prevalent since the lie being discussed became the dominant way in which we understand ourselves. There is also some evidence that the prevalence of the symptoms mentioned is related to the relative equality of the societies concerned. The more unequal they are, the worse the symptoms generated by this dissonance.[13]

Of course, some of these phenomena are inevitably found among other groups within the population, including those in marginal areas. However, marginal communities also face a number of other symptoms of the lie.

Impacts of the 'Lie' in Marginal Urban Areas

In marginalized communities, limited resources mean that there is far less access to the *being* that advertising purports to offer. They can observe but they cannot participate. Those who are poor do not have the means, either in wealth or in access to credit, to be able to join in at anything more than a cursory level. As a result people can come to perceive themselves, their families and their communities as being excluded from the dominant *myth* and so without *being*, while others may feel that they have no or, at best, very limited access to *being* through legitimate means. With no alternative offered with anything like the same intensity, the consequence is that hope dissipates and scepticism (if not cynicism) is the default position adopted whenever interventions are made which seek to bring developmental change.

The dominant anthropology tells the individual and the household that they lack *being*. The solution it offers is that resources be spent on acquiring commodities and experiences. The interventions offered by state and voluntary sector agencies, well-meaning as they are, do not, generally speaking, seek to address the decisive issue. They provide things that are worthy, even necessary, but which do not, indeed cannot, address the root of the problem. There is nothing wrong with family centres, debt advice, health clinics, community rooms, informal education, youth clubs or housing improvement programmes but they cannot promote the changes they seek to generate because they do not address the perceived lack of *being* which can, according to the dominant *myth*, only be addressed by acquisition of commodities and experiences.

There are, of course, some projects that seek to address income and hence capacity for acquisition but they are not of the right order; co-operative development and skills training, for example, rarely, if ever, offer access to fields of work in which income can be significantly increased. Where they do function they impact (some of) the participants and not the community as a whole. Indeed, projects can be counterproductive; they can serve to deepen the sense of listlessness, exclusion and hopelessness that affects so many marginal communities.

The dominant anthropology is consumerist and individualist. So long as it is internalized the crisis in marginal areas will not be resolved by communities as a whole. The salvation offered by the *myth* is in terms of personal consumption and this inevitably means that poor communities are perceived as places to be escaped, something which might be achieved by celebrity, a successful sporting career, winning the lottery or significantly improving one's earning power. Indeed, these issues are profoundly exacerbated by the negative treatment of the working class, particularly the white working class, in the papers, on the television and by politicians of all parties.[14]

Of course, not all marginal communities have been impacted in this way and nor were these things always true of poor communities in the past. Indeed, there is little doubt that absolute poverty was greater several decades ago than it is now. There are clearly other factors to be considered and a number of things might be said about this.

First, the saturation of our senses with marketing messages has taken a long time to reach its present intensity. Until this happened there was more effective competition to the understanding of humanity implicit in most advertising. In other words, functional anthropology remained a contested issue. Views associated with Christianity and with movements like socialism remained influential. These are now effectively relegated to the sphere of the private and the discretionary. Nearly all useful public space promotes the lie of the land.

Related to this, it is clear that alternative anthropologies were once more widely held and acknowledged. It is noticeable that the issues faced by white urban communities where churches are poorly attended are very different from those made up of first-, second- and third-generation migrants. The persistence in these latter communities of different *myths* leads to a different understanding of their circumstances. There are alternative routes to experiencing *being* because institutions like mosques, temples and ethnic-minority churches continue to be significant. Furthermore, although the people from ethnic minorities now appear more frequently in advertising, commercials have for years appeared to be aimed primarily at white people. Most of the actors and models are white as are most of the cultural presumptions of the genre. The consequence of this is that the internalization of the implicit anthropology is most apparent in white communities. These are the communities where church attendance has collapsed.

Next, most urban communities were founded in order to provide a workforce for a major local industry, employer or group of employers. People often had a shared sense of identity, or solidarity and common purpose, rooted in their skills, craft and around their employment.

Finally, many communities across a whole range of social strata had an extensive range of community organizations, such as trades unions, tenants' associations, political parties, social clubs, mutual societies and sports clubs. These advocated and represented a different implied anthropology, one that valued solidarity, mutuality and collective progress.[15] They valued participation and service. These civil society organizations once offered an intermediary between the household and the state. More significantly, for the purposes of the present argument, they offered an intermediary between the household and corporations. All these groups have, in different ways, been undermined. This means that the field is left wide open for the *myth* implicit in contemporary advertising to become dominant.

Provoking the Prophetic Imagination

If it is true that what lies at the root of despair and desolation in marginal communities is the internalization of a false anthropology,

then a major goal to re-ignite a sense of hopefulness will need to
be the promotion of a different understanding of what it means to
be human. If it is to be based on the Scriptures then it must offer a
model that is creaturely, relational and participative. If the distortion
of desire into idolatry and covetousness lies, in the Bible's view, at the
heart of the breakdown of humanity's primal circumstances, then it
must be about embodying an alternative sort of desire around the call
of Jesus Christ who offers the restoration of true human identity and
being.

The prophets of the Bible engaged in all kinds of symbolic activities.
These were not intended to force change but to open up the possibility of another way of understanding the world and of acting within
it.[16] Such activities would deliberately privilege participation over consumption and stress the givenness of *being* over aspiring to remedy its
perceived absence. Churches that mobilize on this issue will need to
consider carefully the kind of model they offer. Many apparently successful congregations offer what is effectively a consumer-orientated
model in which people attend and are offered an experience. In many
ways such models are highly culturally appropriate and fit the expectations of many. However, particularly among marginalized communities, they might serve to reinforce rather than to challenge the
prevailing false anthropology.

This suggests that what is needed can only be offered by communities of people who promote a biblical anthropology and do so in
face-to-face relationships and, within these, key values that speak
hope into the situation are likely to be hospitality and creativity.
Hospitality based on generous sharing is powerful because it suggests that people have worth and *being* without the need to possess
resources; while creativity has the potential to open up new pathways
to participative, relational and purposeful activity.

So the call to prophetic action will involve life in small intentional
communities living hospitably and creatively in marginal places.
Where other interventions look for results and measurable 'outcomes',
these communities will simply offer an alternative understanding of
what it means to be human and the possibility of experiencing *being*

without internalizing the idea that this is something possessed by models who own things and so can be acquired only by the acquisition of commodities. It is much more difficult to state what a call to action might look like at a systemic or macro-level. It is helpful to note at this point that the Scriptures have interesting things to say in relation to economic activity. There is no space for a detailed survey but two themes, the first from the New Testament and the second from the Old, can be picked up here.

In 2 Corinthians 8 the apostle Paul urges the believers in Corinth to make a generous contribution to the collection he is making for the poor in Jerusalem. In order to make his case, he draws on one of the best-known stories in the Hebrew Bible: Exodus. He uses the story to illustrate God's economy. When God fed his people in the wilderness, each could collect enough but none could collect more than they needed. At 8:15 Paul cites Exodus 16:18 and offers as a principle the idea that 'the one who had much did not have too much, and the one who had little did not have too little' (NRSV). Paul insists that there should be *isotes*, a fair balance or even equality. Of course, Paul is arguing that this should motivate arrangements between churches, not between the citizens of a particular country, but it strongly suggests his instinctive reaction to questions of the distribution of resources.

The Jubilee provisions of Leviticus 25 offer an interesting economic model for an agricultural nation where wealth was strongly related to, and understood in terms of, the possession of land. Broadly speaking, the system allowed the hardworking and industrious to be rewarded. However, there was a mechanism to ensure that any inequalities this led to were not ingrained from generation to generation. Every fifty years, at the Jubilee, not only would debts be waived, as they were every seven years, but all the land, the principal means of production, would revert to the descendant of its original owner. While nobody can be sure if these provisions were ever enacted, they do indicate two biblical concerns: that hard work should be rewarded and that inequality should be limited.

These reflections suggest that not only is the dominant anthropology within the UK at odds with the position advocated by the Bible, but so is the prevailing approach to wealth distribution. In the light of these conclusions, what actions might be taken to prophetically keep open the possibilities of other ways of understanding and acting in the world? Unfortunately, many that might be offered tend to sound politically naive or unacceptable and have little possibility of being implemented! However, it is important that they should be named if only to begin a conversation.

One possibility would be to argue for a restriction on the amount and / or content of advertising. For example, if advertising were restricted to the giving of information about products, rather than using the association of models and lifestyles with brands, and promoting the idea that people lack *being*, then the main means by which the false anthropology is promoted would be neutralized. Perhaps such a policy could be advocated on the basis of the need for high standards of truth in public discourse. At the very least, a public debate on the question would allow the issues to be aired.

It is obvious that any such move would be rigorously contested. Companies invest heavily in achieving brand recognition, identity and loyalty. They will be very reluctant to see these accomplishments challenged. It would also be presented as being economically unsound, unnecessary and draconian. We would be told that it would put newspapers, websites, radio stations and television channels out of business. It would also be said that it will limit our right to choose by which would be meant our freedom to choose between products in the market. And I suppose that this is the point. The argument sounds persuasive because this is indeed how we understand ourselves.

Another area would be to keep challenging the understanding of poverty. It is not enough that governments should address absolute poverty, though many might well feel that we could settle for that. Public policy should re-establish the post-war goal of limiting the gap between the poorest and the wealthiest in society. Then again, there are institutions remaining that advocate understandings of humans as relational, purposeful, creative and participative. These include faith communities, some university departments, some museums, national and local arts groups and companies and the BBC in its local and national manifestations. Many of these are under attack and need to be defended. This is not necessarily for the sake of the institutions themselves, for many of them are badly in need of reform, but for the sake of the implied anthropology that they represent.

Finding Hope in Common Ground

The church today finds itself in a novel context. For many years the church in the West has found itself, or a denominational manifestation of itself, in some sort of partnership with the state. One consequence of this is that the state publicly acknowledged and, in some cases, took into account, aspects of a biblical anthropology in the development of its social policy. This is no longer the case though a kind of afterglow remains in some places. This all means that the church, so used to perceiving the state, and accordingly, the prevailing economic system, as an ally, must now learn to engage with it in different ways. Part of this will mean allowing for a critique that will enable it to break with its inherited ways of thinking and also recognizing that biblical anthropology may have more in common with groups which are not necessarily ones to which the church would naturally look for allies; groups that are developing powerful critiques of the dominant anthropology and the forces that sustain it, such as for example, grass-roots movements like the Occupy demonstrations, and those involved with the environmental movement who advocate an understanding of humanity which sees it as integral to, rather than apart from, the rest of the environment.

Finally, of course, hope is found in the work of the Spirit of God who, under the radar of most church and secular commentators, is summoning small communities of followers of Jesus to move into or rise up within Britain's marginal places. Often perhaps unsure of their purpose, they are, whether they know it or not, the embodiment of a biblical anthropology and therefore a source of hope. They are the seed growing secretly to which the reign of God can be compared.[17]

Conclusion

Drawing on the ideas of René Girard, this chapter has sought to argue that western market economies such as the UK have, perhaps unwittingly, allowed a form of advertising to flourish that effectively promotes an understanding of humanity which is profoundly at odds with that found in the Bible, and has serious impact on the framing of hope and aspiration. I call this false anthropology or myth, the lie of the land. Where the Scriptures see humans as created, relational and participative, and having a *being* derived from God, advertising projects an understanding of them as individual consumers who lack *being*, and who are creating themselves through their consumption of commodities, services and experiences. The Bible acknowledges that humanity's original purposes have been distorted and offers restoration, through Jesus Christ, to true human identity and *being*.

Market economies, through the way they provoke covetousness, prompt or play on a human sense of lacking *being* and offer consumption as a remedy. This false anthropology, the lie of the land, has an impact on every part of society but the symptoms vary between them. In poor communities where people lack the resources to engage with the solutions offered by the prevailing myth, the outcomes include a sense of exclusion, desolation and hopelessness. These make helpful interventions extremely difficult. Many are unsuccessful because they do not recognize the fundamental issue.

The chapter then offers some reflections on the nature of a call to action at both local and structural levels and, while recognizing the extent of the intractability of the issues, sees grounds for hope in the small Christian communities that are emerging in surprising ways in Britain's marginal neighbourhoods who, centred around Jesus, seek to embody an alternative anthropology and, in finding creative partnerships with others, are trying to find and arguing for a different way of being human.

Notes

[1] Girard's views are set out in an extensive range of books and articles; the following represent a small selection relevant to the ideas explored here. René Girard, *Deceit, Desire and the Novel; Self and Other in Literary Structure* (Baltimore: Johns Hopkins University Press, 1965); René Girard, *Violence and the Sacred* (Baltimore and London: Johns Hopkins University Press, 1979); René Girard, *The Scapegoat* (London: Athlone Press, 1986); René Girard, *'To Double Business Bound': Essays on Literature, Mimesis, and Anthropology* (London: Athlone Press, 1988); James G. Williams, ed., *The Girard Reader* (New York: Crossroad, 1996); Robert Doran, ed. *Mimesis and Theory* (Stanford: Stanford University Press, 2008); René Girard, *The One by Whom Scandal Comes* (East Lansing: Michigan State University Press, 2014).

[2] Gen. 1:1 – 2:3. All biblical citations in this chapter are from the *New Revised Standard Version*.

[3] Gen. 1:1 and 2:2–3.

[4] Gen. 1:28.

[5] Gen. 1:10,12,18,21,25.

[6] Gen. 1:31.

[7] This is argued, for example, in Girard, *Deceit*.

[8] Matt. 6:21.

[9] Matt. 6:33.

[10] Michael Northcott, 'Girard, Climate Change and Apocalypse' in *Can We Survive Our Origins; Readings in René Girard's Theory of Violence and the Sacred* (ed. Pierpaolo Anatello and Paul Gifford; East Lansing: Michigan State University Press), p. 298. His particular concern is that humanity's apparent inability to act on its knowledge that its actions are causing potentially catastrophic climate change lies in the way in which the market continues to insist on promoting increasing levels of consumption. This analysis, like the one offered in this chapter, suggests that a false anthropology is being promoted which is adversely impacting humanity's capacity to carry out an aspect of its prime mandate, in this case its responsibility to see itself as a part of the created order and with a particular responsibility to care for it.

[11] René Girard in *Anorexia and Mimetic Desire* (East Lansing: Michigan State University Press, 2013) discusses the relationship between imitative desire and eating disorders.

[12] These issues and their relationship to relative affluence are discussed in Oliver James, *Affluenza: How to Be Successful and Stay Sane* (London: Vermilion, 2007).

[13] See the discussions in Richard Wilkinson and Kate Pickett, *The Spirit Level; Why Equality Is Better for Everyone* (London: Penguin, rev. edn, 2010).

[14] This is the argument of Owen Jones in, *Chavs; The Demonization of the Working Class* (London: Verso, rev. edn, 2012). His description is very powerful and effective and his analysis of the political actions taken to weaken the working class is persuasive. However, he does not explicitly address the communications and technological issues that have played a part in enabling a particular anthropology to triumph.

[15] The collapse of community organizations and collective activities in the American context is documented in Robert D. Putnam, *Bowling Alone: The Collapse and Revival of American Community* (New York: Simon & Schuster, 2001).

[16] See, for example, W.D. Stacey, *Prophetic Drama in the Old Testament* (London: Epworth Press, 1990).

[17] Mark 4:26–9.

12

Mission and God: Editorial Conversation

Mike Pears and Paul Cloke

The title of this part of the book indicates that our particular interest is to explore the ways in which the form, essence and life of mission flow from the person of God himself. The order might seem strange – why leave this subject till last when other works on mission would normally take this as a starting point? We hope that the subject of God, made known in Christ and present by his Spirit, has indeed been a central consideration throughout this discussion. However, it has also been our intention to take a fresh view of the landscape in which mission takes place by drawing attention to the particular ways in which patterns of social and spatial exclusion problematize the question of mission. While it is probably fairly safe to assume that there is a broad degree of agreement within mission studies that the form and essence of our mission is predicated on the character and presence of God – that it is he who animates mission and energizes its outworking – there is a much greater diversity of thought about *how* exactly this outworks in practice. We have argued that this 'how' question is best addressed in mission studies by giving primary consideration to the subjects of marginality and otherness – subjects which have been the focus of Parts I and II. In Part III we are seeking to develop the argument by identifying three particular areas which frequently arise in situations where people are struggling to understand how God is present in places and communities that suffer the consequences of exclusion. We invited authors to discuss these in terms of cruciformity (how does the Spirit of God work within the Christian community as it seeks to build bridges across socio-spatial difference?); shalom (what is the nature of God's presence in a marginal place and how do we participate with him?); and hope (how does the presence of God bring hope when, naturally speaking, there seems little cause for hope?).

A compelling point of resonance between the three chapters is the manner in which each of them identifies two distinct sets of narratives. On the one hand there are narratives or discourses which are played out in everyday life and which have a detrimental and often exaggerated negative impact in marginal places. On the other hand there are contrasting 'biblical' narratives which open up new ways of seeing and new spaces of hopeful imagination, which bring into view a range of creative possibilities for ethical and prophetic praxis that are intended to engage deeply with our communities and contexts. How though, are we to understand this idea of conflicting narratives to address the question about 'mission and God'? This is about God because it seeks precisely to understand how he is present in complex and contested marginal places so that even when only 'two or three are gathered in [his] name' (Matt. 18:20) his peaceable presence might be known. Thus for David Purves the narrative of the cross and resurrection of Christ embodied through cruciformity is a radical counter-narrative to that of upward mobility or of colonial expansion. For Juliet Kilpin the power of the 'dominant narrative' which reinforces marginalization through its negative stereotypes of 'the poor' is contested by the biblical narrative of shalom in which the Spirit opens up newly imagined social relationships. And for Stephen Finamore the pervasive power of the 'lie of the land', which presents humans as consumers who lack *being*, is contested by a biblical anthropology that emphasizes the God-givenness of being which is nurtured through relationship and participation in his purposes.

This contrasting or conflicting of narratives is of help in that it brings into view previously hidden values and meaning systems that are embedded and worked out in everyday patterns of life. They draw our attention to the ways in which habits, practices and attitudes, which are a regular part of the life of the communities and places in which these things are lived out, are not neutral but rather are sites impregnated with meaning and power; arrangements of which can be understood in spiritual, social or ideological terms. These located 'powers' function persistently to maintain 'geographies of exclusion' which dehumanize relationships between people of difference and undermine the God-given sense of personhood.

These narratives are not however straightforward, nor are they simple to discern. They are not somehow 'out there' to be viewed and discussed objectively but, as these chapters suggest, they are 'in here' influencing and shaping our own sense of self and view of the world. They are embodied through our daily lives being acted out or 'performed' through our own engagements with the places and people around us and are thus subjectively discerned.

This understanding of 'embodiment' is fundamental to the theory and practice of mission. The very sites through which these conflicting narratives run are in fact our own selves (including our bodies, our sense of self-identity, our inner [gut] and cognitive sense of others and other places) and the communities, including the Christian communities, of which we are a part. One cannot therefore choose to embody a 'biblical' narrative that is 'pure' and somehow unencumbered by other ideological arrangements as if one were somehow above and separate from place and culture. For this reason mission cannot be conceived of as a distinct activity or one which is solely 'done to others'; rather mission is also a deeply inward journey involving personal reflection about the way these narratives dominate and shape our own lives, and an open-hearted acceptance of the transforming work of the Spirit within ourselves as well as in those around us.

It is perhaps this understanding of mission as 'embodied' that we are feeling our way towards when we use terms such as 'authentic' or 'incarnational'. There is a heartfelt sense that mission should involve a real and deep experience of relational connectivity with people of difference, and an acknowledgment of the inevitable costliness of this kind of engagement. The personal spiritual challenge of this is very well expressed in David's discussion about cruciformity. Cruciformity describes the very essence of a mission-shaped spirituality because it is the core praxis (a practiced theology) by which we deal with the conflicts within ourselves, between the biblical narratives with their ideals of embodied convictions and ethical performances, and the ideological narratives whereby we find ourselves participating with dehumanizing beliefs and actions towards self and others.

An embodied approach to mission is therefore deeply challenging. It catches us up in the story of Jesus in profound ways. It does not conceive of mission as an occasional activity, but rather as a way of living that involves our whole selves, profoundly shaping our everyday lives and engagement with others. However it is also deeply hopeful because, in the light of seemingly overwhelming ideological narratives, it offers ethical and prophetic 'strategies' and 'tactics' which reflect both forward-visioned and context-focused ways of being and which invite Christian communities to a faithful and creative improvisation in their own particular neighbourhood. In the missiological terms of *missio Dei*, such a faithful improvisation might be expressed as a participation in peaceable ways of the Spirit in the neighbourhood.

What are the ethical and prophetic strategies and tactics that arise from these chapters and how might they be 'performed' or worked out in practice? We have used this terminology because we want to make sure that this exploration of the theory of mission in marginal places is one that actually connects with real contexts and presents practical approaches for small Christian communities in challenging places.[1] For example, Stephen Finamore's insightful analysis of the dominant anthropology lays out an important theoretical framework for mission in relation to marginality which in turn points to the values of hospitality and creativity as core values needed to engage hopefully and prophetically with the 'lie of the land'. This however leaves the small Christian community with the difficult questions about what the embodiment of these values actually looks like in practice and of course the real issue about whether, in the light of overwhelming powerful narratives of false anthropology, such practices do indeed make any lasting difference or convey any real sense of hope.

There are of course no definitive or 'right' answers to this question. It is intriguing however to see that contextually specific examples of practices are given in the gospels almost as if they were a direct answer to the question, 'What does this look like in practice?' The Sermon on the Mount for example, when talking about being the 'salt of the earth' or the 'light of the world' (Matt. 5:13–14) suggests 'turn the other cheek' or 'walk the second mile' (see Matt. 5:39–41) as tactics which resist the apparently overwhelming ideological power of the Roman imperial system. By refusing to conform to the normal social and cultural arrangements in which the enemy other (in this case the Roman soldier) is accorded the minimum help within the confines of the law, and by instead showing open-hearted hospitality, the social relationship is redefined from occupying enemy to travelling companion; and the power of the Roman Empire to define and dehumanize social relationship is – at least in the immediate circumstance – overcome. As discussed, such an engagement calls both for a reflective and Spirit-led cruciform praxis and also a reflexive and embodied social engagement. In terms of contemporary examples, Juliet presents, in the parable of the two sofas, a situation where one tactic was to expose the way that the media abused images to bolster negative stereotypes of certain groups of people.

Through the course of this book we have outlined a number of characteristics of ethical and prophetic practices. First, in essence they are small; that is they are like 'leaven which a woman puts in a lump of dough' or 'a mustard seed planted in the ground' (see Matt. 13:31–3). They are small in the sense that they are practices which belong to communities that lack social, economic and political power; they belong to the 'two or three that are gathered in God's name' (see Matt. 18:20) or the small Christian community struggling in an overlooked neighbourhood. The smallness indicates a bottom-up rather than top-down approach to transformation and hope. The ambition of the community is not to change the system by gaining positions of power but to refuse its claim to ultimate power by resisting its outworking in the minutiae of everyday encounters.

Second, tactics arise out of 'dilemmas' or 'disjunctures' of everyday life. Mary McClintock Fulkerson describes these sites as 'wounds' which generate new thinking.[2] Wounds give rise to the sense of trouble, dis-ease, of something being wrong or 'out-of-place'. The site of a wound may often be located in a self–other encounter such as those imagined in the phrases 'turn the other cheek' or 'go the second mile'; they are not theoretical but deeply embodied, emotional experiences. They present new redemptive possibility when responses to them are shaped by an inner spirituality of cruciformity. This inner reflective practice of selfless generosity resists conformity to prejudicial judgements which reinforce misrepresentation and stereotype, and makes space for open-hearted humanizing encounter.

Third, ethical and prophetic practices are redemptive and they give embodiment to a newly imagined 'redemptive place'. Specifically they arise out of the space between the self and other, when what transpires is neither as a consequence of assimilation or domination of one by the other, but a newly imagined and newly created 'third space'. Such redemptive places are convened by the Spirit and associated with newly imagined ethical and prophetic practices. Thus, in 'going the second mile' or 'turning the other cheek', neither the culture of the oppressor or oppressed makes provision for what happens next! Rather the subversive tactic opens up a new situation where one-time enemies are now invited to respond to each other as neighbours. A new set of ethical and relational practices is called for which will enable them to live in this newly discovered redemptive place.

All of these actions involve a level of choice and perhaps one of the most important choices – particularly for those immersed in difficult contexts – centres around holding on to a sense of hopefulness.

Indeed the confrontation between narratives of cynicism and hope is a key ethical and political choice in contemporary times.[3] But how can hope be practised? This is a difficult question to grapple with. In part it concerns reflection about and sensitivity to the need for prophetic utterances about and responses to the injustices and calamitous orthodoxies of the current order. Echoing Steve Finamore's chapter, Walter Brueggemann[4] presents a powerful picture of the American church as being so encultured to the ethos of consumerism that it has little power to act on its faith traditions. Brueggemann's call is to nurture, nourish and evoke an alternative and energizing consciousness and perception that challenge the dominant surrounding culture. Such energizing counteracts social despair with prophetic hope. It recognizes that God is on the move among the darkness of contemporary inequality and marginalization – not the bloated comfortable God of the capitalist and consumerist empire, but a God whose doxology cuts through the current ideology allowing compassion and justice to emerge.

Brueggemann speaks of hope being allied to the prophetic imagination and thus to conclude we follow Brueggemann by presenting three imaginative manoeuvres through which hope vested in the subversive power of spiritual belief can be recognized:[5]

- The possibility of the prophetic – the introduction of fresh hopeful ideas and practices into the dominant culture.
- The possibility of engaging spiritual interiority – discerning and diagnosing the problems inherent in the current order in terms of its spiritual as well as material core.
- The possibility of an alternative consciousness, perception and emotion, opening up ruptures in the seemingly hegemonic spaces of the current order, producing new lines of flight and new spaces of hope.

Through socially active faith, some will get to understand and follow the message of Jesus, but everyone will benefit from an expression of hope in wider society.

Notes

1   The language of 'tactics' is drawn from Michel de Certeau, *The Practice of Everyday Life* (Los Angeles and London: University of California, 1984).

2   Mary McClintock Fulkerson, *Places of Redemption: Theology for a Worldly Church* (Oxford: Oxford University Press, 2007) p. 13.

3   Jim Wallis, *God's Politics: Why the American Right Gets It Wrong and the Left Doesn't Get It* (Oxford: Lion Hudson, 2005).

4   Walter Brueggemann, *The Prophetic Imagination* (Minneapolis: Augsburg Fortress, 2001).

5   Brueggemann, *Prophetic Imagination*. For discussion of Brueggemann in the context of faith-based organizations see: Paul Cloke, Justin Beaumont and Andrew Williams, *Working Faith* (Milton Keynes: Paternoster, 2013), pp. 5–7.

Author Biographies

Stuart Christine

Stuart is a physics graduate from Oxford. After completing theological studies at Spurgeon's College, he and his wife Georgie went to Brazil with the Baptist Missionary Society, spending ten years churchplanting. In 1988 Stuart became New Testament Tutor at Spurgeon's for four years before returning to Brazil with his family to teach mission studies at the São Paulo Baptist Seminary while working in the city's favela slums. In 2012, they moved to the Wythenshawe estate, Manchester, to pastor Brownley Green Baptist Church where Stuart is currently concluding PhD studies in mission in deprived urban communities, with a view to further writing, teaching and mission consultancy.

Paul Cloke

Paul Cloke is Professor of Human Geography at the University of Exeter. His recent research has examined the role of faith in combatting social exclusion and marginalisation, and is published in *Faith-Based Organisations and Exclusion in European Cities* (Policy Press) and *Working Faith* (Paternoster Press). Paul has written widely on the intersection of faith and social science. He is Fellow of the British Academy and Academician of the Academy of Social Sciences, and is highly experienced in publishing having produced more than thirty books and more than 220 academic articles and chapters. Paul is part of Exeter Vineyard Church.

Stephen Finamore

Steve is Principal of Bristol Baptist College. He is a minister of the Baptist Union of Great Britain and has experience of mission initiatives on three continents. He trained for ministry at Regent's Park College and holds a degree and a doctorate in theology from the University of Oxford. In the past Steve has worked as a lawyer, a pastor, and in community development in inner London and the Peruvian Andes. He was involved with Tearfund for twenty years including ten as a trustee. Steve is married to Becca and they have two daughters.

Juliet Kilpin

Juliet Kilpin is a founding member and co-ordinator of Urban Expression, an urban mission and church-planting agency which prioritizes the inner cities and the margins. She works as a freelance trainer and consultant, most recently project-managing the relaunch of the Fishermen's Chapel in Essex and co-ordinating a peacemaking initiative in the informal refugee camp in Calais. Juliet is also a Baptist minister and has published *Urban to the Core: Motives for Incarnational Mission* (Leicestershire: Matador, 2013), a series of reflections on the values and experiences of those involved in Urban Expression teams.

Sian Murray Williams

Sian is a Baptist minister and part of St Mark's Baptist Church, a multicultural community in Easton, Bristol. After gaining a BA and an MBA, Sian worked for twelve years with the Baptist Missionary Society. She went on to train for ministry and led Littlemore Baptist Church, Oxford, until 2006 when she joined the staff of Bristol Baptist College as Tutor in Worship Studies, and latterly as Co-ordinator of Ministerial Formation. She has co-authored *Multi-Voiced Church* (with Stuart Murray Williams; Authentic Publishing, 2012), published a prayer book for Urban Expression, *Praying Our Values* (Urban Expression, 2007), and been a contributing author to other publications.

Mike Pears

Mike is the director of Urban Life, a learning and research network which develops innovative and pioneering approaches to ministry and mission in marginalized and deprived places. He has been involved in urban mission for over thirty years in a variety of contexts including Peckham (London), Vancouver (CA) and Bristol, and is currently a member of a small intentional community in a large urban estate. Mike completed his doctoral studies at the International Baptist Theological Seminary Centre (VU Amsterdam) in theological and ethnographic studies of place and is a tutor in missions studies at Bristol Baptist College.

David Purves

Revd David Purves is the pastor of Collydean Granary Baptist Church in Glenrothes. He is also a steering group member of and outreach co-ordinator for Teen Challenge, Edinburgh, an organization engaging with people with addiction issues. David has a degree in international relations with Arabic, a Masters in theology, and during his studies at Oxford University held a studentship with the Oxford Centre for the Study of Christianity and Culture.

Cathy Ross

Dr Cathy Ross is Tutor in Contextual Theology at Ripon College, Cuddesdon, Lecturer in Mission at Regent's Park College, Oxford, and MA Co-Ordinator of Pioneer Leaders at the Church Mission Society. She has previously worked in Rwanda, Congo and Uganda with New Zealand Church Mission Society. Her research interests are in the areas of contextual theologies, world Christianity, feminist theologies and hospitality. Her most recent publications include *Life-Widening Mission: Global Anglican Perspectives* (Oxford: Regnum, 2012); *Mission in Context* (with John Corrie; Ashgate, 2012); *The Pioneer Gift* (with Jonny Baker; London: SCM, 2014); *Mission on the Road to Emmaus* (with Steve Bevans; London: SCM, 2015); and *Pioneering Spirituality* (with Jonny Baker; 2015).

Andrew Williams

Dr Andrew Williams is a lecturer in the School of Geography and Planning, Cardiff University. His research focuses on the relationships between religion, welfare and neoliberalism, with particular regard to food banks, homelessness and faith-based drug services. His latest book is *Working Faith: Faith-Based Organisations and Urban Social Justice* (co-edited with Paul Cloke and Justin Beaumont; Paternoster, 2013).